Subjective Experiences of Interactive Nostalgia

This book is part of the Peter Lang Media and Communication list.
Every volume is peer reviewed and meets
the highest quality standards for content and production.

PETER LANG
New York • Bern • Berlin
Brussels • Vienna • Oxford • Warsaw

Subjective Experiences of Interactive Nostalgia

Edited by Ryan Lizardi

PETER LANG
New York • Bern • Berlin
Brussels • Vienna • Oxford • Warsaw

Library of Congress Cataloging-in-Publication Data

Names: Lizardi, Ryan, editor.
Title: Subjective experiences of interactive nostalgia /
edited by Ryan Lizardi.
Description: New York: Peter Lang, 2019.
Includes bibliographical references and index.
Identifiers: LCCN 2019002415 | ISBN 978-1-4331-6242-8 (hardback: alk. paper)
ISBN 978-1-4331-6243-5 (paperback: alk. paper) | ISBN 978-1-4331-6244-2 (ebook pdf)
ISBN 978-1-4331-6245-9 (epub) | ISBN 978-1-4331-6246-6 (mobi)
Subjects: LCSH: Nostalgia. | Social media—Psychological aspects.
Social media—Social aspects. | Computer networks—Social aspects.
Classification: LCC BF575.N6 L59 2019 | DDC 302.23/1019—dc23
LC record available at https://lccn.loc.gov/2019002415
DOI 10.3726/b14765

Bibliographic information published by **Die Deutsche Nationalbibliothek**.
Die Deutsche Nationalbibliothek lists this publication in the "Deutsche Nationalbibliografie"; detailed bibliographic data are available on the Internet at http://dnb.d-nb.de/.

29 Broadway, 18th floor, New York, NY 10006
www.peterlang.com

Table of Contents

Introduction

RYAN LIZARDI

Nostalgia is a tricky subject to tackle, considering the ways in which it has not only changed in conception over time, but also in the recent burgeoning and rich scholarly explorations. This collection seeks to work in concert with, and in complement to, the many scholars who have come before and looked at what it means to long for a past time, place, object, country, media, or even state of mind. Where this collection seeks to differ is in its approach, or more appropriately approaches.

There are as many varied experiences of nostalgic longing as there are varied approaches to studying nostalgia. A deep deconstruction of nostalgia's beginnings as a description of a literal homesickness amongst the Swiss army, progressing to a memory malady for the likes of Freud to analyze, and then to a postmodern intertextual concept might be necessary in some chapters of this collection, while others will choose to focus on the history of the term only briefly. And this choice, in some ways, is entirely the point of why this particular focus on subjective experiences of interactive nostalgia is necessary. Recent scholars have done a masterful job of exploring many aspects of the term, Janelle Wilson, Paul Grainge, Svetlana Boym, Stephanie Coontz, Alastair Bonnett, Emily Keightley, Michael Pickering, and Tim Wildschut representing just a few. Emmanuelle Fantin, Ekaterina Kalinina, Manuel Menke, and Katharina Niemeyer even created the International Media and Nostalgia Network, while researching the term themselves, in order to come to a better understanding of nostalgia's evolving presence in our culture.

From Johannes Hofer to Sigmund Freud to Svetlana Boym to Stephanie Coontz, our understanding of what it means to long for the past has changed and morphed over time and, as such, our methodological approaches have needed to morph in kind. Although impossible given the space appropriate for an introduction such as this one to fully explore what subjective experiences of interactive nostalgia could entail, that is where the chapters come in, it will be helpful to briefly discuss the positioning of this collection as it pertains to each word in its title. To start with, the concept of subjective experiences, or subjective positioning, is crucial to understanding the goals of this collection, as many of us have been studying nostalgia in its various forms differently for some time now. Similarly, people have always experienced feelings of nostalgic longing for times, places, things, and events, whether or not they were always explicitly labeled as such. In this sense, this collection is not necessarily labeled as about subjective experiences because it deals solely with subjective qualitative methodologies, though instances of subjective analysis occur during moments of textual analysis, but deals instead with how people actually experience feelings of nostalgic longing. Yes, the media might want us to experience certain kinds of nostalgia, but people have to be the ones to do the actual longing in the end. This collection seeks to honor the agency of those feeling nostalgic, which Jeff Malpas describes as "indispensable to human subjectivity, and so its locatedness via bodily movement becomes essential to this subjectivity" (Malpas 2018, x). From chapters dedicated to understanding what kinds of nostalgia are encouraged in video gamers to chapters that look at the specific feelings of longing engendered by virtual museum tours, the idea is to look at the subjective nostalgic experiences of people in the contemporary media landscape.

The concept of interactivity is directly connected to these subjective experiences, as many of the chapters in this collection address how making consumers feel as if they are a part of the longing process moves them into a subjective position, as opposed to a more objective and passive position. Early research on interactivity often dealt with instruction, such as a focus on learner-interface interaction (Hillman, Willis, and Gunawardena 1994) as well as a focus on interaction attributes like "interaction with content" and "collaboration" (Northrup 2001, 31). It did not take long for the concept of interactivity to be applied to gaming and play, as "choice and its consequence are part of the interactivity and intrigue of the game … which creates high engagement" (Hedberg, Brown, and Arrighi 1997, 52). As technology becomes more sophisticated, such as in the case of virtual reality, this connection between interactivity and engagement grows as does the "sense of presence to a world that arises from the inscription of the body in the VR system" (Ryan 2015, 53). Interactive, in this sense, is part of "being there" or, in the case of nostalgia, wanting to go back there. Although this has been the traditional, or at least the initial, thinking about interactivity as it pertains to gaming, which is why the first section of this collection works within this interactivity subset, the definition is far more complicated. Seeking to "delimit" the term,

Erik Bucy says that "[i]nteractivity, first and foremost, should be reserved to describe reciprocal communication exchanges that involve some form of media, or information and communication technology" (2004, 376). Bucy connects this concept back to the subjective experience of consumers saying, "audiences may perceive a communication setting as interactive even when it lacks apparent control" or "communicative reciprocity" (2004, 377). In this way, the conception of interactivity in this collection is one of reflexivity, as authors present case studies where the feelings of longing that are encouraged lead to subjective experiences of nostalgia amongst consumers.

This encouragement of nostalgia, our final titular word, within contemporary media seeks to make our past eternally relevant, but our experiences in reaction to this encouragement are varied. To be nostalgic, or to be encouraged to feel nostalgia, is a sentiment of longing, a broadly defined feeling of emotional connection to the past. This thread connects the earliest research on the subject to the most recent. Johannes Hofer pioneered its discussion as a feeling of homesickness (Kessous and Roux 2008, 194). In the eighteenth century it was described as manifesting in symptoms of melancholia and depression (Wildschut et al. 2006, 975). Often, contemporary scholars look to its qualities of reminiscence and recollection (Wilson 2005, 25). Even when the focus is on how technologies encourage nostalgia, connections are made between the materiality of media and the subjective experience of longing (van der Heijden 2015, 105). Nostalgia is felt, experienced, which is why this collection seeks to connect it to a subjective positioning. At the same time, increasingly the encouragements to long for the past have asked us to engage with our memories interactively. Whether in the form of physical haptics, sonically, visually, or mentally, we are being asked to become a part of our individual, and our cultural, memory recollection. Combining these three concerns together, the subjective, the interactive, and the nostalgic, is the primary goal of this collection. We as consumers and researchers have different subjective experiences of longing for the past, especially in regards to our interactive media like video games, applications, and other digital content, and this collection seeks to honor those differences. In search of a more interdisciplinary understanding of the various forms and experiences of interactive nostalgic longing, this collection contains ruminations that explore these subjectivities of nostalgia from methodologically diverse perspectives (from the historical to the philosophical, from autoethnography to political economy). We hope that the benefits of such an approach is not only that this collection will appeal broadly within the already popular genre of nostalgia studies, but also function as a text that can speak across academic borders.

Section 1: Playing Through Nostalgia

The first section will lay the groundwork for the foundational understanding of interactivity described above as it has often been conceived, through play and gaming experiences that seek to create communicative reciprocity in regards to the past. There are many ways to combine subjectivity and interactivity, but looking at how games encourage particular subjective nostalgic experiences, while foreclosing others, seemed like a logical place to begin to explore our understanding of how interactive nostalgia can be achieved.

The first chapter of this collection, by Ashley P. Jones, looks at a classic and contemporary gaming franchise, *Tomb Raider* (1996-present), and the ways a series reboot can influence the nostalgic longing associated with the original, thereby influencing our present interpretations of the series as a whole. This chapter combines historical and textual analysis to explore everything from Lara Croft's changing looks, character agency, and player experience. The result is a vivid reconstruction of the changing, and sometimes unchanged, subjective player experience made possible by the interactive nostalgic elements of the franchise.

Chapter Two, by Sebastian Felzmann, turns its attention to the very process of technical advancements in video games, a production imperative, that has led to an industrial retrogaming counter reaction designed to appeal to the sensitivities of users who grew up with video games. A combination of industrial study, audience study, and definitional work, this chapter, which is a revised and adapted version of a German published lecture given at Humboldt University in 2013, looks directly at the how and the why of the contemporary retrogaming trend within the video game industry and is a significant addition to the interactive nostalgic focus of this collection.

Shifting to a look at a more hands-on form of interactive play, Chapter Three, by Jonathan M. Bullinger, discusses a form of idealized play and nostalgia present in LEGO collections. The LEGO Group, with its varied offerings in digital and physical brick form, does not sell sets that depict nation-based warfare, and this chapter seeks to explore the LEGO customizer collector groups who fill in this gap in transgenerational nostalgia. Performing an ethnography of groups who create custom LEGO war pieces and sets, this chapter looks at the difference between an idealized construction of childhood and imagination preparation and the long legacy of war toys.

My chapter comes next with an autoethnographic look at the development of video game console emulation technologies, communities, and commodifications, and connects them to the industry's revival of dormant catalogs through virtual console DLC and the eventual repackaging and "re-consoling" of popular properties. I contrast my own subjective experiences seeking out hard to find Nintendo Classic Edition consoles with my engagement in inventive methods of DIY emulation and the communities that support both endeavors. The experiences of these disparate methods of retro gaming are quite varied, and speak to the different nostalgic subjectivities encouraged through the practice of either buying a rare pre-packaged version of the past and building one for yourself.

Section 2: Digitally Nostalgic

The second section moves beyond the gaming experience, but still within the interactive realm of the digital, these chapters look at nostalgia through the lens of online subjective interactivity, and still within the parameters of subjective experiences of communicative reciprocity. From social media to virtual tours to streaming content, the experiences of nostalgia in this section are highly interactive and subjective, and demonstrate the variations of the experience of interactively longing for the past.

This section begins with a rhetorical analysis, by Raymond Blanton, of the Netflix monster hit, *Stranger Things* (2016-present), as an embodiment of nostalgic longing indicative of a swell of late 1980s Cold War nostalgia in media today. Methodologically, this chapter utilizes autoethnography, critical-cultural analysis, and of course rhetorical analysis to determine how nostalgic longing functions interactively, subjectively, and rhetorically as a meaning making practice, through the lens of *Stranger Things* and its retro synth soundtrack.

The next chapter is a tour-de-force exploration of online virtual plantation tours and their use of white nostalgia as a tool to direct the historical narrative and reinforce the white nostalgic narrative of the Old South. Examining eight different Southern plantation virtual tours, Alexandra Lippert and Carson S. Kay argue that interactive digital media allow these plantations to selectively choose the voice, perspective, and memory of the pre-Civil War era in a manner that maximizes profit from white nostalgia and cultural glorification. Describing these virtual tours as a form of public memory, the result of this analysis is an exposition of interactivity as a means to promote a sanitized version of history.

Turning the collection's attention to the increasingly nostalgic world of social media, JeongHyun Lee's chapter on social media's automated nostalgia of the digitally archived past looks at the ways in which Facebook, among other social media platforms, has transformed our everyday memories into nostalgic triggers. For Lee, the encouragement of longing for the past is achieved through the active construction of nostalgic subjectivities by selecting, organizing, and reanimating memories.

Still focusing on social media and Facebook, but in a very different manner, Alexandra Bardan and Natalia Vasilendiuc's chapter on the representations of communist nostalgia amongst those born in Romania after 1989 explores both Facebook communities dedicated to the communist period as well as an online pool of respondents from selected Facebook communities to determine the level of displaced nostalgia that exists for a time period before they were born. This chapter adds to the growing scholarly conversation about second-hand, or imagined, nostalgia not based on direct experience, and presents an important discussion about what it means to experience subjective longing through the lens of generational curiosity and post-communist nostalgia.

Section 3: Rethinking Nostalgic Experiences

Still sometimes digital, and still always interactive, the next section looks to reframe our thinking about our subjective nostalgic experiences. These chapters move beyond traditional views of longing, and explore nostalgia as material decay, part of a radical revolution, and part of a growing notion of longing for the past as a political tool for change.

This section begins with a chapter, by Mani Mehrvarz and Maryam Muliaee, that has a novel approach to the study of nostalgia, that of a focus on failure. Mehrvarz and Muliaee look to the ways in which obsolete technology, media archaeology, and decaying media lead to the conception of "media-as-things" as opposed to a culturally transparent object and argue that the "thingness" in media could potentially encourage nostalgic experiences of longing regardless of their historical placement and reference. This truly unique perspective on mediated nostalgic longing examines how grainy film images, failure in digital and analog media, and scratched records encourage viewers' engagement with the disintegrating materiality of the media, thereby focusing their attention on the loss represented in the decay.

The final two chapters in this collection look towards the current and future potentials inherent in nostalgia, starting with Emily Truman's look at iconic popular culture representations and their ability to encourage viewers to experience forms of radical nostalgia. Building from Alastair Bonnett's work on nostalgia's ability to engender these kinds of progressive feelings, Truman extends the conversation by focusing on three revolutionary icons, Marie Antoinette, Rosie the Riveter, and Barack Obama, for the way their imagery has not been depoliticized through nostalgia but has been re-framed as symbols that reflect a mode of thinking about the future rather than a sentimental orientation to an ideal past. Through in-depth image analysis, Truman deftly argues that the emergence of the radical nostalgia aesthetic seeks to re-define contemporary and future cultural and political values.

In the final chapter of this collection, Sally J. Spalding takes direct aim at critics of nostalgia who view it is solely an emotion that would distract and idealize by presenting nostalgia as capable of encouraging prosocial and productive action. Utilizing social scientific and rhetorical theories of nostalgia, Spalding examines which types of nostalgia promote and which discourage political engagement with contemporary issues by analyzing two interactive public art installations that encourage participation through the evocation of nostalgic longing. Through deep readings of these installations, Spalding demonstrates that the coupling of nostalgia and depoliticization is not inherent, but contextual.

References

Bucy, Erik. 2004. "Interactivity in Society: Locating an Elusive Concept." *The Information Society* 20: 373–383.

Hedberg, John, Brown, Christine, and Arrighi, Michael. 1997. "Interactive Multimedia and Web-based Learning: Similarities and Differences." In *Web-based Instruction*, edited by Badrul Huda Khan, 47–58. Englewood Cliffs, NJ: Educational Technology Publications.

Hillman, Daniel C. A., Willis, Deborah J., and Gunawardena, Charlotte N. 1994. "Learner Interface Interaction in Distance Education: An Extension of Contemporary Models and Strategies for Practitioners." *American Journal of Distance Education* 8, no. 2: 30–42.

Kessous, Aurélie, and Roux, Elyette. 2008. "A Semiotic Analysis of Nostalgia as a Connection to the Past." *Qualitative Market Research* 11, no. 2: 192–212.

Malpas, Jeff. 2018. *Place and Experience: A Philosophical Topography.* New York: Routledge.

Northrup, Pam. 2001. "A Framework for Designing Interactivity into Web-Based Instruction." *Educational Technology* 41, no. 2: 31–39.

Ryan, Marie-Laure. 2015. *Narrative as Virtual Reality 2: Revisiting Immersion and Interactivity in Literature and Electronic Media.* Baltimore, MD: Johns Hopkins University Press.

van der Heijden, Tim. 2015. "Technostalgia of the Present: From Technologies of Memory to a Memory of Technologies." *European Journal of Media Studies* 4, no. 2: 103–121.

Wildschut, Tim, Sedikides, Constantine, Ardnt, Jamie, and Routledge, Clay. 2006. "Nostalgia: Content, Triggers, Functions." *Journal of Personality and Social Psychology* 91, no. 5: 975–993.

Wilson, Janelle. 2005. *Nostalgia: Sanctuary of Meaning.* Lewisburg, PA: Bucknell University Press.

Section 1

Playing Through Nostalgia

1. *Reconstructing Lara: The* Tomb Raider *Reboot as Nostalgic Experience*

Ashley P. Jones

Full disclosure requires that I tell you that my heart holds the *Tomb Raider* video game series near and dear as this was the first console game I truly enjoyed playing. It was my brother's game and I distinctly remember watching him get stuck on a particular sequence and turning the console off. After he left the room, I booted the PlayStation back up and proceeded to beat that sequence and continue on with the game. Later, when my brother returned, he was very confused when he realized the game save was not where he had left it. Thus began the feud between the two of us as to who would finish the game first.

The situation makes me smile looking back on it now, but the experience is not a unique one. My fondness for the *Tomb Raider* video game series is just one example of how video game nostalgia manifests itself for an entire generation of gamers. Video games have become what Sean Fenty has described as "powerful nostalgic artifacts" that open a state of being for players to return to (Fenty 2008, 20). While the games themselves are the portal to this nostalgic memory, the immersive experience of the video game is really what holds the nostalgic pull. In other words, the gameplay provides the opportunity for players to re-experience their first time immersing themselves in what the game offers (Fenty 2008, 23). When a game series covers several iterations over the course of multiple decades, this provides an opportunity to explore how the games as nostalgic artifacts become interpreted and re-imagined by the game's producers. The *Tomb Raider* series provides precisely this opportunity.

The *Tomb Raider* video game series has been categorized into three different generations over the course of the more than two decades the series has been around (Han 2014, 33). The first generation of the series the six earliest games, spanning from the original release in 1996, *Tomb Raider*, to *Tomb Raider: The Angel of Darkness* in 2003 (Core Design 1996–2003). The video game developer, Core Design, was responsible for this generation. The second generation of the series began when Crystal Dynamics took over as the game developer and covered the games released from 2006 to 2008 which included *Tomb Raider: Legend, Tomb Raider: Anniversary,* and *Tomb Raider: Underworld* (Crystal Dynamics 2006–2008). Audiences appeared to be burnt out on the series however, and Crystal Dynamics stopped developing the games for a few years after the final release in 2008. *Tomb Raider: Angel of Darkness*, the final game of the first generation of *Tomb Raider* sold a mere 2.5 million copies worldwide. *Tomb Raider: Underworld*, the final game of the second generation, sold only 2.6 million copies worldwide. Both games together failed to sell anywhere close to the 7 million copies of Core Design's original 1996 *Tomb Raider* (Marshall 2013). In 2013 the third generation of the series kicked off with the release of *Tomb Raider* as an origin story for the protagonist, Lara Croft (Crystal Dynamics 2013). A sequel to this new timeline was released in 2015: *Rise of the Tomb Raider* (Crystal Dynamics 2015). Early in 2018 Crystal Dynamics announced a third release for later in the year: *Shadow of the Tomb Raider* (Eidos Montreal 2018). *Shadow of the Tomb Raider* was released in September 2018. The game series has spawned its own cultural artifacts including two different film adaptations and a comic book series.[1] The plethora of texts associated with the video game series provides evidence that the game series has been able to capture the hearts of players for over two decades now.

Lara Croft and the *Tomb Raider* franchise offer an important case study in how nostalgia informs contemporary choices of video game characters and development. Exploring the elements that have been maintained throughout the different releases of the narrative games and adopted into the additional texts associated with the series provides evidence that certain aspects of the game create the essence, and thus the nostalgic immersion, that the game developers have capitalized upon. These elements include aspects such as Lara's dress, body style, weapons, and the story choices that have continued to be used throughout the series. Analyzing these elements will build a profile of one of the longest-running video game series efforts to appeal to both existing and new players in a fast-changing video game landscape.

Nostalgia is a unique point of view that allows for more flexibility in how we understand the experiences of consuming a text. Psychologists agree that nostalgia operates as a yearning or desire to return to a different time or state in which pleasant or happier experiences were had (Madigan 2016, 57). The term is far more complex than just a yearning or desire, however. Nostalgia is cognitive, performative, and provides an interpretive framework (Cook 2005, 3–4). Through each of these layers, nostalgia presents the opportunity to see history from multiple perspectives.

Nostalgia does not operate in the sense of bringing the original back from the dead. On the contrary, nostalgia works merely on the opportunity to recreate the circumstances under which the original created the memory. The original never truly repeats itself. This linearity of time is one condition that Malcolm Chase and Christopher Shaw argue is a requirement for nostalgia to take place (1989, 3). Recognizing and accepting that the nostalgic artifact is simply a trigger for the circumstances of the original experience is the cognitive aspect of nostalgia. This would most likely be playing the video game itself. The original can never be copied in its exact form or state of being as this would not create the nostalgic experience with the text. The linearity of time is forever propelling experiences forward. Players may be able to go back to a game but they will never be able to truly recreate the experience that invited nostalgia in the first place. Each play-through of a game creates a new experience of the game. If the initial experience creates the recipe for the nostalgia in the succeeding play-throughs, those play-throughs do not recreate the initial experience through the very existence of the nostalgia. Instead, those succeeding play-throughs create representations of the original nostalgic experience.

In this sense, nostalgia works as a simulacrum of the original experience (Dika 2003, 3). Nostalgic playing of a game such as *Tomb Raider* (1996–2018) acts as a representation of the original play-through which created the nostalgia in the first place. Baudrillard argues that simulacrum presents a representation with no original (1981/1994). Nostalgia creates simulacrum through the affectionate urge to recreate an original experience that ultimately will never occur. Nostalgic players of a video game will recognize that this is not their first experience with the game if it already holds a nostalgic memory for them. Instead, the game is a portal to that first and original experience of a game that becomes the ideal, thus reifying the role of nostalgia that Chase and Shaw argue for.

The second requirement that Chase and Shaw argue of nostalgia is that our current experiences are not living up to our expectations (1989, 3). This incites the nostalgic memory since nostalgia is associated with what has been interpreted as happier or better times (Madigan 2016, 56). This requirement also lends itself to the understanding that nostalgia operates in an interpretive manner. Our memory acquires nostalgia through the player's interpretation of their original experience with a video game in addition to the player's current experiences, presumably with what has been interpreted as a deficient video game. In other words, as Pam Cook argues, the existence of the nostalgic memory shows that players understand there is a gap that exists between the two experiences (2005, 4). The experiences of the original play-through of the video game inciting nostalgia and the current experience of playing that video game create two sides of that gap. The bridge between the gap is the experience of nostalgia. By attempting to bridge the gap, players enact the performance aspect of nostalgia by enacting a recreation of the original immersive experience. However, performative acts are not a repeatable occurrence. Therefore, this gap is never one that can be crossed but instead remains a pull toward the singular and original experience.

The final requirement of nostalgia that Chase and Shaw argue for is that remnants of the original experience must remain in some form (1989, 4). The ephemera of the original immersive experience of a game becomes the tangible link to the nostalgic memory.[2] Since this is often seen as the replaying of a game, a player literally re-enacts their original experience to the best of their ability (Cook 2005, 4). However, these re-enactments as performances are a once and done concept. As much as a player can try to recreate their original experiences with a video game, it is an impossible feat. This also lends itself to the idea of nostalgia operating as simulacrum again. The remnants of that original experience that become the nostalgic artifacts and triggers simply act as layers of copies that become the foundation of the nostalgia. The performativity of the nostalgic memory reinforces the nostalgia itself without ever satisfying the desire the nostalgia created in the first place. Indeed, the performativity aspect of nostalgia ensures its continued existence.

These different aspects and requirements of nostalgia all lend themselves to the idea that Chase and Shaw put forth that nostalgia is a recreation of history from a subjective point of view (1989, 4). Cook argues along a similar vein that history and nostalgia work on a continuum that provide the poles of how we create our understanding of our experiences through memory: "In that sense, it produces knowledge and insight, even though these may be of a different order from those produced by conventional historical analysis, and may be experienced in different ways" (Cook 2005, 3–4). History is multi-sided and must be recognized as being so. Nostalgia is one way of doing this.

Using a concept called re-vision, Adrienne Rich argues that looking back upon a text can provide fresh insights and an avenue of critical analysis that was not apparent before (1972, 18). Nostalgia can act as a form of re-vision, particularly through what Tim van der Heijden (2015, 103) proposes as technostalgia. Technostalgia is a term Heijden uses to refer to the cultural memory shift of digital technologies emulating analog technologies in a performative act. For Heijden, nostalgia is moving away from subjective experiences and into the materiality of performance and presence. Nostalgia becomes an action or practice undertaken that allows the medium itself to act as a form of nostalgia. For a video game player, this can take the form of playing games that can be nostalgia-inducing. In terms of how *Tomb Raider* (1996–2018) does this, the re-boot of the *Tomb Raider* series calls upon the iconicity of the original trilogy, thus recreating the experiences of playing the original games, through modern technologies.

Video games are particularly adept at being able to tease out this historic constructivism as both the technology and the narratives tend to build upon themselves (Taylor & Whalen 2008, 3). Both ludological and narrative elements contribute to the nostalgic effect within video games. The ludological elements of a game are the examination of the play activities associated with a game (Mayra 2008, 8). This often involves the game mechanics and rules of play that enable a game to be played and experienced. Narratology, on the other hand, derives from literary studies. Narratology explores the fictive, "representation of events" in a game that mechanics and rules ultimately coordinate (Mayra 2008, 8). Both elements are cooperative within gaming studies. These elements are used to create nostalgia within games as well. Even though gaming interfaces and hardware continue to update, ludologically a game can recreate a mechanic in newer games that first appeared in the original game experience that created the nostalgia. For example, in *Tomb Raider* (Core Design 1996) Lara is known for a simple, yet elegantly done swan dive into deep pools of water from incredible heights. This mechanic has continued through the game series and is most recently featured in *Shadow of the Tomb Raider* (Eidos Montreal 2018) with a quick reminder of which buttons to press for Lara to engage in the iconic action. Similarly, the narrative elements are easier to recreate across a gaming series since they are often one of the reasons the game series continues. Video games embody all three requirements that Chase and Shaw put forth in that the immersive experiences "offer the seduction of a perfect past that can be replayed, a past within which players can participate, and a past in which players can move and explore" (Fenty 2008, 22). The cognitive, performative, and interpretive layers all coalesce in the video game experience. This offers a truly unique experience of nostalgia.

Nostalgia in video games can be explicitly or implicitly done. An explicitly nostalgic game manifests as a remake or a port to a new platform. An implicitly nostalgic game presents the same narrative throughout several games or uses the same button configurations to create a continuous experience over several games (Lizardi 2015, 85). In the case of the *Tomb Raider* game series, it would qualify as an explicitly nostalgic video game. Several elements of the gameplay and narratives continue to be used and recycled through the various games. This continues to the point that an expectation of what Lara Croft should look like, sound like, and act like emerges in subsequent games and other texts associated with the game series.

One of the most recognizable aspects of the *Tomb Raider* game series is Lara Croft. The leading lady of the series has evolved over the last 20 years from a busty but blocky polygonal tomb raider into an athletic, svelte and more realistic-looking tomb raider. Part of this must be attributed to the technology of video games becoming smoother and as close to real-looking as we've ever been. The third generation games even featured motion-capture technology of the actress Camilla Luddington (Campbell 2015). However, there are several aspects of the character that have become iconographic for the series as a whole. Indeed, Lara Croft has become a metonymy for the game series itself.

When Lara first debuted in 1996, she rocked long brunette hair held back in a braid, short and impractical shorts, a blue tank top, hiking boots, twin pistols, and a stoic facial expression (Core Design 1996). Noticeably, she was well-endowed with large breasts that, due to the polygonal structure of the technology of the time period, were pointed and hard to miss. Over the years, her outfit and looks has changed a few times, even several times throughout a single narrative. But as many cosplayers have shown, the tank top, braided hair, and short shorts have become the mainstay for the Lara Croft character. Evidence of this is also shown in the first *Tomb Raider* film starring Angelina Jolie (West 2001). Jolie's version of Lara included the signature short shorts, tank top, and thigh-strapped twin pistols. It was so convincing that the signature look even became the image used for the movie poster and DVD cover.

In the 2013 game series reboot, *Tomb Raider*, the origin story of Lara Croft is featured for the narrative (Crystal Dynamics 2013). As players first encounter Lara, it is hard to mistake the iconography. Although noticeably younger and more expressive looking, Lara is still in her signature tank top, hiking boots, and is still featuring well-rounded breasts.[3] She even has long brunette hair, although it is now tied into a high ponytail. As the game progresses, it becomes a goal to find and wear the twin pistols. All of this is to say that the look of Lara Croft has become a nostalgic expression that the game developers have capitalized upon. In the sequel to the 2013 game release, Lara has the option of changing her outfit at her first save point in a cold, tundra-like landscape. One of the options is the first outfit from the 2013 game featuring the nostalgic elements of classic Lara Croft. Despite the outfit being not practical in the landscape at that moment in the second game's narrative, the nostalgic pull of the first rebooted game is presented to the player, and by extension the nostalgia of the original 1996 game as well. Additionally, the third game, *Shadow of the Tomb Raider* (Eidos Montreal 2018), the nostalgia of previous games is pushed even harder. Early in the game, players again have a choice of switching out Lara's outfit for earlier games' versions including the iconic outfit from *Tomb Raider 2* (Core Design 1997) and Lara's cover look from *Tomb Raider: Angel of Darkness* (Core Design 2003). In fact, changing Lara's outfit to one of these earlier generation choices not only changes Lara's clothes, but also changes Lara's overall design to match the game the outfit derives from. You can play as sharp-edged, polygonal Lara in the *Tomb Raider 2* outfits or you can play as the svelte, still comically large-breasted Lara from *Angel of Darkness.* Despite playing the most recent game on the most up-to-date platforms, long-time players can still be tethered to their original nostalgic experiences through Lara's look.

The voice of Lara Croft works in a similar manner to link a player to their first experience of Lara in the early games (Core Design 1996–2003). Lara voice has, while not heavily featured in the early games, always been distinctly British and enunciated. This has continued into the films and later games as well. Jolie's depiction of Lara Croft required the actress to speak with a British accent instead of her American one to keep with the character's origins in the game series (West 2001). The second film version released in 2018, starring Alicia Vikander, a Swedish actress, also required a British accent (Uthaug 2018). Camilla Luddington, the actress who was motion-captured and did the voice acting for the rebooted third generation video games is British and maintained the accent. Lara's voice is as iconographic as her clothing and physical appearance is to maintain the nostalgia of the gamer's experience. Even for gamers that may just be joining the series in 2013, the use of the same voice actress and the option of the outfit choices reinforce the nostalgic pull of the first rebooted game.

Another major example of the explicit nostalgic elements that have been used throughout the *Tomb Raider* game series is narrative tropes that keep popping back up. I will examine two of them in detail: the first is the use of Lara Croft's father as character motivation; the second is the use of the supernatural.

Lara Croft's father holds a reprising role throughout the game series and in additional texts as a motivator for why Lara decides to lead the lifestyle that she does. While known by many names throughout the series, the title of Lord Croft or name Richard Croft appears to be the most consistent. The narrative that continues to pop up repeatedly is that Lord Croft is either missing or is presumed dead.[4] In search of what happened to him, Lara becomes a renowned tomb raider that searches the world for clues.

Versions of this story became prevalent after the first film adaptation with Angelina Jolie (West 2001). The second generation of video games ran with a similar storyline as well. In *Tomb Raider: Legend* (Crystal Dynamics 2006) Lara's mother goes missing and is presumed dead after a mysterious experience in a lost tomb. Lara's father becomes obsessed with discovering what happened to her mother and begins researching ancient legends and myths in hopes of finding Lara's mother. Lara takes over her father's research after his death to eventually discover that her mother is still alive and Lara can possibly save her. The third generation of games did not start with the father as motivator narrative but decided to pick it up in the 2015 game release, *Rise of the Tomb Raider* (Crystal Dynamics), as well as bringing back the recurring villain corporation of Trinity. At the end of *Rise of the Tomb Raider*, Lara discovers that her father's supposed suicide was actually a hired hit from Trinity. In *Shadow of the Tomb Raider* (Eidos Montreal 2018), a flashback sequence shows a nine-year-old Lara traversing Croft Manor, discovering a hidden room and artifacts of her dead mother. A sudden shot rings out as Lara runs from the hidden room to her father's study to find the body of her father lying over his desk, gun in his hand. This pairs with Lara's repeated drive to get ahead of Trinity and complete her father's work, a major plot push within the game. The second film adaptation also incorporated the storylines of both the 2013 *Tomb Raider* game release and the 2015 *Rise of the Tomb Raider* game release into a single narrative by focusing on how Lara Croft became an adventuring tomb raider through finishing her father's last quest before he went missing (Uthaug 2018). Lara's relationship with her father and his legacy is one she must confront and choose to embrace within the plot of the film.

This narrative provides evidence again that different elements of the story continue to be copied and recycled from different texts associated with the game series. While not as iconographic or metonymic of the game series as Lara Croft's physical appearance, the narrative of Lord Richard Croft being the character motivation behind Lara's actions and reasons for tomb raiding is strong. The use of the narrative in later generations of the game series and associated texts provides an additional layer of nostalgic interpretation to the more limited games of the first generation.

The use of supernatural phenomena is also a narrative element that continues to be repurposed in the game series as well as the associated texts. Elements such as resurrected tyrannosaurus rex dinosaurs, immortality, Nordic sea serpents, and undead Asian goddesses run rampant throughout the narrative worlds of Lara Croft. While not the same supernatural phenomena in every game is present, the use of the supernatural as a narrative structure that moves the plot forward and fills in plot gaps is noticeable. It has become a mainstay in the series to bridge the incredible physical feats of Lara as she adventures around the world and to keep the world from getting too small. If aliens and dinosaurs exist in this narrative world, who is going to stop Lara from conquering anything our imaginations can dream up?

A specific example of the supernatural phenomenon being ported from one text to another is the use of the Himiko storyline in both the rebooted 2013 game *Tomb Raider*, and the 2018 *Tomb Raider* movie starring Alicia Vikander. Himiko is an ancient Asian goddess that is said to hold amazing and terrible supernatural powers. In the 2013 game, Lara races to save her friend from becoming the human sacrifice necessary to release Himiko from her tomb (Crystal Dynamics 2013). In the 2018 film, Lara searches, finds, and destroys Himiko's tomb before harm comes to the world (Uthaug 2018). This storyline is also similar to the *Tomb Raider: Cradle of Life* film adaptation that Jolie starred in 2003 (de Bont 2003). In this narrative, instead of Himiko, Lara is attempting to track down Pandora's Box and keep its power out of the wrong hands.

As Lara often stumbles into situations she can't anticipate, similar storylines with supernatural consequences have popped up throughout the *Tomb Raider* game series. In *Tomb Raider: The Last Revelation* (Core Design 1999) Lara pulls an amulet from a sarcophagus, ultimately releasing a dark god named Seth from his entrapment and setting off a series of battles, including possession, undead creatures, and strange weather patterns charged by the power of Seth. The game ultimately ends with Lara sealing Seth back into tomb while also sacrificing herself as the Great Pyramid of Giza collapses upon her. In *Shadow of the Tomb Raider* (Eidos Montreal 2018), again Lara takes an artifact that sets off a series of catastrophic events to wipe the world clean. Immediately, Lara is caught up in a tsunami and later has to battle against a freak storm in Peru, earthquakes, and mudslides as she fights against Trinity to reclaim the artifacts causing such destruction and save the world from falling into the wrong hands.

The unexplained, hard to believe, or out of this world is a common trope that continues to lend itself to the *Tomb Raider* series. This can be traced back to when Core Design was creating the first game in a similar fashion to their earlier, Indiana Jones-inspired game *Rick Dangerous* (Deuber-Mankowsky 2005). *Tomb Raider* takes the storyline of an adventurer and freshens up the graphics with our now iconic Lara and keeps the adventure elements I have outlined above.

With the recent reboot of the series by Crystal Dynamics in 2013, we see what elements have managed to stick around since the game's inception twenty years earlier. These elements act as the tools to create nostalgia in players who know the game, and specifically the character of Lara Croft, from earlier iterations. These tools also end up establishing both ends of the gap between the original nostalgic experience and the new experience of the rebooted game series. The existence of the gap between the original experience and the nostalgic triggers embedded in the rebooted game series indicate the simulacrum of the nostalgia at play here. Long-time or repeat players interpret the rebooted game series through triggers such as those I've presented here that remind them of their first experiences of with Lara. Despite the best game design or tributes to earlier games, it is an impossibility to ever recreate that nostalgia-inducing performance, however. The performativity of nostalgia doesn't allow for it. Playing a game is never done the same way twice for a single player. Instead, what we are left with is the simulacra of an experience in the reboot of the game series. Players can perform Lara through recreated actions, dialogue, outfits, and narrative storylines, but they can never truly experience Lara Croft as an original ever again. That original only exists as a form of a memory inside of the player.

All three dimensions of nostalgia are present in the third-generation reboot of the game series as well as in the 2018 film adaptation. The rebooted series has successfully shown that nostalgia is evident in the choices made to reconstruct the game. The performativity is shown in the players working their way through the game, recognizing the nostalgic triggers, and then interpreting them. Cognitively, players are made aware from the onset of the 2013 game that this is a reboot to the entire series they had known. The game is designed to act almost as a prequel to the Lara older gamers grew up with, hence the decision to pull in strategic outfits, actions, and narrative tropes from earlier games. Creating a connection between the original nostalgic moment for the players, whether that is in the first or second generation of the series, to the continuation of these elements into the third generation was a strategic choice that proved the right decision. In the first month of *Tomb Raider's* release, 3.4 million copies sold. Eventually the game became the best-selling release in the series' history (Matulef 2015). Players were drawn back into the franchise.

The success of the 2013 game also provides evidence that the interpretation of the game series was favorable as well. Players appeared to be able to not only make the connection between the Lara they knew and the Lara they saw successfully, the game provided enough of a connection that player's interpretations of the game appeared to link to that nostalgic memory. Reviews of the game reflect this interpretation. Matt Miller of the gaming magazine *Game Informer*, called the game "a fresh start to an old series" with enough of a balance between the needs of contemporary gamers while staying true to what the *Tomb Raider* series is all about (Miller 2013). Also of *Game Informer*, Matt Helgeson called the game "nearly flawless" (Helgeson 2014). The interpretive framework applied to the game by players (and reviewers) alike appear to approve of the game as nostalgic without being a remake.

Regardless of the success of the game, the developers made distinct choices that reflected their understandings of the fan base surrounding the game series and essence of what *Tomb Raider* was meant to be for players. Incorporating nostalgic elements into the reboot of the series allowed them to reconnect with older players that had been fans of the earlier generations of the game as well as create a new generation of players that will now be looking for their own nostalgic elements as the series continues and becomes adopted into other textual forms. The *Tomb Raider* series has been revamped, but the spark of the original Lara Croft and *Tomb Raider* franchise has been far from lost. The series and Lara have been reimagined for a new generation of gamers.

Notes

1. Simon West directed the first film adaptation released in 2001 with a sequel released in 2003. Roar Ulthaug directed the second film adaptation that was released in 2018. The comic book series was created by Dark Horse Comics and follows the 2013 reboot of the game.
2. This can be the game itself but may also include texts such as screenshots, music, sound effects, or even paratexts such as fan culture items like t-shirts or fan fiction.
3. Although Lara's breasts are much more proportional in this generation of the games.
4. Versions of this narrative pop up in the second and third generations of the game series as well as both film adaptations.

References

Baudrillard, Jean. *Simulacra and Simulation*. (Ann Arbor, MI: University of Michigan Press) 1981/1994.

Campbell, Colin. "The Reconstruction of Lara Croft" in *Polygon.com*. July 10, 2015, https://www.polygon.com/features/2015/7/10/8925285/the-reconstruction-of-lara-croft-rise-of-the-tomb-raider.

Chase, Malcolm & Shaw, Christopher. "The Dimensions of Nostalgia" in *The Imagined Past: History and Nostalgia*. ed. Christopher Shaw & Malcolm Chase. (Manchester: Manchester University Press) 1989.

Cook, Pam. *Screening the Past: Memory and Nostalgia in Cinema*. (New York: Routledge Publishers) 2005.

Core Design. *Tomb Raider.* Produced by Mike Schmitt (Eidos Interactive, 1996). Video Game.

Core Design. *Tomb Raider 2.* Produced by Troy Horton (Eidos Interactive, 1997). Video Game.

Core Design. *Tomb Raider 3.* Produced by Troy Horton (Eidos Interactive, 1998). Video Game.

Core Design. *Tomb Raider: The Last Revelation.* Produced by Troy Horton (Eidos Interactive, 1999). Video Game.

Core Design. *Tomb Raider: Chronicles.* Produced by Andrew Watt (Eidos Interactive, 2000). Video Game.

Core Design. *Tomb Raider: The Angel of Darkness.* Produced by Andrew Watt (Eidos Interactive, 2003). Video Game.

Crystal Dynamics. *Tomb Raider: Legend.* (Eidos Interactive, 2006). Video Game.

Crystal Dynamics. *Tomb Raider: Anniversary.* Produced by Lulu LaMer (Eidos Interactive, 2007). Video Game.

Crystal Dynamics. *Tomb Raider: Underworld.* Produced by Alex Jones (Eidos Interactive, 2008). Video Game.

Crystal Dynamics. *Tomb Raider.* Produced by Kyle Peschel (Square Enix, 2013). Video Game.

Crystal Dynamics. *Rise of the Tomb Raider.* Produced by Rose Hunt (Square Enix, 2015). Video Game.

Deuber-Mankowsky, Astrid. *Lara Croft: Cyber Heroine.* (Minneapolis: University of Minnesota Press) 2005.

Dika, Vera. *Recycled Culture in Contemporary Art and Film: The Uses of Nostalgia.* (New York: Cambridge University Press) 2003.

Eidos Montreal. *Shadow of the Tomb Raider.* (Square Enix, 2018). Video Game.

Fenty, Sean. "Why Old School Is 'Cool': A Brief Analysis of Classic Video Game Nostalgia" in *Playing the Past: History and Nostalgia in Video Games.* ed. Zach Whalen & Laurie N. Taylor. (Nashville, TN: Vanderbilt University Press) 2008, 20.

Han, Hye-Wan. 2014 "Characterization of Female Protagonists in Video Games: A Focus on Lara Croft". *Asian Journal of Women's Studies* 20. no. 3. 27–48.

Heijden, Tim van der. 2015. "Technostalgia of the Present: From Technologies of Memory to a Memory of Technologies". *NECSUS, European Journal of Media Studies* 4. no. 2. 103–121.

Helgeson, Matt. "Tomb Raider: Definitive Edition: Lara's Never Looked Better". *Game Informer.* January 24, 2014. http://www.gameinformer.com/games/tomb_raider_definitive_edition/b/xboxone/archive/2014/01/24/tomb-raider-definitive-edition-review-game-informer.aspx

Lara Croft: Tomb Raider. Directed by Simon West. (Burbank, CA: Paramount Pictures) 2001. DVD.

Lara Croft: Tomb Raider-The Cradle of Life. Directed by Jan de Bont. (Burbank, CA: Paramount Pictures) 2003. DVD.

Lizardi, Ryan. *Mediated Nostalgia: Individual Memory and Contemporary Mass Media.* (Lanham, MD: Lexington Books) 2015.

Madigan, Jamie. *Getting Gamers: The Psychology of Video Games and Their Impact on the People Who Play Them.* (Lanham, MD: Rowman & Littlefield Publishers) 2016.

Marshall, Rick. "History of Tomb Raider: Blowing the dust off 17 years of Lara Croft". *Digital Trends.* March 9, 2013. http://www.digitaltrends.com/gaming/the-history-of-tomb-raider/

Matulef, Jeffrey. "Tomb Raider Reboot Has Sold 8.5m Copies". *Eurogamer.* June 4, 2015. https://www.eurogamer.net/articles/2015-04-06-tomb-raider-reboot-has-sold-8-5m-copies

Mayra, Franz. *An Introduction to Game Studies: Games in Culture.* (Los Angeles, CA: Sage Publications) 2008.

Miller, Matt. "Tomb Raider: Old Name, Remarkable New Series". *Game Informer.* February 25, 2013. http://www.gameinformer.com/games/tomb_raider/b/xbox360/archive/2013/02/25/tomb-raider-review.aspx

Rich, A. 1972. "When We Dead Awaken: Writing as Re-Vision". *College English* 34. no. 1. 18–30.

Taylor, Laurie N. & Whalen, Z. "Playing the Past: An Introduction" in *Playing the Past: History and Nostalgia in Video Games.* ed. Zach Whalen & Laurie N. Taylor (Nashville, TN: Vanderbilt University Press) 2008.

Tomb Raider. Directed by Roar Uthaug. (Burbank, CA: Warner Bros. Pictures) 2018. Motion Picture.

2. "Been There, Done That!": An Examination of Media Nostalgia as a Creative Practice for Creating New Retro Games

SEBASTIAN FELZMANN

Note: An earlier version of this chapter was included in the German publication *Shift Restore Escape: Retrocomputing und Computerarchäologie*, ed. Stefan Höltgen (Winnenden: CSW-Verlag, 2014).

Introduction

Media nostalgia and thus retro gaming or gaming nostalgia have become an increasingly important branch of the computer game scene in recent years and are attracting ever-growing attention—not only on the part of recipients and users who have grown up with the medium, but also on the part of producers. The basis for this development is certainly the specific composition of the computer game medium: "A videogame is a game which we play thanks to an audiovisual apparatus and which can be based on a story" (Esposito 2005a, 2). The audiovisual apparatus is the technical basis of the game: without it, it cannot take place and it determines its respective media constitution. As a result, the game is logically subject to specific changes when the technological foundations change. Compared to other, older media, where technological development takes place in much slower cycles, this is without a doubt a genuine characteristic of computer games.[1] There exists a constant pressure to outperform the technically possible; the user is caught in a treadmill of planned digital obsolescence of hardware manufacturers and platform sellers, which forces him to constantly adapt and keep pace with the developments of the medium.

Gaming Nostalgia Is Interconnected With the Technological Advancement of the Video Game Apparatus

The more the technological advancement accelerated, the stronger the forces that opposed it became. Svetlana Boym caught this mechanism in one sentence: "Progress didn't cure nostalgia, but exacerbated it" (Boym 2001, XIV). A problematic understanding of the concept of immersion fueled this development. Contrary to the active concept, as postulated by Jane Murray (1998), the game producers understood it primarily as a passive process of being taken prisoner by a world that is presented as credibly—and therefore as photorealistic—as possible (Rosenfelder 2008).

Therefore, the cycles between the individual epochs, i.e. the phases in which one console generation or a specific PC configuration is dominant and ruling the marked, became shorter and shorter, resulting in constant pressure on manufacturers to innovate and the need to upgrade even faster on the part of media recipients, if they do not want to lose track. On the one hand, this technological development has produced increasingly credible digital game worlds. On the other hand, however, it also caused a constant loss of users' "digital home." Every new epoch left the previous users who grew up with a system, gained formative experiences with it, and matured on it, homeless in some way: "Modern Nostalgia is a mourning for the impossibility of mythical return, for the loss of an enchanted world with clear borders and values" (Boym 2001, 8). The media nostalgic player longs for his "digital home," which was determined by a very specific media composition of the medium shaping him. At the same time, there is the fiction that this digital home could be visited again at any time, as long as a copy of the program code of any kind existed. But the medium of video games in particular is characterized by the constant loss of its earlier technical forms of manifestation—considered obsolete in retrospect in the respective current epoch (Lowood et al. 2009). It is almost impossible to experience older games in their original form after a certain epoch threshold, because the systems on which they were played simply no longer exist or have died due to technological detritus and/or old age. Although there is the possibility of forms of replication or emulation, the cultural heritage of digital culture is largely lost. Even an exact emulation of the original system can often not convey the same "game feeling" that the user remembers—or believes to remember (Payne 2008).

This is also due to the fact that the reception situation of games (Figure 2.1) is a special one: The gameplay takes place within a virtual realm, which is defined by the rules of the game, and in which the player acts with some sort of avatar—may it be a simple mouse cursor, a crosshair of an egoshooter or the elaborated character of a RPG. This virtual world, which takes place on

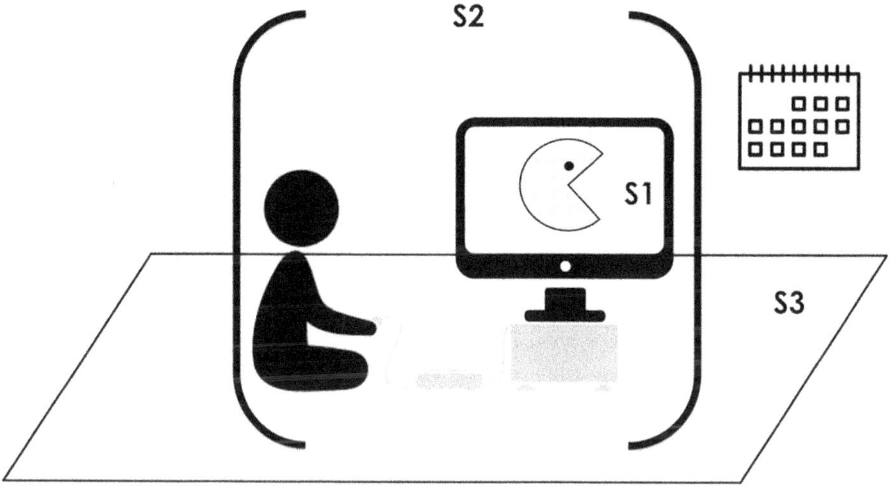

Figure 2.1: The typical reception situation of a video game[2] (own creation).

the screen and unfolds within the diegese of the game, can be labeled as S1. It is surrounded by the specific reception situation in which the player deals with the medium in a gameplay session provided by a specific technological audio-visual apparatus and which can be called S2,[3] enveloped by his every day's life and broader social context, S3, defined by his own individual situation, biography and age.

If Huizinga's theses concerning the *magic circle* were valid in their full depth (Huizinga 1955), S3—and to some lesser extend S2—would have no control over the player. But this is not the case: "We cannot say that games are magic circles, where ordinary rules of life do not apply [...]. Games are created through the act of gameplay, which contingents of acts by players. Those acts are always, already, contextual[4] and dynamic" (Consalvo 2009, 415–16). Thus the nostalgically minded player is denied a return in every respect, because it may be possible for him to restore the game (S1) under certain circumstances and despite the described difficulties, and even re-create the specific media dispositive (S2), but the context (S3) can no longer be restored in the remembered form, because: "We as players are different. We have changed, and the games themselves have helped us to change" (Fenty 2008, 22).

This is the important interconnection to the process of media-nostalgic transfiguration—the social integration of playing in an original context:

> When talking about certain play experiences, it often turns out that they are remembered in a context with other biographical experiences. [...] It was noticeable here that these memories often contain the detailed circumstances around

> the purchase of the first computer, for example the Commodore 64, and the played games. Detailed memories of dates and the friends with whom the games were played are also characteristic. (Herlyn and Meister 2009, 36)

Playing is therefore also a social phenomenon, especially in the early ages of gaming, because players did not occasionally deal with the medium alone, but often played in smaller groups or communities. One reason for this was the fact that the technology was too expensive to be purchased by one solely or that many games could be played in 2-player-mode on one device: "Many players report that they sat in front of a computer game together with several other people [...]. On the one hand, players watch each other while playing, on the other hand, they play with and against each other" (Butler 2007, 129). At the same time, the exchange of copied data carriers (floppy discs, datasette tapes, etc.) was very common among the early adopters of the home computers of the 80s. By sharing copied games and tools a self-perceived avant-garde of media users was formed, which represented a society with its own rules and defining "texts" (Bennahum 1998). The creative memory is not only about the game itself, the context, which was or is in effect by the creation and retrieval of memorial images, becomes important, too. This context is defined by S3 in connection to S2. Thus, with the first coinage by the respective media product, an experience emerges which is determined both by the conditions of the medium as such and by the entire dispositive (Debray 2002), and is supplemented by the social integration / context of the first-time recipient. The player can therefore not solemnly remember the feelings he had while playing and what moved him at this point of time earnestly but also always mixes the circumstances of the context to which he was subjected to (Williams 2006).

However, the nostalgia of the individual recipients or players of a particular epoch in the medium allows them to find themselves in a larger context: It generates a connection between the individual memories of a single player and the collective memory of an entire group of recipients. This in turn is determined by the composition of the medium: The players gain experience in dealing with the game on level S2, i.e. technical obstacles that need to be overcome, and experience the flow of the game itself in the concrete realization of the gameplay on level S1. Games are thus a collective medium that brings together entire groups of players, since the structure of the games is designed in such a way that different users share the same or very similar experiences:

> No matter how the characters may be designed, no matter how individually and profoundly crafted they may be with background history and cutscenes [...]. In

> the end, hundreds of thousands of people can slip into them without any problems. No trace of individuality, the heroic tale is only a lure to attract and engage an army of single players. (Mertens 2004, 285)

The media-nostalgic longing for the "classic" games of the past is therefore always longing for a common basis of identification, based on experiences that one has gathered individually, but from which one can assume that they are automatically shared by all other participants of the group, determined and ensured by the structure of the games.

Nostalgia and thus technology-related media nostalgia (Böhn 2010) as a subcategory is—according to Maurice Halbwachs's thesis of the sociogenesis of memory (Marcel and Mucchielli 2003)—a social phenomenon. It lives from the communicative exchange of recipients about events that can be shared. Through this, the respective group creates a specific group identity in which the individual can fit in. The feeling of a common, identity-creating past arises through the foundation texts that they share: "These resources mediate the commonly held experiences of its members, lending credence to a group's claims of collective identity" (Payne 2008, 53). At the same time, this group provides the framework for the different individually-shared memorial pictures, i.e. the way in which something can be remembered: "Remembrance that corresponds to the group's self-image and interests. Particular emphasis is placed on similarities and continuities that demonstrate that the group has remained the same. Participation in collective memory indicates that the remembering individual belongs to the group" (Erll 2005, 17). This has to be seen in connection with: "Memorial pictures are thus preserved by being 'inserted' into a broader frame of meaning. This frame has the status of a *fiction*. Remembering means giving meaning to experiences within a specific individual framework" (Assmann and Assmann 1994, 118).

The framework for remembering is the nostalgic return to earlier times as the basis of a common identity. The media-nostalgic users transfigure the experience already gained in and with the games (Salen and Zimmerman 2003, XIV). By doing so they hide the often unnerving technological problems, the sometimes frustratingly high level of difficulty and the mostly very simple game principles in their memorial pictures in favor of a transfigured, yearning recollection. This specific form of social interaction can be observed very nicely within the phenomenon of retrogaming if the definition of Petri Saarikosi is applied: "A general term for subcultures that appreciate old computer games. This phenomenon includes collecting old games and game devices as well as their active playing" (Suominen 2008).

Retro Gaming Players Are Longing for an Impossible Return and Try to Preserve Their Home

In a first, superficial investigation, three different fields of activity on the side of the media recipients can be distinguished for the media-nostalgic occupation with retro games—apart from the direct reception/replay of the games:

On the one hand, the aforementioned exchange of gained experiences and the associated comparison of individual experiences, which are synchronized and harmonized (freed of any disruptive or distortive elements) on a collective level (Halbwachs 1985). It is possible to observe here the—sometimes very heated—discussions in Internet forums about experiences had with certain games. Interesting here is the transfiguration of the simple game principles of the earlier days, the often-frustrating high degree of difficulty, the frequently occurring technical obstacles and the rather simple audiovisual presentation. Overcoming technical problems is therefore not an object of negative experiences, it is perceived in an absolute contrary way: overcoming these barriers and finally gaining access is rather portrayed in a heroic and transfigured way. This can be interpreted at this point as a kind of reference to "insider knowledge," which makes it possible to create a kind of micro-group on the Internet by jointly recalling the solution to these problems and overcoming the technological barriers to access. An excerpt from a forum may serve as an example for the almost typical discussion about the technological obstacles of the past that are now cast in a very positive light. The excerpt below deals with the specifications and knowledge needed by the players to run LucasArts' *TIE Fighter* on a computer with MS-DOS as an OS:

> >>Dies. Und NC (Norton Commander). Und so viele andere Sachen. Die
> >>Leute von heute wissen gar nicht, was wir schon alles für einen Spaß hatten.
>
> Himem.sys, emm386.exe, autoexec.bat, config.sys, DOS = HIGH, DEVICEHIGH und LOADHIGH ... das waren noch Zeiten, als man mit 640 kb Speicher hantieren und manuell zuweisen musste, um bestimmte Programme oder Spiele überhaupt zum Laufen zu bringen. Dagegen war es mir damals absolut schleierhaft, wie zur Hölle man jemals eine gigantische Festplattenkapazität von 21 Megabytes füllen können sollte.

The above shown excerpt can be roughly translated like this:

> >>This. And NC (Norton Commander). And so many other things. Today's
> >>people don't even know what fun we've had.
>
> Himem.sys, emm386.exe, autoexec.bat, config.sys, DOS = HIGH, DEVICEHIGH and LOADHIGH ... those were the days when you had to handle 640 kb of memory and assign it manually to get certain programs or games running at all.

> On the other hand, it was absolutely incomprehensible to me how the hell you could ever fill a gigantic hard disk capacity of 21 megabytes. (Source: https://www.gamestar.de/xenforo/threads/tie-fighter.126823/page-2, last accessed on 14th of May 2018)

On the other hand, the retro gamer scene is characterized by a strong impulse to preserve and to port games and game content by the users themselves to other and mostly new platforms and systems: "Most significant, though, is the sense of custodianship that is coming from the field of digital media itself" (Slovin 2001, 152). These efforts are often completely independent from the original media producers and are implemented in small user groups. Slovin sees also a strong nostalgic influence on users influenced by the medium as the driving force for these efforts to preserve original game systems and content. Private initiatives such as RetroGames e.V. and the MAME project, but also the Computerspielemuseum in Berlin, could be seen as concrete expressions of this conservation impulse, which have made it their task to preserve outdated games—measured by the current state-of-the-art—and to transfer them—at least partially—to new systems. An example of the latter is the fan-made development of scummVM, which allows classic LucasArts adventures to be played on current systems without any problems.

One can consider the attempt of restaging experiences already had as a third occupation with nostalgia. These restaging of experiences include fan efforts in the field of retro remakes or total conversions of current titles in the guise of an earlier game. A retro remake is a computer game that is a new staging of the original, which does not take into account the technological advancement of the medium, but rather reproduces the game with modern means in its almost original appearance and enriches it with new contents. The game principle (Game Mechanics / Rule Set) and control system remain untouched. Thus this examination of the original material contradicts both the general line of advancement of the medium and the concept of remake itself (Felzmann 2010, 2012).

For the practice of the retro remake, the term *Formzitat* (which could be loosely translated as "quotation of forms") could be applied, which Andreas Böhn shaped in relation to textual imitation strategies and intertextual phenomena. The newer media product, thus, always refers to the possible predecessor(s) through the chosen form with its specific distinctive features: "Through the strategy of the intermediary quotation of forms, conveyed through the form of the quotation's context and through the cited form, the corresponding media are shown in their differences" (Böhn 2003, 7). Of course, it must be said that the remake does not overcome any intermedia boundaries, since it is still a computer game. However, technical progress has led to further development of the medium itself. It has therefore created new possibilities in the creation of specific products, so that one can almost speak of different media. Thus, the retro remake is caught between the restorative and reflective nostalgia in Svetlana Boym's diction (Boym 2001, 41): On the one hand, an attempt is made to restore the original home, thus placing the emphasis on the restorative moment. At the same time, however, the power of the reference is emphasized and the passed time between the original and the remake, including the social and cultural changes associated with it, is clearly mentioned and made evident. Retro remakes are often written by interested and talented laymen, media users who have been socialized with computer games and who have experienced their advancement in connection with their own biography. The users themselves create a media product that tackles and reflects their nostalgic longing at the same time.[5] The same applies to total conversions, which represent a transfer of old game content—the aesthetics, the rule system and the story with its narratives—into the guise of a new game. The current title thus becomes the host to which the old is grafted parasitically. This often happens out of the desire to make games that are no longer executable on the current systems in their prior form due to technological limitations available again.

The Industry Answers With Old Games in Re-usage and New Games That Feel Somehow Old

By switching perspective from the user scene to the side of the media producers in the investigation of the retro phenomenon, one can observe two main strategies by which the industry reacts to the sensitivities of the users: Republishing and recycling on the one hand, retro (re-)development on the other.

Bundling titles that are already published in a kind of recycling effort is not a specific novelty of the current retro boom. Rather, this has been common practice since the first game consoles in the 1970s and 1980s (Swalwell 2007). More profitable than a pure re-usage of already known contents and forms (e.g. compilations of major series or titles), however, is a remediated recreation (Bolter and Grusin 2000), a conscious design and creation of new games that refer to the prior state of the media dispositive, but carry within them the chance to provide the player with new experiences. This avoids the nostalgic disappointment that inevitably comes to the recipient, who hopes to be able to perceive old titles in exactly the way that he has in mind in his transfigured memory: "In this sense, the nostalgia felt for video games is not nostalgia for a past state before the trauma of the games disrupted us, but a desire to recapture that mind-altering experience of being in a game for the first time. It is a yearning for liminality itself—for the moment of transition"[6] (Fenty 2008, 23).

But this liminality, the longing for the feeling of transition, the moment of the first contact and original experience and—at the same time—the sought formative contact can no longer be achieved. Users grow by and with the media they use. They acquire new knowledge and new experiences and thus also change the already mentioned spaces S2 and S3, i.e. both the specific reception situation and the surrounding context of the reality of one's every-day-life. In this respect, a return to the old place is only possible at the price of a deep disappointment.

To avoid this disappointment and the moment of transition into something unknown at the same point of time, it is necessary to create something new, to offer the players new experiences that they had not or cannot have made yet in this way. This can only be achieved by creating new retro games that were previously unavailable in their specific form. This is achieved through the quotation of forms: It produces a computer game that refers in its media composition to an earlier state of the medium. The game is, for example, in a certain tensely relationship to the current state of the disposition within which it appears anew. It is a new (and never before published) title, but it feels somehow familiar and retro. This feeling of ambivalence is created by recourse to earlier forms of mediality in contrast to the current state of the art. In its otherness, the new retro game thus becomes a pointer onto the former state and constitution of the dispositive.

But which elements of the medium video game can now be or become nostalgically transfigured or designed in such a way that they appear as a memorial pointer to a prior reception context? Nicolas Esposito's definition attempt, as already mentioned, helps here once again: "A videogame is a game which we play thanks to an audiovisual apparatus and which can be based on a story" (Esposito 2005a, 2). The key words here are *game*, *play*, *audiovisual apparatus* and *story*—each one of them is an important constituent and therefore a defining element for the specific disposition of a specific game. For a more detailed investigation, it is useful to transform Esposito's definition into a triadic schema with the cornerstones aesthetics, narration and game mechanics, that captures the powerful expressive sides of the pluri-medial super-sign computer game (Figure 2.2). These sides of expression of the games are therefore:

1. the aesthetic design, i.e. the specific audio-visual composition of the game in relation to the game itself, the packaging and the enclosed material;

2. the game mechanics constituted by the specific rule set in terms of ambition and complexity as well as game principle and mode of operation; this also includes the genre within which the game is positioned;
3. the story underlying the game, i.e. the plot that is conveyed within the game and the design of the narrative structures and the fictional universe.

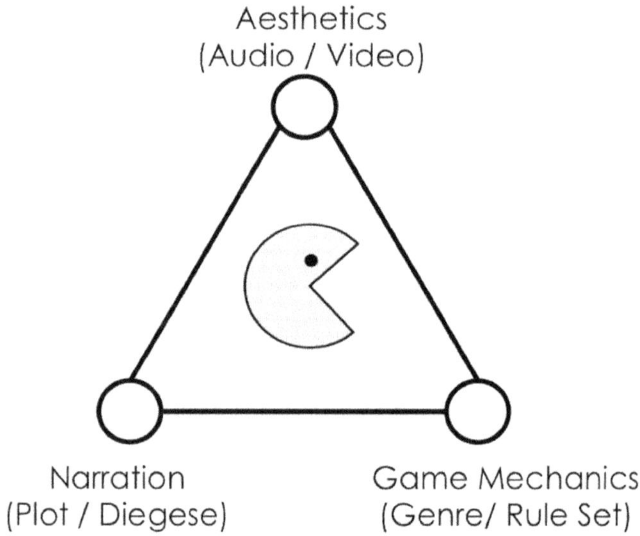

Figure 2.2: The expressive sides of the "super sign" video game, based on Esposito's definition (Esposito 2005a) and integrating several aspects of the MDA framework (Hunicke, LeBlanc, and Zubek 2004) (own creation).

For the reproduction of these elements, however, it is important that the source texts to which reference is made are known and shared by the recipients; otherwise it is not possible to see it in contrast to its origin and the nostalgic addressing fails. It is therefore to be assumed that only those games serve as foundation texts whose relevance is declared by consent, as one can thus rely on the broadest possible basis of foundation texts. In other words, it is imperative that there is a canon of high-quality and well-known games that can be referred to in the creation of new "old" games. A superficial observation of the current titles can already establish a conscious re-medialization or retro design trend and finds a popular example for each side of expression of the super sign.

Quotation of Forms I: Mega Man 9 (Aesthetics)

Here one can observe the adoption of a specific aesthetic, which was influential in its distribution for a specific period or epoch in the history of the game. This is expressed, for example, in a lower screen resolution, a reduced color depth and a more minimalist sound than current technical possibilities provide, in order to refer to the 8-bit era of early consoles and home computer systems. The technological constitution thus becomes a marker in connection with the biography of the user. The current titles of the *Mega Man*-series (esp. 9 and 10) are concise examples of this. Their aesthetics and cover artworks (Gogolin 2004) are not state-of-the-art of the current technological development but rather show the typical visual design of the late 1980s. Nevertheless, they are titles from 2008 and 2010 for Nintendo's Wii, Microsoft's Xbox 360 and Sony's Playstation 3, but the way the titles are presented remains dramatically below the possibilities of these consoles—the Retro Remake successfully recreates the original aesthetic of the prior game in a new title. The developers made this decision deliberately, because the game "is for the people who played it back then. Now they're older, of course, but this game is for them. We hope they can remember the fun they had when they played it in their childhood, and that by playing it now, they recall that, and it's still just as fun to them" (Nutt 2010).

They wanted to address exactly that nostalgic vein of the users already socialized at a prior point of their individual gamer biography with the game. At the same time, the self-chosen limitation in the way of presentation was also an artistic decision with which one hoped to stand out from other titles: "It's another type of creative expression, because nowadays, everyone wants surround sound and 3D graphics and things like that, and they get too caught up in that" (Ibid.). Thus, the retro reference also represents a new possibility of escaping the constant overbidding gesture of the games and created a unique selling point.

Quotation of Forms II: Bionic Commando Rearmed (Game Mechanics)

Current retro games can also take up a genre that has already been out of fashion or adopt its control system. In the field of computer games, the realization of the underlying set of rules is understood as a genre. Because in the design of the underlying rules, which make a game such in the first place and which structure the process similar to the program code, the games are strongly influenced by technological development. What is feasible regulates what is done. With the expanded possibilities of the medium, caused by technological development, new forms arise which exploit these possibilities to the disadvantage of older genres, which are slowly being disregarded or completely forgotten (Costikyan 2005; Montfort and Bogost 2009).

Bionic Commando Rearmed is a good example of a reappearance of an already known but no longer popular game principle. On the level of the control system and the game mechanics, this is a skillful reproduction of the original from 1987, but combines this (while retaining the original 2D gameplay of the Run 'n' Gun) with an updated graphics that, although hinting at a three-dimensional depth, merely makes usage of the full potential of modern 3D engines. Ironically, this actually quite simple game[7] received a much better metascore (86 points) than the actual triple-A remake of *Bionic Commando* from 2009 (69 points). The triple-A remake tried to attract attention mainly through a complete three-dimensional world and a state-of-the-art game engine—but failed to supply the player with an engaging gameplay and did not use any references to the original game from the 80s.

Quotation of Forms III: Monkey Islands 2 HD (Narration)

Monkey Islands 2 Special Edition from LucasArts presents a remake that is in its form close to the mechanisms of the already mentioned retro remake. Here the game was upgraded with a slightly modernized version of the graphics engine and thus made available on current systems and consoles. However, the plot itself has not undergone any changes. Although this is not really a peculiarity, the genre of the adventure game lives from the tricky stories that, similar to the genre of RPGs, motivate the recipient to deal with it. So the question arises: Why is the same story told here with the same figures in an almost identical, only better and cleaner resolution, graphic presentation? With this design decision LucasArts tried to attract players who have never been in contact with the fictional pirate world before as well as those who already played the 19-year-old predecessor title.

The latter are addressed with a specific build-in feature that—in contrast to the technical design and thus artistic decision in *Mega Man 9*—is not based on a conscious commitment to a reduced appearance: The player can switch between the current presentation with high-resolution images and smooth animations and the original presentation with its coarsely pixelated shape at any time during the game. Here the reference to the past is consciously designed as such in order to bring the game on the level of graphics into a connection line with its predecessor and to use it in its outdated appearance as a nostalgic pointer to the earlier reception context of the players. The difference between the two modes of representation is shown to the player and, in connection with technological progress, the elapsed time is also made evident.

At the same time, however, one is not necessarily dependent on them. Rather, it is possible to enjoy the game in its new form without being disappointed in its nostalgia. LucasArts produced a hybrid product that stands between classic remake and retro remake and not only defines itself through nostalgic references but also brings something new in the form of presentation while delivering something familiar in its content at the same time.

Further Nostalgia-Fuelling Methods of Game Design and Production Are Already Emerging

In addition to these concrete realizations of individual aspects in the form of the remake and the retro remake, hybrid forms can also be observed, which engage in a constructive play with the expressive sides of the game and the references to earlier forms of manifestation. Benjamin Beil distinguishes here between *integration*, *combination* and *transformation* (Beil 2013).

The *integrative form* uses an integration of different elements, which, form a unique form—the contrast arises through the ambivalence between the surrounding game and the stored retro elements, an approach that has also been used in the form of many Easter Eggs in well-known game series and is therefore not really new. The *Super Adventure Box*, an add-on for Guild Wars 2, which was designed in a specific 8-bit style, is a perfect example for the integrative form. The add-on comprised 4 zones and could be only entered through the main game, keeping the original gameplay whilst adjusting the user interface and the presentation to the before mentioned 8 bit-style.

The *combinatorial form*, in turn, seeks a connection of disparate elements—the contrast is permanently present to the player, since the various media forms stand directly next to each other and are presented together. It thus shows clearly stronger media breaks than the integrative form and is thus also much more obvious in its referential character to the mediality of the games. This effect can be witnessed in *Super Paper Mario*, which combines 2D- and 3D elements and allows the player to switch the view by 90° steps.

The *transformative form*, on the other hand, realizes an extension of the possibilities: The media composition, which is used in the presentation and usually refers back to an earlier form, has an impact on the control mechanics or the gameplay of the game. The nostalgic references and/or the interactions with it changes and/or establishes new possibilities to play and new rule sets. An example can be found in *3D Dot Game Heroes*. The graphic presentation, which strongly resembles the *Zelda* franchise, is a three-dimensional one, but the individual elements are composed of square basic polygons, giving the impression that it is an originally 8-bit graphic, which has only been expanded into the third dimension.

The individual blocks that make up the world look like oversized pixels—a strong reference not only to *Minecraft* but also to the voxel-technology that was discontinued in its development almost 15 years ago. At the same time, this nostalgic look also has a massive impact on the gameplay: For example, the length of his sword determines the strength of the protagonist's attack. During the course of the game, the player has the opportunity to have new pixels forged on his sword by a blocksmith and by doing so to increase his power. Thus, the chosen presentation method also determines the rule set and thus the realized gameplay.

Conclusion

An initial overview of media-nostalgia in the field of computer games has shown that this phenomenon is now abundantly represented both on the part of the recipients and on the part of the producers. However, while the users are initially looking for a return to the already-known, which provides them with a familiar basis of identification for defining their own self within a modern age marked by constant and rapid change, the manufacturers often act differently. For them, nostalgia serves as a tool either to resell content already created or to give their products an emotional unique selling point beyond the hardware hype and thus generate revenues. As a by-product of both efforts, a kind of canon can be derived by observing the preserved games thematized in the nostalgic acts that shaped the users at specific times. Another study of this could finally provide an answer to the question of what makes a game a classic that is still part of players' cultural memory far beyond its life cycle—which is assumed to last at least 18 to 24 months (Swalwell 2007).

Notes

1. Here we should refer to the more than 100 years of history of the film. Video games, on the other hand, took just under 40 years to develop into their current form (Kent 2001).
2. This schematic is a detail-reduced derivation of Frans Mäyrä's Contextual Game Experience Model (Mäyrä 2007).
3. How important this Space S2 can be for the game experience is shown in the research work of Nicolas Esposito (2005b), who tries to preserve specific reception situations of the game experience.

4. The importance of the game's context is also shown by J. C. Herz's observations during a review of the exhibition Hot Circuits at the American Museum of the Moving Image (AMMA) in 1989 (Herz 1997) and the experiences of the exhibition curator Rochelle Slovin (Slovin 2001).
5. See Postigo (2007) for more details on the convergence between recipients and producers in the fan programmer scene.
6. Gerrit Herlyn and Helle Meister also refer to the special significance of the first moment in their observation of the bibliographic influence of computer games (Herlyn and Meister 2009).
7. Here the problem arises that a recourse to an earlier and often simpler game principle could theoretically not only produce a retro game, but also simply a casual game. These are generally determined by lower demands on the recipient (Pearce 2008).

References

Assmann, Aleida, and Jan Assmann. 1994. "Das Gestern Im Heute. Medien Und Soziales Gedächtnis." In *Die Wirklichkeit Der Medien. Eine Einführung in Die Kommunikationswissenschaft*, edited by Klaus Merten, Siegfried J Schmidt, and Siegfried Weichsenberg, 114–40. Wiesbaden: Springer Fachmedien Wiesbaden.

Beil, Benjamin. 2013. "Die Sehnsucht Nach Dem Pixelklumpen Retro-Gaming Und Das Populärkulturelle Gedächtnis Des Computerspiels." In *Performativität Und Medialität Populärer Kulturen*, edited by Marcus S Kleiner and Thomas Wilke, 319–36. Wiesbaden: Springer Fachmedien Wiesbaden. doi:10.1007/978-3-531-19023-5_14.

Bennahum, David. 1998. *Extra Life: Coming of Age in Cyberspace*. New York: Basic Books.

Böhn, Andreas. 2003. "Intra- Und Intermediales Formzitat Im Film Als Medienreflexion." In *Formzitat Und Intermedialität*, edited by Andreas Böhn, 13–44. St. Ingbert: Röhring Universitätsverlag.

———. 2010. "Mediennostalgie Als Techniknostalgie." In *Techniknostalgie Und Retrotechnologie. Karlsruher Studien Technik Und Kultur Band 2*, edited by Andreas Böhn and Kurt Möser, 149–66. Karlsruhe: KIT Scientific Publishing.

Bolter, Jay D., and Richard Grusin. 2000. *Remediation: Understanding New Media*. Cambridge: The MIT Press.

Boym, Svetlana. 2001. *The Future of Nostalgia*. New York: Basic Books.

Butler, Mark. 2007. *Would You Like to Play a Game? Die Kultur Des Computerspielens*. Berlin: Kadmos.

Consalvo, Mia. 2009. "There Is No Magic Circle." *Games and Culture* 4 (4): 408–17. doi:10.1177/1555412009343575.

Costikyan, Greg. 2005. "Game Styles, Innovation, and New Audiences: An Historical View." In *Changing Views: Words in Play. Proceedings of DiGRA 2005 Conference*. Tampere: DiGRA.

Debray, Regis. 2002. "Für Eine Mediologie." In *Kursbuch Medienkultur. Die Maßgeblichen Theorien von Brecht Bis Baudrillard*, edited by Claus Pias, Lorenz Engell, Oliver Fahle, Joseph Vogl, and Britta Neitzel, 67–72. Stuttgart: DVA.

Erll, Astrid. 2005. *Kollektives Gedächtnis Und Erinnerungskulturen. Eine Einführung.* Stuttgart / Weimar: Metzler.

Esposito, Nicolas. 2005a. "A Short and Simple Definition of What a Videogame Is." In *Changing Views: Words in Play. Proceedings of DiGRA 2005 Conference.* Tampere: DiGRA.

———. 2005b. "Immersion in Game Atmospheres for the Video Game Heritage Preservation." In *Changing Views: Words in Play. Proceedings of DiGRA 2005 Conference.* Tampere: DiGRA.

Felzmann, Sebastian. 2010. "Playing Yesterday: Mediennostalgie Und Videospiele." In *Techniknostalgie Und Retrotechnologie. Karlsruher Studien Technik Und Kultur Band 2*, edited by Andreas Böhn and Kurt Möser, 197–215. Karlsruhe: KIT Scientific Press.

———. 2012. *Playing Yesterday: Mediennostalgie Im Computerspiel.* Boizenburg: vwh Verlag.

Fenty, Sean. 2008. "Why Old School Is 'Cool'. A Brief Analysis of Classiv Video Gaming Nostalgia." In *Playing the Past. History and Nostalgia in Video Games*, edited by Zach Whalen and Laurie N Taylor, 19–31. Nashville: Vanderbilt University Press.

Gogolin, Heiko. 2004. "Wenn Weniger Mehr Ist." *GEE - Game Entertainment Education* 2 (8): 64–68.

Halbwachs, Maurice. 1985. *Das Gedächtnis Und Seine Sozialen Bedingungen. Forschung.* Vol. 538. Suhrkamp: Suhrkamp-Taschenbuch Wissenschaft.

Herlyn, Gerrit, and Helle Meister. 2009. "Notes on the Biographical Meaning of Games and Online-Games." *Eludamos. Journal for Computer Game Culture* 3 (1): 33–41.

Herz, J. C. 1997. *Joystick Nation: How Videogames Ate Our Quarters, Won Our Hearts, and Rewired Our Minds.* Boston/New York/Toronto/London: Little, Brown & Company.

Huizinga, Johan. 1955. *Homo Ludens: A Study of the Play-Element in Culture.* Boston: Beacon. doi:10.1007/BF02382925.

Hunicke, Robin, Marc LeBlanc, and Robert Zubek. 2004. "MDA: A Formal Approach to Game Design and Game Research." *Workshop on Challenges in Game AI* 44 (8): 1–4. doi: 10.1.1.79.4561.

Kent, Steven L. 2001. *The Ultimate History of Video Games: From Pong to Pokemon—The Story Behind the Craze That Touched Our Lives and Changed the World.* New York: Three Rivers Press.

Lowood, Henry, Andrew Armstrong, Devin Monnens, Zach Vowell, L. Judd Ruggil, Ken McAllister, Rachel Donahue, and Dan Pinchbeck. 2009. "Before It's Too Late: Preserving Games across the Industry/Academia Divide." In *Breaking New Ground: Innovation in Games, Play, Practice and Theory. Proceedings of DiGRA 2009 Conference.* Tampere: DiGRA.

Marcel, Jean-Christophe, and Laurent Mucchielli. 2003. "Eine Grundlage Des Lien Social. Das Kollektive Gedächtnis Nach Maurice Halbwachs." In *Maurice Halbwachs – Aspekte Des Werks*, edited by Stephan Egger, 191–228. Konstanz: UVK.

Mäyrä, Frans. 2007. "The Contextual Game Experience: On the Socio-Cultural Contexts for Meaning in Digital Play." In *Situated Play, Proceedings of DiGRA 2007 Conference*, 810–14. Tampere: DiGRA.

Mertens, Mathias. 2004. "Computerspiele Sind Nicht Interaktiv." In *Interaktivität. Ein Interdisziplinärer Schlüsselbegriff*, edited by Christoph Bieber and Claus Leggewie, 272–88. Frankfurt/New York: Campus.

Montfort, Nick, and Ian Bogost. 2009. "Random and Raster: Display Technologies and the Development of Videogames." *IEEE Annals of the History of Computing* 31 (3). IEEE Educational Activities Department: 34–43.

Murray, Janet Horowitz. 1998. *Hamlet on the Holodeck: The Future of Narrative in Cyberspace*. Cambridge: The MIT Press.

Nutt, Christian. 2010. "He Is 8-Bit: Capcom's Hironobu Takeshita Speaks." *Gamasutra: The Art & Business of Making Games*. http://www.gamasutra.com/view/feature/3752/he_is_8bit_capcoms_hironobu_.php?print=1.

Payne, Thomas. 2008. "Playing the Deja-New. 'Plug It in and Play TV Games' and the Cultural Politics of Classic Gaming." In *Playing the Past. History and Nostalgia in Video Games*, edited by Z Whalen and L N Taylor, 51–68. Nashville: Vanderbilt University Press.

Pearce, Celia. 2008. "The Truth About Baby Boomer Gamers: A Study of Over-Forty Computer Game Players." *Games and Culture* 3 (2): 142–74. doi:10.1177/1555412008314132.

Postigo, H. 2007. "Of Mods and Modders: Chasing Down the Value of Fan-Based Digital Game Modifications." *Games and Culture* 2 (4): 300–13. doi:10.1177/1555412007307955.

Rosenfelder, Andreas. 2008. *Digitale Paradise. Von Der Schrecklichen Schönheit Der Computerspiele*. Köln: Kiepenheuer & Witsch.

Salen, Katie, and Eric Zimmerman. 2003. *Rules of Play: Game Design Fundamentals*. Cambridge: The MIT Press.

Slovin, Rochelle. 2001. "Hot Circuits. Reflections on the 1989 Video Game Exhibition of the American Museum of the Moving Image." In *The Medium of the Video Game*, edited by Mark P. Wolfe, 137–54. Austin: University of Texas Press.

Suominen, Jaakko. 2008. "The Past as the Future? Nostalgia and Retrogaming in Digital Culture." *Fibreculture* 11 (September): 1–13.

Swalwell, Melanie. 2007. "The Remembering and the Forgetting of Early Digital Games: From Novelty to Detritus and Back Again." *Journal of Visual Culture* 6 (2): 255–73. doi:10.1177/1470412907078568.

Williams, Dmitri. 2006. "Why Game Studies Now? Gamers Don't Bowl Alone." *Games and Culture* 1 (1): 13–16. doi:10.1177/1555412005281774.

Mentioned Games

3D Dot Game Heroes (Silicon Studio 2009)
Bionic Commando (Capcom 1987)
Bionic Commando Rearmed (GRIN 2008)
Bionic Commando (GRIN 2009)
Guild Wars 2 (ArenaNet 2012)
Mega Man 1 (Capcom 1988)
Mega Man 9 (Inti Creates, Capcom 2009)
Mega Man 10 (Inti Creates, Capcom 2010)
Monkey Island 2: LeChuck's Revenge (LucasArts 1991)
Monkey Island 2: LeChuck's Revenge Special Edition (LucasArts 2010)
Super Paper Mario (Intelligent Systems, Nintendo Software Planning & Development 2007)

3. *Lego Historical War Sub-Cultures: Idealized Play and Nostalgia*

Jonathan M. Bullinger

Introduction

Digital interactive environments are fertile areas to raise new questions about the experience of nostalgia. Particularly as these simulations become more familiar, and thus, more convincing to users. However, there is a unique analog both resilient to such digital overtures and one that is also fertile ground for questions of nostalgia: the eighty-six-year-old Danish toy manufacturer, The Lego Group. Specifically, one aspect of human society the company has chosen never to replicate for play: nation-based warfare. As outlined below, interactive nostalgic longing occurs within Lego war toy fan communities at three different levels. I draw upon established academic theory and research on nostalgia, toy soldiers, and Lego's system of play to illustrate it.

Play is free, ordered, but not ordinary, life (Huizinga 1980). First, Lego's construction bricks are an organized system of play that provides materials during the idealized childhood to imagine through, and create from. Lego invokes a longing for a type of childhood that may never have existed. A childhood spent constructing an idealized communal future. Second, the larger adult collector market (Adult Fans of Lego or AFOL) for both official Lego products, and the sizeable second-hand customizer Lego market, indulges nostalgia for this individual romanticized childhood. The third level of nostalgia is to look at World War II as the last "ludic" war (Campbell 2008). All three of these levels (Lego's idealized childhood, the individual's romanticized better time, and WWII as the last ludic war) are wrapped in a transgenerational container understanding of nostalgia as encouraged, available, and economically rewarding (Lizardi 2017).

This chapter presents research on the Lego customizer collector groups who fill a space not provided officially by Lego's idealized construction of childhood and imagination preparation for future and past aspects of our culture (e.g. "Town," "City," and historical imagination, "Castle"). This is to better understand the intersection between toys on one side, simulating universal humanism, community, and constructive imagination and on the other side, the long legacy of war toys and weapon fetishization, with trans-generational nostalgia for both acting as a bridge.

Literature Review

Nostalgia

The twentieth century began with utopia, but it concluded with nostalgia, as optimism fell out of fashion while nostalgia always remained in vogue, according to Harvard comparative literatures scholar Svetlana Boym (2007). The past, and our nostalgia for it, is comforting. The past is familiar, it can reaffirm and validate, provide us both guidance and identities, and particularly through nostalgia, an escape mechanism from the present when we require one (Papageorgiou 2015, 478). Often these escapes feel pressing because great change has occurred, or as Boym states "outbreaks of nostalgia often follow revolutions" (2007, 10). Historian David Lowenthal hints at nostalgia's perceived utility when he explains the lure of the past: "we crave evidence that the past endures in recoverable form. Some agency, some mechanism, some faith will enable us not just to know it, but to see and feel it" (1985, 14). For example, Duyvendak (2011) shows how the rise of populist politicians and their discourse of nostalgic sentiment in both the U.S. and Western Europe are both tied to fear of losing homes or a homeland.

However, contemporary scholarship evolves nostalgia's definition, understanding it to possess multiple longings with numerous cognitive and emotional investments behind each nostalgic desire (Berliner 2012, Angé and Berliner 2015). Nostalgia, rather than a "debilitating imposition upon our consciousness of the past" (Atia and Davies 2010, 181), possesses a complicating critical potentiality (Glazer 2005, Kalinina 2017), particularly through material culture (Cashman 2006) and temporal associations (May 2016).

We want what we cannot possess; and we know we cannot truly go home again. The reason for this is because we mistake nostalgia for a place, when really it is for a time, "the time of our childhood, the slower rhythms of our dreams" (Boym 2007, 8). This craving or desire was originally a pain or longing due to a physical displacement from one's homeland. Swiss medical student, Johannes Hofer, first used the term in his 1688 dissertation. At the time this medical condition was believed to be curable. Afterwards, the meaning of nostalgia continued to evolve. From this pain from physical displacement noted as a medical ailment, it transformed to a disease of the mind, and then eventually to a personal psychological phenomenon (Sprengler 2009, 11). Modernity, industrialization, and urbanization acted as strong stimuli for the evocation of nostalgia due to the anxieties it produced. Historian Gary Cross (2015) specifies consumed nostalgia as a reaction to latter twentieth-century personal experience of living within fast capitalism. For Cross, identity is formed, and nostalgically reaffirmed, in this fast context, through the purchase of specific goods. More generally, for nostalgia to work, the observer must forget certain historical contradictions. Our imperfect memories and raw desires idealize the past; it is one imagined for the most part, rather than actually experienced.

For our purposes regarding war, toy soldiers, and Lego's unique play and brand identity, it is the restorative form of nostalgia that possesses interesting consequences because it often confuses a real home with a romanticized or imaginary one. Many young men throughout military history have given their lives for these romanticized homelands. Furthermore, as historical enthusiasts, we can be unreflexively nostalgic for those misinformed crusades and fictitious motherlands. Boym expresses this tragic sentiment beautifully when she writes "unreflective nostalgia can breed monsters" (2007, 9).

However, today, digital interactive communicative media, and social media in particular, has allowed nostalgic communities to find one another and share artifacts from a particularly beloved era. In the common vernacular, we often hear of "vintage", "retroists", "classic", "'90s kid", etc. It possesses a meaning beyond just fashion, an ephemeral trend, or blatant money-grab. The interplay of nostalgia and memory can be seen as helping to maintain one's identity (Wilson 2005), and increasingly psychological studies of nostalgia view it as a constructive personal psychological state, rather than a destructive one (Tierney 2013). For many young men, early vicarious identity experimentation is conducted through some form of toy soldier.

Toy Soldiers

Author and lecturer, Daniel J. Foley, writes in the opening to his book *Toys Through the Ages* that collectively, toys "tell the story of civilization in miniature" (1962, 1). That sentiment still rings true today, and the company that best exemplifies it, Lego, began its contemporary form around the same time as Foley's words. Children enact their desire to imitate their worlds through toys; objects whose nature are, as British author Antonia Fraser described, "compounded of pleasure, fantasy and imitation" (1966, 8). Here, I use nostalgia as an entry point for pleasure and fantasy within toys for the adult enthusiast.

For many adult enthusiasts, toys represent "the nostalgic charm of childhood" (Fraser 1966, 11), a recreational escape, or brief illusions of control over that "civilization in miniature" Foley referenced. This embracement of toys by both child and adults is *not* a new phenomenon. The transition from only military men and nobles commissioning toy soldiers, to post-World War II, lifetime mass media fan markets indulging in nostalgic war, *is* new.

This blurred line between adult and child enthusiast began from "prehistory to at least the late eighteenth century" (Fleming 1996, 81). Media critic and author, Ed Halter (2006, 5) notes "As long as humans have waged war, they have also played it" and quotes play theorist Huizinga who wrote "Ever since words existed for fighting and playing, men have been wont to call war a game" (2006, 95). Horses and warriors, created as either souvenirs or toys have been found during excavations and dated to both Ancient Greece and Rome (Foley 1962, 62–63). During medieval times, children would play with wooden mounted knights. Author of American collectibles and antiquities, William C. Ketchum Jr., writes one of the appeals of the military miniature is their "exactness of detail and dress" (1981, 85).

Frederick the Great's rule as King of Prussia (1740–1786) captured the public's imagination. His exploits in war set off the introduction of *tin* soldiers in Nuremberg beginning in 1760. Toy soldiers constructed from tin, rather than more expensive materials, allowed for their mass embracement by children. The creation is credited to Nuremberg craftsman, Johann Gottfried Hilpert. Daniel J. Foley notes this mass embracement (1760) turned to mass popularity of the tin soldier, lasting nearly two hundred years. No longer just royals commissioning toy soldier sets, the everyday man and child could strategize a sanitized version of war. During this time, ultimately metal would give way to plastic in the post-WWII toy soldier market.

Beginning with these "little green Army men" (early 1950s to present) and continuing through G. I. Joe (1964–1976) "action figures" (NOT dolls) with Kung Fu grip, and on to the 3 ¾ inch scale G. I. Joes (1982–1994) of my own 1980s Reagan/Rambo/*Top Gun* (1986) militarized childhood, plastic soldiers were truly the troop replacements for the tin warriors begun way back in Nuremberg. This same post-World War II market of plastic toys for children symbolized by little green soldiers, also birthed the modern form of Lego so easily recognized today.

Lego

It feels silly to "introduce" Lego due to its near ubiquity in our culture. Nonetheless, the Danish company, began by Ole Kirk Christiansen began building wooden toys in 1932. The company name "Lego" is a contraction of the Danish phrase "leg godt" (play well). Due to the affordability of plastic injection molding machines, toy companies began switching from metal and wooden toys to plastic. By the late 1940s, Lego followed suit, in conjunction with developing their "system" of interlocking construction bricks. The branding, plastic production process, design of the brick, and embracement of selling a "system" evolved during the 1950s and was in place by the early 1960s (Lipkowitz 2009, 17–21).

This chapter really couldn't be written about another toy. Lego was, and is, unique as both a toy and a brand. I will briefly outline five areas that support this assertion. Even though their competition has increased since the last of Lego's original brick patents expired back in 1989, Lego still sets itself apart since its toys are a legacy system. Lego bricks bought today, theoretically, should link together with bricks from 1958, 1968, 1978, etc. This rewards buyer investment—the more you buy, whenever you buy, the more you can build. Additionally, this legacy system also helps to support lifetime fandom, transgenerational fandom and nostalgia (parents teaching and playing with their children with Lego).

Second, through their January 28, 1958 patent (Lipkowitz 2009, 21) for their interlocking principle, quality control, and corporate brand identity, Lego has established its uniqueness within the toy industry. Yes, their competitors (such as K'Nex, Kre-O, and Mega Bloks) use a similar design principle, but they lack both the quality and legacy within their systems. Their corporate brand identity—still in place but slightly challenged due to increased licensing and vocal online audience feedback—is supported by the inherent creativity and positivity that comes from the act of building. This leads into my third point—it was, and for the *most* part, still is, a toy not about destroying (e.g. toy guns, toy grenades, tanks) but rather about using a child's imagination to construct anything.

While not all products of a child's imagination are altruistic, Lego's original "system" offering (1955s Town Plan) was built around communal or civic construction (Lipkowitz 2009, 18). The idea of building better communities, or at least a miniature, idealized version of an existing one, is one of the cornerstones of Lego's unique brand foundation. This type of play comprises my fourth point, that this system encourages play between parent and child together (Fraser 1966, 234). Finally, more recently, Lego construction systems offer both pre-established licensed themes and the ability to show off your own creativity. While building to pre-established narratives (Fleming 1996) can be problematic, the inherent customization of Lego mitigates this slightly.

When Lego transitioned from wooden to plastic systematic construction toys, it created a uniqueness both in toy and brand. Its unique attributes include working as a legacy system, the inherent creativity and positivity of building toys, their focus on Town-based themes advocating for civic engagement, and the mini-figure as focal point for a child's play of imitation. Both Lego as legacy system and building as civic engagement buttress transgenerational play between parents and children. These attributes help to construct the idealized childhood Lego sells, in part, through its inherent project of building better contemporary and future idealized communities.

Equally important for this present research is an innovation from 1978—the introduction of play themes (Lego Town, Castle, and Space) from Lego. Since then, Lego has created themes as diverse as: Arctic, Duplo, Disney Princess, Mindstorms, Ninjago, Bionicle, Aqua Raiders, NBA, Lego Baby, Dino Attack, Homemaker, Monster Fighters, Pharoah's Quest, Pirates, Time Travels, and Vikings—just to name a few. If we go back to Daniel J. Foley's statement that toys "tell the story of civilization in miniature," it seems as though Lego has tried to do so both via fact and fiction. Seemingly, no geographic location, era, or fictionalized play scenario has been left uninterpreted into the magical world of Lego. However, there is one that has never officially been interpreted. It is Lego historical war, and it is the focus of this chapter.

Lego and War

The answer to the question "Why doesn't Lego sell historical war sets?" is easily found within the company's 2010 Progress Report on page twenty-six under the heading *Guideline for weapons and conflict in LEGO experiences.* Here, the company notes that a large number of their mini-figures use weapons and children most likely put them in battle with other armed mini-figures. Also, such play is prevalent among four-to-nine year-old boys. Such experimentation in play allows children to recognize such conflict in non-play situations. So, Lego actually sees conflict play as "perfectly acceptable" (The Lego Group 2010, 26).

The report continues by stating while Lego believes children can differentiate between play and reality, they are nonetheless using the 2010 report to record previously unwritten rules Lego has always followed. Lego states "The basic aim is to avoid realistic weapons and military equipment that children may recognize from hot spots around the world and to refrain from showing violent or frightening situations when communicating about LEGO products" (The Lego Group 2010, 26). In addition, Lego writes that the brand is "not to be associated with issues that glorify conflicts and unethical or harmful behavior" (The Lego Group 2010, 26). So, for the purposes of this chapter, Lego finds "conflict play" perfectly acceptable but abstains from "glorify[ing] conflicts." A quick browse through their product offerings substantiates that position.

For example, the Lego Castle theme, beginning in 1978, armed mini-figures with swords, lances, and axes. To a lesser extent, Lego Space, beginning in 1982 offered part number 4360 "camera with side sight" that many children used instead as a "space gun." While Lego offered police cars since 1978 and a police station since 1979, no Lego officer was outfitted with a firearm (just walkie-talkies and eventually megaphones). Lego firemen use hand axes. The bow and arrow also made its appearance in the Castle theme, most prominently in the 1987–1990 Forestmen sub-theme. The closest Lego comes to historical war (albeit fictionalized) was the popular Pirates (1989–2002) theme. The faction the Lego Pirates were attacking were "loosely based on the French and British naval seaman" (Martell 2009, 33) and were first introduced as Imperial Soldiers, then Imperial Guards, and eventually just Imperial Armada. They came armed with spring-loaded cannons, muskets, swords, and flintlock pistols. A similar arsenal and play scenario appeared in the 1996–1997 Western theme that pitted cowboys versus cavalry soldiers in a vaguely nineteenth century U.S. frontier. Fans could outfit these mini-figures with rifles, pistols, cannons, pick axes, and cutlass swords. Editor-in-Chief of the popular online Lego news site, *The Brothers Brick*, Andrew Becraft, also notes similarities to military vehicles in sets 4953 (F-14 Tomcat fighter plane), 7475 (Humvee), and 7477 (Russian Mi-24 helicopter) (2008). The *Indiana Jones* (2008–2009) licensed theme also contained generic cartoonish depictions of German soldiers wearing green or tan fatigues and caps.

On the truly fantastical side, various sci-fi and fantasy themes (both licensed and original) incorporate swords, old-timey pistols, or rayguns of one sort or another. The most popular of which, of course, is the ongoing *Star Wars* license (1999-present). Also, Lego interpreted one of its plastic toy predecessors by way of Pixar's *Toy Story* (1995), when it released set 7595 Army Men on Patrol including rifle, walkie-talkie, and minesweeper accessories. Also, the Disney/Marvel licensed Lego theme parallels Disney/Marvel films' character transformations: Nazi "The Red Skull" and German soldiers become merely "The Red Skull" and his Hydra foot soldiers.

Looking through these product examples and Lego's official policy leaves one to wonder whether it is a temporal limit as much as a fantastical restraint regarding imitation of conflict. As Lego wrote, conflict play is perfectly acceptable, but, perhaps, only if it is also roughly at least two hundred and fifty years ago (the Pirates' Imperial Soldiers). Though even this rule is broken when considering the 1996–1997 Western theme approximating the nineteenth century. With this rule broken, combined with the limits of fantastical restraint, we're left with nostalgia or an idealized version of the past through play—Imperial Soldiers versus Pirates and Cowboys versus Calvary Soldiers—as the logic for Lego historical conflict offerings.

Together, nostalgia and memory as transformative imagination provide a foundation for our study of war play and Lego's unique brand identity. Again, we can contextualize nostalgia around the Lego historical war sub-culture with the levels provided in the introduction: Idealized Past & Future [Lego's civic focus]; Romanticized Childhood; Last Ludic War [nation-based war had rules], and Transgenerational Nostalgia [same toy experiences]. So, with Lego's conflict policy in place, and the company only dipping their toes in the water of fantastical versions of historical war, many third party vendors have filled in this gap by offering high quality war scenario customization using existing high quality genuine Lego pieces. It is a mixture of aesthetically accurate models built on the idealized past (nostalgic) version of both "good" and forgotten wars. The Lego Historical War sub-culture provides a rich environment to explore all variations of these nostalgic enthusiasms.

Lego Historical War Sub-Culture: Market Context

Fan creations most assuredly are born when what fans want is not offered officially. We see this with traditional fan fiction, fan movie posters, fans photoshopping DC and Marvel characters onto the same cover, and remix and extended versions of pop songs—just to name a few. Since Lego does not offer historical war sets, fans—in particular AFOLs—take it upon themselves to recreate personnel, vehicles, and battle scenarios from the U.S. Revolutionary War, the U.S. Civil War, World War I, World War II, the Korean War, the Vietnam War, and contemporary U.S. wars in the Middle East.

A typical AFOL relationship to Lego, as of the time of this writing, would be: first Lego set received as a child during the early '80s. Then, fandom dipped during high school and college, then reignited during the late '90s/early 2000s. Also during childhood, AFOL would put together plastic models of cars, planes, ships, and HO scale train accessories, while playing with green plastic army men and G. I. Joe 3 ¾ scale action figures. Yet, we also see that the allure of Lego historical war extends beyond AFOLs. For example, in 2014, a Kickstarter began to help realize a nine-year-old's "vision" for a Lego World War II diorama in anticipation of attending that year's World War Brick convention. Beyond this military sub-culture, historical enthusiast creators such as Brendan Powell Smith publish books using Lego to recreate secular and biblical historical scenes.

The current market for Lego historical war is comprised of an assortment of online storefronts, foreign companies producing Lego-competing sets, and a wide variety of smaller online sellers mostly focusing on custom mini-figures sold through eBay. The larger foreign competitors to Lego, who fill the niche of historical and contemporary war include Chinese company Sluban, Korean company Oxford, and also Polish manufacturer Cobi. Military-themed sets have been Cobi's best selling since 1999, considered their "key product" (Schmidt 2015), in part, because it does not compete directly with Lego offerings.

Regarding the larger online storefronts, customizer Brickmania is the current market leader in terms of reach, offering two physical retail locations, their online component, regular attendance at various regional Lego festivals, and for five years, an annual convention titled World War Brick. One of the most popular Lego-compatible accessories within this sub-culture is produced by the Seattle-based company Brickarms run by Will Chapman. Chapman produces historical guns, helmets, and equipment vests for minifigs, and currently the customizer Brickmania is the number one reseller of Chapman's work.

Some new buyers, ignorant of official Lego sets' relatively high price point, receive "sticker shock" when they first see most Lego customizers' prices. Due to the labor involved in parting out genuine Legos, designing kits, acquiring inventory from other online sellers, and for some, making their own plastic accessories, stickers, and custom paint applications onto existing Lego, these customized kits are expensive. For example, a small vehicle with no figures can cost $30, a large vehicle set $200, and an ornate TV show set recreation even higher. Relative scarcity of certain colors offered officially by Lego increases costs to the customizer and is often passed on to the customer. Identical builds with differing (and scarcer) colors could result in as much as a $25 difference between kits. The larger online storefronts strive for "museum quality" with their kits and want to provide the same level of quality for both kids and AFOLs, at all price points. Sellers are very aware their "stuff is not for everybody, be it with price or subject matter" (Seller interview #3).

The current Lego historical war sub-culture is enabled via multiple factors. Internet commerce, specifically Lego parts clearinghouse Bricklink.com, allows a viable secondary market for genuine Lego reselling. New Lego parts are purchased on Bricklink, a "virtual mall of Lego reselling" (Seller interview #1). Lego sets are also purchased and parted for resale on Bricklink. However, due to the value and popularity of Lego, Bricklink has been flooded with users who sometimes mix colors and mislabel parts. This leads to inefficiencies and headaches for some historical war custom sellers who rely on Bricklink for their business. The Internet, connecting robust databases, has also allowed for a convenient and thick reference for Lego products (sets, instruction manuals, parts, reviews, and community forums). Together, these two online elements form the digital infrastructure for this fan sub-culture.

Adult Fans of Lego (AFOL) grew up on Lego and know they can rely on the quality of their legacy system, even when Lego as a company is losing money. In 1998, Lego lost $24.5 million and in 2000 lost $105 million (Tagliabue 2001). Legos are a relatively expensive toy, and their rebound with phenomenal sales figures from the aughts were achieved through a combination of inventive new themes, digital presence via video games, increased marketing, and licensed sets; the economic value of Lego sets also rose on the buying and collecting market. This helped to buttress the sub-culture's digital infrastructure.

In addition to the ability for secondary sellers to buy Lego parts as needed for their creations, there is also the affordability of producing high-quality compatible Lego accessories as well as custom printing on the mini-figures themselves. Due to Lego's understandably aggressive trademark monitoring (The Lego Group 2011), each seller is diligent in placing a variation of the following language on their online shop's page: "This is not a LEGO® Product. These are re-used LEGO® elements that have been repackaged or altered from their original form. LEGO® is a trademark of the LEGO® Group, which does not sponsor, authorize or endorse this product. The LEGO® Group is not liable for any loss, injury or damage arising from the use or misuse of this product."

Through online store fronts and Lego fan conventions, these sellers connect with their fans and buyers. In addition to historical war, most of these custom Lego secondary sellers also offer some form of popular culture Lego product not currently offered officially by Lego. These popular culture offerings are not the focus of this present chapter. However, they are mentioned here due to their connection to the larger theme of nostalgia, since much of the popular culture offerings are also from buyers' childhoods.

Along with regional Lego festivals displaying builds, providing activities for kids, and numerous vendor booths including those companies selling customized Lego historical war kits, there are also many online fan communities as well. The sets and mini-figures lend themselves to photography, and as such there are Lego WWII Flickr pages, Facebook pages, and Pinterest boards. These posts and galleries, along with the online sellers, international company kits, Bricklink, and physical conventions, comprise the Lego historical war sub-culture.

For this present chapter, I've interviewed sellers and surveyed buyers regarding questions of nostalgia, the intersection of Lego's creative, civic-minded brand identity and historical war, and their perspective on Lego's uniqueness via IRB approved instruments. Admittedly, the number of interviews and survey responses can not support generalizable statistical significance. However, as a small sample of both sides of this sub-culture, they provide valuable introductory insights on these two questions. First, what role does nostalgia play within Lego historical war? Second, how do members of the sub-culture navigate the potential tension between Lego's unique brand mythos and the impulse for continued militarism via history? Presented here is the data from those interviews and surveys, followed by an interpretative discussion and conclusion built around the theme of interactive nostalgia.

Lego Historical War Sub-Culture: Sellers & Buyers Data

As a way to transition to the data I collected from buyers and sellers, here I begin by noting buyers' survey responses regarding *where* they purchased either custom Lego historical war sets or non-Lego competitors' sets. Nine options, including international companies like Sluban, were presented to respondents with the ability to write in other sellers if the respondent wished to do so. The overwhelming seller of choice for these respondents was Polish manufacturer Cobi. This was followed by Brickarms, then Brickmania, with Chinese company Sluban and American company Citizen Brick tied for fourth.

Similar to other fandoms, some Lego historical war super collectors will buy one of everything from a seller to display in their home, marveling at the design and detail. Online survey results show my participants to be mostly international (Germany, UK, and the Netherlands), all male, majority Caucasian, late 40s to late 50s in age, and a majority possess an income of $70,000 a year or higher. Even with relatively higher incomes, a majority reported only purchasing one to five Lego historical war toys per year, with only a quarter of respondents purchasing within the range of eleven to twenty-five. However, for all time purchases, across years, a majority of respondents have purchased ten or more items in total. Here I present the results organized into four categories: nostalgia, war & history, childhood & generations, and Lego's uniqueness as a toy.

Nostalgia

One seller noted that it is almost like making up for certain items that were unavailable during childhood. This is commonly phrased to the seller from buyers at Lego festivals as "Oh my God, where were you guys when we were kids?" (Seller interview #3). When asked directly whether nostalgia for Lego played a role in his interest in these sets, one online seller's response provided an illustrative example. For him, nostalgia for Lego only occurs when he sees a set he himself owned when he was a child. In regards to the Lego historical war sets, it is not nostalgia but just the joy of building itself that provides pleasure. Further, to interpret the real life object through both the systematic and aesthetic constraints of Lego, brings great satisfaction. When asked whether there was a nostalgia for war, or at least "good wars", inherent in these sets, his response was "Yeah, a little bit" but "nostalgia" isn't quite the correct word. Rather, it was the precision, detail, and (as much as is possible working in Lego) accuracy of the custom creation of a real life object, in this case a "tool that was designed for combat" (Seller interview #2). This particular seller also expressed he felt more for kits representing Vietnam or recent conflicts, rather than WWII because the stories customers tell him are newer, fresher, and perhaps more dynamic than the WWII stories his grandfathers either told too often or not enough.

Online buyer survey responses overwhelmingly replied "yes" they do feel nostalgia plays a role in their interest in Lego historical war sets. When asked what they were nostalgic for, and given three options plus a write-in option, respondents equally responded nostalgia for both "playing with Lego" and "putting together military models." Only one respondent chose nostalgia for "Good wars in our history like WWII". Though, one other respondent wrote in "Having grandfathers who fought in WW2" (Buyer response #7). For sellers we see a nostalgia for their own childhoods, and a fascination and possible fetishism for the tools of war. Whereas, for buyers it was for their childhood models and less so for good wars. Family history with war, and stories about it showed through in both.

War & History

These narratives about military history and technical specifications continued for most sellers; they held twin interests in history and Lego, and selling such sets sate them both. Short quotes both from interviews and online sellers' storefronts help to summarize their perspective: "Personally if I buy or build a World War era model out of LEGO it all comes down to history. Ever since I started learning about the Civil War in school I was hooked on military history. Therefore I loved to recreate some of the iconic vehicles and scenes from important battles from different military conflicts" (Seller interview #4). Another seller, Combat Brick, explains on their website "I have a strong interest in military history of WWII, Vietnam and current events of low-intensity conflicts of Modern Warfare. I also truly enjoy playing with LEGO. CombatBrick was born as a fusion of those two" (Combat Brick 2018).

Often fans within this sub-culture enjoy creating small combat scenes or much larger displays showing off both their great design ability using the medium of Lego, and their eye for great detail within a dramatic scene of war. Some buyers, even in spite of such high price points for most Lego historical war sets and figures, will continue to customize the kit after they purchased it either through additional bricks or sticker decals. Usually the impulse for this comes from a desire for even greater accuracy (technical specificity) or as one seller notes "so it looks a little more realistic and authentic. For me, the details, that's what I like. And other people have done some more stuff" (Seller interview #3).

In regard to purchasing custom mini-figure soldiers and also purchasing Brickarms accessories, the rationale for doing so can vary widely among customers. Some just want what looks aesthetically pleasing ("looks cool") while others specifically ask "what weapon and equipment did this type of soldier use *EXACTLY*?" (Seller interview #1). Sellers, on the other hand, tend to stick with genuine Lego parts—especially for vehicle kits—due to their reliability, high quality control, and parts inventory.

The main interpretation from respondents of my phrase *Lego historical war* is to emphasize the former, and downplay the latter. As one of the online sellers who responded to my survey phrased it, "We at [customizer name] don't promote war, we promote history." He goes further by interpreting this as Lego's mission as well, "the word is they don't want to promote war as child's play. They want to promote history." Continuing on, he states their position as: "We're not war profiteers. We're not anything, we're a business that's found a niche market on something that we do very well" (Seller interview #2). So, while not specifically addressing the word *nostalgia*, or phrase *nostalgia for previous military engagements*, we see in the section the umbrella term *history* to frame buyer and seller enthusiasms.

This seller also provided an anecdote about large dioramas they contributed to an Army museum depicting World War II's Battle of the Bulge that further illustrates his perspective on toys and history. Parents who brought their children interpreted the dioramas as an educational visual rather than just a toy. The few remaining World War II veterans on hand were surprised such battlefield settings could be recreated from Lego and the diorama inspired the vets to tell stories. This led my participant to conclude "To see us have the ability to connect with a total stranger and have them just strike up a conversation about personal experiences from some of the worst places/events in the history of our world, there is just something about that ... it's an amazing experience" (Seller interview #2). Here history is engaged again, but this time framed as educational. Unfortunately, the exact lessons from such a curriculum are not specified.

Some sellers have had customers who voice an opinion that can be summarized as feeling "They [sellers] promote violence and killing people" or "You make these giant destructive toys. You take guns and make them into toys" (Seller interview #3). While most sellers set up shop online or travel to regional Lego festivals to set up a booth for a day, one popular seller, Brickmania, also features two physical retail stores. In their Illinois store, they feature various Lego tile mosaics of personalities from World War II. One of them is German General Erwin Rommel (1891–1944). One customer took offense at it and said so via social media. Brickmania's position is that Rommel hated the Nazi party and may have been part of a plot to kill Hitler; his loyalty was to the country and its military, not to the ideological principles of The Third Reich. Again, this displays an interest in the historical record of a major war and also a curiosity and nostalgia for previous nation-state based warfare.

This emphasis on history, rather than war, is echoed by online buyer responses. When given a choice to characterize their interest in Lego historical war sets as one for warfare, history, or Lego, the majority chose the option "history". In a later open-ended question, where respondents could write anything else they felt was important for me to know about the sub-culture, two respondents both justified their interest in different but nonetheless roundabout ways. The first emphasized he was only interested in "the technical aspect of the military models ... I collect and build from all war parties, axis as well as allies" (Buyer response #5). The other wrote "Nostalgia, creativity, and history that leaves the LEGO groups moral high ground intact is a win for everyone" (Buyer response #1).

An interesting subtopic of war, history, video games and toys was revealed during interviews. I highlight it briefly here because it connects with previous work I've published on video games and war history (Salvati and Bullinger 2013). Various military-themed popular culture representations of war often overlap and "speak" to each other; if not directly, then certainly through an audience's exposure. Here, it is video games and Lego historical war. When the customers are asked how they knew about a particular piece of equipment, the customers will often reference the popular video game series *Call of Duty* (2003-present). One seller believes "I think that's [video games] actually had a big influence on kids being interested in the game history and military history. Games like *Call of Duty*, games like *Battlefield* (2016). I can't tell you how many kids I've talked to love *Battlefield* and have become fascinated with

World War One as a topic and a conflict because of that game." The seller finds these interactions positive because "it's encouraging kids to think more about history and learn" (Seller interview #1). The pattern the seller recognizes is: exposure to video games first, this helps to build a love of the topic second, resulting finally in this historical scenario replicated in the unique building toy of Lego.

Childhood & Generations

There seems to exist a generational difference within the Lego historical war sub-culture. Younger fans who have grown up during Lego's resurgence look to Lego as the primary building tool beyond traditional plastic and glue models. They also played with wooden train sets (e.g. Thomas the Tank Engine) rather than traditional model trains. Whereas older fans' childhoods more heavily relied on traditional models and model trains; most said they had put together "MANY models". We also see this for some regarding toy soldiers. Some children spent more time with Star Wars toys then they did with little green plastic Army men. Nonetheless, the love for Lego, and subsequent nostalgia for it, begins early for both generations during childhood. Survey results showed an almost equal split between respondents for whom Lego was "fun, but just one of many toys played with" and "It was my favorite; I could definitely have been called a 'fanatic.'"

Lego's Uniqueness as a Toy

Lego's modularity and its ability to be rebuilt are both seen by sellers as its core advantages over traditional "plastic and glue" models. Also, while traditional models may have more detail, they are considered by some "a one and done" toy. Also, for some respondents, if traditional models are painted, then they become a display piece rather than a toy. Also, Lego's versatility and compatibility as a legacy system make it unique. Comparing a Lego historical war tank set to a traditional model tank kit, sellers said: Lego is cleaner than a plastic/glue tank, faster to build, provides more colors, offers more decals and aftermarket add-ons. Plus, mooring it in Lego's uniqueness—its versatility to be rebuilt—is for some respondents, "something no other toy provides" (Seller interview #2). This is most prevalent in the online responses. The online survey choice, "Lego is different from all other toys. There is a purity of imagination the brand embodies that makes it both unique and special," was chosen the most of three choices. The other two choices for core attributes of Lego's brand were (a) Lego's creativity, and (b) value as a building toy. Though, when later asked to write an answer in their own words to the question “What does the Lego brand mean to you?” there was heavy emphasis on creativity and endless possibilities. However, one respondent explained the appeal of either technological fetishism or great love for WWII toys, when he wrote in “They [Lego] were first, but my [sic] hart goes to Cobi, for the WW2 tanks” (Buyer response #3).

Conclusion: Lego, War, Nostalgia, & History

An interesting idea was introduced by Antonia Fraser in her book *A History of Toys* when she hypothesized “if toys are the starting-point of dreams” (1966). If this is true—toys are a key material object children use as a focal point for their imaginations—then what does this mean for the concepts of war and nostalgia? The answer is simple for children like Louis XIV and his toy soldiers. His dream would be to transfer what he learned in silver miniature to flesh-and-blood armies, as a leader of men, a student of war. So too, do today’s children, who hope to serve their countries one day as military personnel and who begin by playing with war toys.

We, however, are left with one variable not accounted for—nostalgia. Nostalgia for the toys of our youth and nostalgia for “good wars” long past. “If toys are the starting-point of dreams”, and some of these toys are nostalgic representations of long-ago wars, then is our starting-point already a reflection? Of course, a nine-year-old boy can not be nostalgic for something he is ignorant of, but the toy designed for him to dream, is perhaps, a nostalgic design from an adult creator. As we have seen from the data, the sub-culture’s focus and understanding is to extend the lesson of history, not nostalgia. For even the adult designers themselves can not truly be nostalgic for certain wars, for they too, are too young to possess firsthand experience.

However, it is the culture of war, buoyed in part by a traditionalist “great men and war” historical perspective, that is passed down generationally, and generates a nostalgia all its own. It is combined with a technological fetishism for the tools of war. Together, nostalgia for great men / great wars and the technologies of war are couched in the language of “history” by participants. The effect is augmented when this history is conveyed through one of the most optimistic, unique, and civic-minded toy systems of a generation. Anyone can build anything they desire when using the Lego brick system. There is an inherent creative objectivity to the system’s design of play. So, to explore “history” through Lego is perceived as a neutral, educational experience.

Nonetheless, Lego’s foundation has been the child’s imagination, bounded by a system, and projected through the prism of present civic worlds, future outer space explorations, and far past medieval adventures.

The Lego historical war sub-culture harnesses that imaginative projection and refocuses it through the lens of nostalgia on to a real past—not just *a* past war, but an entire previous culture of nation-based war. As the data reveals, sometimes it is a conversational medium for the minutiae of military strategy. Other times, it is just the beloved medium for preferred ("cool") aesthetics of assertive warrior poses from wars that hold meaning for a culture nostalgic for war tools.

However, Boym (2007) notes, nostalgia can be either restorative or reflective. The former is narrow, and longs for a transformation that can never occur, while the latter is more complex and meditates on the longing itself. The interactivity of Lego play across generations, its brand mythos, and the perceived objective version of *history* combine for buyers and sellers of Lego historical war to form a bridge between restorative and reflective forms of nostalgia. Buyer respondent number one succinctly summarized this perspective on the sub-culture when he answered "Nostalgia, creativity, and history that leaves the LEGO groups moral high ground intact is a win for everyone".

References

Angé, Olivia, and David Berliner, eds. 2015. *Anthropology and Nostalgia*. New York: Berghahn.

Atia, Nadia, and Jeremy Davies. 2010. "Nostalgia and the Shapes of History." *Memory Studies* 3 (3): 181–186.

Becraft, Andrew. 2008. "Should LEGO Release Modern Military Sets?" *The Brothers Brick* (blog). July 6, 2008. https://www.brothers-brick.com/2008/07/06/should-lego-release-modern-military-sets-editorial/.

Berliner, David. 2012. "Multiple Nostalgias: The Fabric of Heritage in Luang Prabang (Lao PDR)." *Journal of the Royal Anthropological Institute* 18: 769–786.

Boym, Svetlana. 2007. "Nostalgia and Its Discontents." *The Hedgehog Review* 9 (2): 7–18.

Campbell, James. 2008. "Just Less than Total War: Simulating World War II as Ludic Nostalgia." In *Playing the Past: History and Nostalgia in Video Games*, edited by Zach Whalen and Laurie N. Taylor. Vanderbilt University Press.

Cashman, Ray. 2006. "Critical Nostalgia and Material Culture in Northern Ireland." *Journal of American Folklore* 119 (472): 137–160.

Combat Brick. 2018. "Combat Brick: About Us." May 21, 2018. http://combatbrick.com/index.php/home.

Cross, Gary. 2015. *Consumed Nostalgia: Memory in the Age of Fast Capitalism*. New York: Columbia University Press.

Duyvendak, Jan Willem. 2011. *The Politics of Home – Belonging and Nostalgia in Western Europe and the United States*. London: Palgrave Macmillan.

Fleming, Dan. 1996. *Powerplay: Toys as Popular Culture.* Manchester: Manchester University Press.

Foley, Dan. 1962. *Toys Through the Ages.* Philadelphia, PA: Chilton Company.

Fraser, Antonia. 1966. *A History of Toys.* New York: Delacorte Press.

Glazer, Peter. 2005. *Radical Nostalgia: Spanish Civil War Commemoration in America.* Rochester, NY: University of Rochester Press.

Halter, Ed. 2006. *From Sun Tzu to XBox: War and Video Games.* New York: Thunder's Mouth Press.

Huizinga, Johan. 1980. *Homo Ludens: A Study of the Play-Element in Culture.* Boston, MA: Beacon Press.

Kalinina, Ekaterina. 2017. "Beyond Nostalgia for the Soviet Past: Interpreting Documentaries on Russian Television." *European Journal of Cultural Studies* 20 (3): 285–306.

Ketchum Jr., William C. 1981. *Toys & Games.* Washington, DC: The Smithsonian Institution.

Lipkowitz, Daniel. 2009. *The Lego Book.* New York: DK Publishing.

Lizardi, Ryan. 2017. *Nostalgic Generations and Media: Perception of Time and Available Meaning.* Lanham, MD: Lexington Press.

Lowenthal, David. 1985. *The Past Is a Foreign Country.* Cambridge: Cambridge University Press.

Martell, Nevin. 2009. *Standing Small: A Celebration of 30 Years of the Lego Minifigure.* New York: DK Publishing.

May, Vanessa. 2016. "Belonging From Afar: Nostalgia, Time and Memory." *The Sociological Review* 65 (2): 401–415.

Papageorgiou, Georgios C. 2015. "Heritage in Consumer Marketing." In *The Palgrave Handbook of Contemporary Heritage Research*, edited by Emma Waterton and Steve Watson. New York: Palgrave Macmillan.

Salvati, Andrew J., and Jonathan M. Bullinger. 2013. "Selective Authenticity and the Playable Past." In *Playing with the Past: Digital Games and the Simulation of History*, edited by Matthew Wilhelm Kapell and Andrew B. R. Elliott. New York: Bloomsbury Academic.

Schmidt, Gregory. 2015. "Lego's Success Leads to Competitors and Spinoffs." *The New York Times*, November 20, 2015. https://www.nytimes.com/2015/11/21/business/legos-success-leads-to-competitors-and-spinoffs.html.

Sprengler, Christine. 2009. *Screening Nostalgia: Populuxe Props and Technicolor Aesthetics in Contemporary American Film.* New York: Berghahn Books.

Tagliabue, John. 2001. "Lego Tinkered with Success, and Is Now Paying a Price." *The New York Times*, December 25, 2001. https://www.nytimes.com/2001/12/25/business/lego-tinkered-with-success-and-is-now-paying-a-price.html.

The Lego Group. 2010. "Progress Report." Billund, Denmark. https://www.lego.com/r/www/r/aboutus/-/media/aboutus/sustainability/progress-report/progress_report2010.pdf.

———. 2011. "Fair Play Brochure." Billund, Denmark. https://www.lego.com/en-us/legal/legal-notice/fair-play.

Tierney, John. 2013. "What Is Nostalgia Good For? Quite a Bit, Research Shows." *The New York Times*, July 8, 2013. https://www.nytimes.com/2013/07/09/science/what-is-nostalgia-good-for-quite-a-bit-research-shows.html.

Wilson, Janelle L. 2005. *Nostalgia: Sanctuary of Meaning*. Lewisburg, PA: Bucknell University Press.

4. *The Development of Video Game Emulation and Its Subjective Nostalgic Experiences*

RYAN LIZARDI

Introduction

This chapter explores the development of video game console emulation technologies, communities, and commodifications, and connects them to the industry's revival of dormant catalogs through virtual console DLC and the eventual repackaging and "re-consoling" of popular properties as well as the impetus to create more reliable and inventive methods of DIY emulation. Building from a variety of scholarly threads, from video game emulation and archive studies such as Guttenbrunner, Becker, and Rauber (2010) and Newman (2012b) to nostalgia studies like Coontz (1992) and Whalen and Taylor (2008), this paper tracks the history of video game console emulation through to a comparison of Nintendo's "Classic Edition" releases and DIY versions such as the "Pi Cart." The experiences of these disparate methods of retro gaming are quite varied, and speak to the different nostalgic subjectivities encouraged through the practice of either buying a rare pre-packaged version of the past and building one for yourself. Exploring online fan communities from both experiences, such as those hunting for the elusive NES Classic Edition in 2016 and SNES Classic Edition in 2017 versus those discussing the best methods of building an emulation machine inside of an old NES cartridge, helps to broaden our understanding of what it means to experience and interact with our nostalgia in a digitized world. Much like Walter Benjamin was concerned with what unpacking his library says about us as collectors and our life's continuity (1968), so too is this chapter concerned with the implications of different forms of experiencing our resurfaced video game pasts. If the predominant lens through which players are encouraged to long for, archive, and maintain our vintage video game libraries is through false scarcity and commodification, the lasting version of our digital histories becomes quite different than if we were encouraged to curate our own connections to our gaming pasts.

Emulation History

Wanting to play 8-bit (and 16-bit) classic video games is not solely a twenty-first century phenomenon, as gamers barely let their early consoles get dusty before they looked to replay them, assuming they were not broken already. Then, along came the concept of console emulation on a personal computer, and suddenly all the titles, good and bad, were available in digital form, assuming of course that you had the technological know-how to find and maintain an emulator and ROMs. Video game emulation refers to "a piece of software that allows one platform (e.g. a PC) to run the program code and potentially deal with inputs and outputs through various peripheral devices (e.g. joysticks and pads) of another platform (e.g. a Nintendo console)" (Newman 2012b, 48). Though not a perfect process, emulation represented for those without a working Nintendo what James Newman describes as "the most viable, possibly only, means of accessing commercially unavailable titles" (2012b, 48). When Newman says "only" he is really referring to another important argument he has made that "for all this apparently manifest growth, innovation and diversification, the simple fact remains that videogames are disappearing" (2012a, 3). Newman means that the preservation of video games as cultural artifacts is not on par with other art forms like film or even television. Discussing the inability to truly recapture the experience of playing Donkey Kong exactly as it originally existed, complete with narrative, graphics, and precise gameplay, Newman says that "[i]t is clearly not impossible to resurrect Donkey Kong in some form or other, but given how significant this game is. … I would contest that it is astonishingly difficult and the results surprisingly variable" (2012a, 8). There are many strategies to intervene in the case of degradation and obsolescence, such as emulation referring to the "capability of a device or software to replicate the behavior of a different device or software" and "may prove the most promising solution for console video games" (Guttenbrunner et al. 2010, 77). This argument for emulation is one-sided and academic, as "the acquisition of system boot ROMs or executable code very often involves practices that most charitably can be described as existing in a legally grey area … but which the videogame industry unequivocally positions as piracy" (Newman 2012b, 138). The companies that own the rights to these systems and games are, unsurprisingly, narrowly focused on the economic impact of emulation, but Newman argues "overlook a host of other practices that rely on precisely the same processes of copying and ripping but which, by contrast, are dedicated to celebrating and lengthening the life of games," such as is the case with video game preservationists (2012b, 138). This is not to say that all of the gamers running emulation software in the mid to late 1990s, when this non-commercial practice was at its zenith because of the unavailability of vintage games and technological advancements in computing, were all altruistic preservationists. Most just wanted to play *Super Mario Bros.* again.

Legally speaking, there are a few court cases worth mentioning because of the way they counterpose the interests of companies like Nintendo against emulation practitioners, which lays the foundation for their presentation of the Classic Edition consoles as the only true way to be a nostalgic gamer. In 1990, the company Codemasters developed a product that worked as an intermediary between video game cartridges and the NES, or Nintendo Entertainment System, allowing players to circumvent game rules like the amount of lives or the speed of their protagonists, in other words "cheat." The product was sold a few times, and eventually Lewis Galoob Toys changed the name to Game Genie and attempted to release the product in the US. Nintendo sued Lewis Galoob Toys in 1991 for copyright infringement. Much to Nintendo's dismay, the court sided with Galoob saying, the "[u]se of the Game Genie by consumers to temporarily alter copyrighted video games for their own enjoyment does not create a derivative work" and that, important for later emulators, "a game owner who has fairly acquired a Nintendo game has a right to use the entire work" (Lewis Galoob Toys, Inc. v. Nintendo of America, Inc., 780 F.Supp. 1283, 1991). The pertinence to emulation of the 1990s to the present is that this case affirmed that the rights of the consumer to alter a product after its purchase extended to the altering of code as long as it did not produce a derivative work. This could cover someone creating an emulator and ROMs in the "very narrow limitation relating to a copy being made by the rightful owner of an authentic game to ensure he or she has one in the event of damage or destruction of the authentic" (Nintendo 2016a). This equivocation does actually put Nintendo more in line with Newman's thoughts on the video game preservationist, but only in a case where the emulator/ROM creator owns the system and the games and does not distribute these products Nintendo feels violate their copyrights. Nintendo, perhaps more than any other existing video game company, has every reason to protect these rights given their historical and continued reliance on characters from this vintage gaming era. In this way, Nintendo has embodied the tenet that their series should be used to sell the "older segment of the audience its own memories" (Gordon 2017, 79). So while the emulation battle was being waged in the courtroom and in 1990s cyberspace, Nintendo continued to cultivate brands and characters like Mario, Link, and Donkey Kong, and eventually tapped into the very same vintage catalog that had been the subject of emulation enthusiasts. Starting with the Wii console, Nintendo began a path that led to the Classic Editions, starting with the launch of their wildly successful "Virtual Console" that made many 8 and 16-bit games available commercially for the first time in over a decade. Nintendo tested the limits of this re-commodification of their past catalog with the *NES Remix* series (2013–2014), and I have previously argued that these "medium transitions serve to reify normalized and codified modes of video game consumption that were once free and potentially contemplative" subverting "a form of agency and ownership for fans who were contributing to the historical archive of these games, which content owners found economically problematic" (Lizardi 2017, 34).

Theory/Methodology

The crucial argument is that there is a big difference between the nostalgia experienced when producing, curating, and playing your own device and collection when compared to the experience of procuring, paying for, and playing Nintendo's commodified version. To explore this split in nostalgic experiences spurred by varying emulation conditions, I will be looking at the ways in which particular forms of nostalgia are encouraged or discouraged in myself and the communities that support these forms of emulation. This will entail an engagement with nostalgia studies theoretical material, as well as heuristics I have developed to examine types of encouraged and discouraged longing for a mediated past, such as the difference between mourning and melancholic attachments. Considering the subjective experiences at play within this split in nostalgic longing, and the aims of this collection, an autoethnographic approach seemed the most appropriate methodological perspective to utilize.

In previous works, such as my exploration of mediated nostalgia as a perpetual, individual force and my examination of intergenerational mediated nostalgia concerns (Lizardi 2014, 2017), I have developed a helpful heuristic that uses the Freudian dichotomy of mourning and melancholia as a way to more deeply understand how media texts specifically ask consumers to be nostalgic. The difference between the two types of longing, combined with considerations of economics, ownership, and production, rely on determining whether a particular media text encourages comparison, contemplation, and release of an object of desire, or discourages this type of longing in lieu of a goal of recreation and perpetuation. Mournful longing refers to a process where "gradually and painfully, libido is withdrawn from the lost object … when the mourning process is completed" while melancholic longing refers to continual attachment "to a lost object, and the pain of loss does not lessen in the normal way" over time (Dickinson and Erben 2006, 229). What will be shown in this comparison of two forms of emulated nostalgia is the, sometimes literally painful, process of creating a Pi Cart encourages critical contemplation and comparison of the past and present, whereas the difficulties contained within the search for the Nintendo Classic Editions are contained within the realm of commodification and that any past/present contemplation is mitigated by the glossy recreation and idealization in the gameplay itself. Fredric Jameson worried about what happens when postmodernism represents history and its objects with the goal of obscuring the differences between the then and now, or what he called the "disappearance of the American radical past" (1991, 24). When media encourage a form of nostalgia that smooths over the rough edges of the past, either through omission or through changing the original experience and context, it can lead to a reduction in viewing the past as unique and radical. Susan Strasser advances a similar tenet by encouraging us to view the past as "alien" so as to avoid thinking of it as a "static realm of sentimental remembrance" (2003, 376).

Methodologically speaking, I knew that bringing in communities of those searching for, building, and ultimately playing these systems would be integral to understanding these encouraged nostalgic longings, but also wanted to leverage my own experiences doing these same things. Shifting from an ethnographic approach to an autoethnographic one, or at the very least blending the two, comes with particular assumptions. Leon Anderson argues that autoethnographies bring with them a recognition of subjectivities and connectedly "reject traditional realist and analytic ethnographic epistemological assumptions" (2006, 377). As observer and participant, any claim to pure objectivity would stand on tenuous ground at best. Leon describes the history of the descriptive literary approach of evocative autoethnographers, like Carolyn Ellis and Arthur Bochner, arguing "that narrative fidelity to and compelling description of subjective emotional experiences create an emotional resonance with the reader that is the key goal of their scholarship" (2006, 377). This mode of inquiry, as with many other critical theoretical positionings, "shares postmodern sensibilities—especially the skepticism toward representation of 'the other' and misgivings regarding generalizing theoretical discourse" (Leon, 377).

Heewon Chang's work on the methodology of autoethnography helps to move from the recognition of an openly subjective researcher and participant to a set of criteria and structures to ensure robust explorations. Chang presents five criteria for a full autoethnography: "(1) complete member researcher (CMR) status, (2) analytic reflexivity, (3) narrative visibility of the researcher's self, (4) dialogue with informants beyond the self, and (5) commitment to theoretical analysis" (378). Conceptualizing and positioning myself as fulfilling these autoethnographic criteria was more than simply looking at my extensive past gaming experiences and my desire, encouraged or innate, to "[r]emember your first Goomba stomp" by playing *Super Mario Bros.* again (Nintendo 2016b). Sure, I am exactly the demographic Nintendo had in mind when they said on the NES Classic website to "pick up that gray controller" and to "rediscover the joy of NES games" (2016b). However, "complete member researcher" status is deeper than being in the consumer pool, but must rise to the level of being "a complete member in the social world under study" (Leon 2006, 379). Being this CMR meant that I participated fully in the online forums beyond my role as a researcher (i.e. I actively sought the systems, advice on how to build my own, and helped others achieve these same goals), all the while never losing sight of the theoretical analysis taking place. I kept extensive notes, logs, and screenshots of my interactions in the forums as well as when I was at the various physical store locations, but as an active participant I was also always there as more than a researcher. Standing in front of dark and frigid storefronts, I was always there for the consoles. Steering into its subjectivity, as an autoethnographic researcher you should see value in and "openly acknowledge your personal memory as a primary source of information in your research" (Chang 2008, 71). However, in this particular exploration of encouraged nostalgic longing I am cognizant of the "pitfall of over-relying" on "personal memory" as a "single tool without other measures for checks and balances" (Chang 2008, 55). To this end, the exploration is not exclusively insular, as there is an expectation that "the stories of autoethnographers" will be "reflected upon, analyzed, and interpreted within their broader sociocultural context" as well as associated online communities (Chang 2008, 46).

Much of what is described above covers the autoethnographic elements of the search for and production of these emulation systems, however, the added element of video game player as researcher and participant adds another layer of complexity to this particular topic. Speaking specifically about videos games as a potential site for ethnographic research, Seth Giddings presents the case for autoethnographic elements in line with Chang's CMR status, with the argument that "some understanding and analysis of the forms, aesthetics and conventions of video games as popular digital media is very useful, as is the acknowledgement and description of the physical and social context in which these forms and conventions are realized, vivified" (2009, 147). Calling this instances of play "microethnographies," Giddings posits they "describe a nonscientific, improvised, opportunistic approach to recording, describing, and analyzing brief moments of everyday technocultural activity" (2009, 149). Giddings refers not only to the players themselves, but takes the next step in labeling "the computer hardware, software, and human bodies, their parts, and their coming together in the intense and intimate circuits of gameplay" all as "part(icipants) of central concern" in these microethnographies (2009, 149). Taking this fully inclusive look at the ways in which video games, their players, and the social context all work in concert to produce meaning in a technocultural environment is quite helpful in thinking about how different emulation conditions would encourage or discourage particular forms of nostalgic longing.

Getting the Systems

One benefit of connecting with online communities that support searches for limited edition products is that there is no shortage of concern about availability. The undertone of paranoia in forums ahead of the NES Classic Edition launch, specifically Nowinstock.net, was backed up by well-sourced rumors and statistics, which led me to consider the possibility that I would not actually get one through retail and should look for alternatives. Nintendo's strategy to germinate a sense of urgency about a product that recreates game experiences from thirty years ago worked, for me, which explains why I felt the need to pursue building an emulator system despite the technology for doing so existing long before 2016. In fact, I had already delved into the world of retro gaming emulation in the late 1990s, but now sought to come closer to the type of product that Nintendo was releasing in stores. Research on NES Classic Edition alternatives led directly to the "Pi Cart," which crams an entire emulation-dedicated system into a hollowed out NES cartridge. Developed by Zach Levine and posted on the website HowChoo, there were incredibly detailed instructions on how to remove the original innards of a chosen grey NES cartridge and replace them with a minature Raspberry Pi computer, USB inputs for controllers/power, and an HDMI output (2016) (Figure 4.1). Levine also links to instructions on loading the open-source RetroPie software onto your Raspberry Pi, which compared to my experiences curating emulators and roms in the late 1990s streamlined the entire process.

The experience of acquiring the parts for, and building, the Pi Cart system was markedly different from what was eventually needed to secure my Classic Editions, and consequently the nostalgia encouraged by these disparate

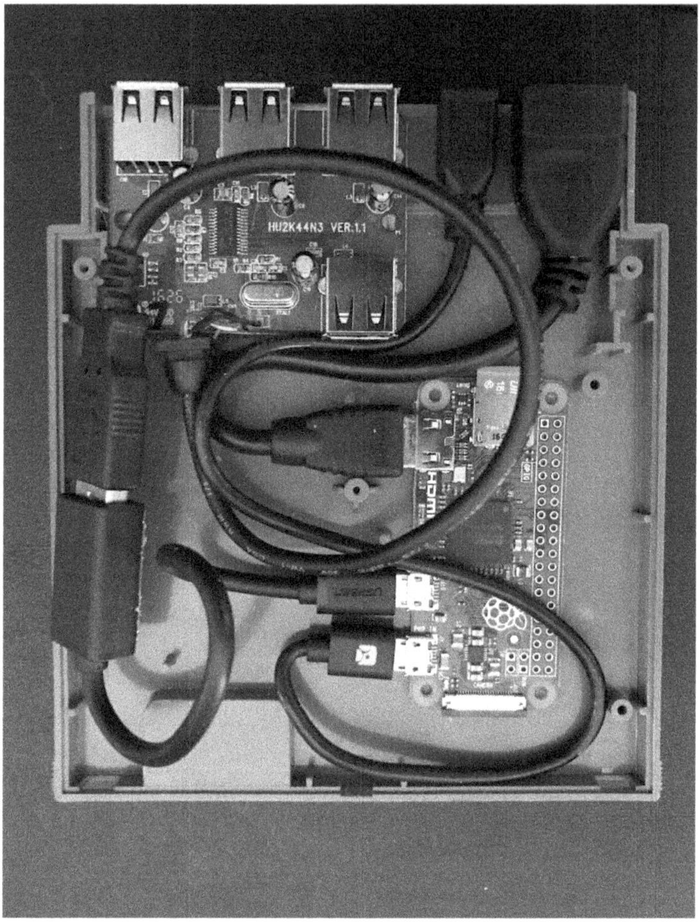

Figure 4.1: Author photo of the complicated space management and wire routing involved in Pi Cart construction.

experiences was completely different. After purchasing my list of materials needed from Amazon, I took a trip to two local flea markets in search of the perfect NES cartridge to hollow out. My goal was to use one of the rare gold *The Legend of Zelda* (1986) cartridges, but when faced with the prospect of ruining this icon of vintage gaming, I opted instead for a copy of *Back to the Future* (1989) for its more pointed nostalgic connections. Once all materials were in hand, the whole process took about three hours, including loading the emulation software and roms onto the cartridge. Though complicated to fit and route all of the required components, and despite a small cut acquired when removing the internal cross supports that held the original cartridge chip board, creating my own Pi Cart was simple thanks to the level of detail and support provided by the community of Raspberry Pi enthusiasts. Before I could begin my search for the NES Classic Edition in earnest, I had built a system capable of playing every game included in Nintendo's commercial release, as well as titles from systems like Gameboy, Sega Genesis, and Super Nintendo. In fact, nearly one year ahead of the eventual release of the SNES Classic Edition, my Pi Cart could play all of the games that would be released on this system, which makes my extensive search for it all the more proof of the successful nature of Nintendo's encouragement of perpetual commodified nostalgia.

Despite having a Pi Cart in hand, I did not stop my dogged pursuit of the Nintendo NES Classic Edition, and was eventually successful at procuring not just one console but two with the help of a tracker website called Nowinstock.net. This site, along with others of its kind, are designed to provide a simple service, a real time look at the stock levels of a given item at chain stores like Walmart, Target, and Gamestop. Some sites, like Brickseek.com, work by having the consumer plug the SKU number into the site and are given the number of items in stock nearby, but Nowinstock.net creates pages for each of its hot items and provides information for each store, such as links to the product page, last time in stock, browser alerts for when something changes on a page, and the all-important comments section. What sets Nowinstock.net apart is the community that has sprung up around the search for hard-to-find consumer items, even if it was not the original intention of its founder, Justin Vavrick.

In an interview with Vavrick on October 18, 2017, Justin described why on a site that is unique in the stock-searching community, the Nintendo Classic Editions are even more unique onto themselves. Vavrick remarks that the Nintendo Classic Edition consoles garnered a significant amount of comments when compared to other Nowinstock tracked products. At the end of the SNES Classic's launch cycle, its page received 293,000 comments in four months, second only to the combined Nintendo Amiibo Super Smash Bros. page, which had received 680,000 comments over the course of a few years and technically was spread across over 60 different products. Vavrick estimates that the average comment volume of a popular item on his site is 1500–5000 comments, and so his evidence that the NES and SNES Classic Editions were "obviously something special" seems well-reasoned (2017). With that volume of engagement, Vavrick, unsurprisingly, describes an environment conducive to much more than just rare item hunting, with "people of a like mind" finding "comradery" and feeling "much more connected" than in the other product forums on the site (2017). The crucial proof of this connection for these users, who Vavrick describes as the "core family of the site," exists in their persistence and engaged commenting long after they secured their own Classic Editions (2017). Vavrick posits that "they become friends" and then stuck around for the aforementioned comradery or to help each other secure consoles (2017). One potential alternate explanation is that many of the users "started to notice scalping," which Vavrick considers "the dark side of my site," especially with the SNES Classic launch as they had seen similar developments in the NES Classic page (2017). Though Nowinstock has rules and moderators in place to curb this type of behavior when it is explicit, certain users took to internally policing members who they suspected were actually scalpers by keeping track of how many a particular user said they were looking for, and if they continued to seek more after that number was attained. An imperfect system, to be sure, but it points to the group's feelings about the true nature of the page. Users, including myself, continued on the site long after securing orders for each Classic Edition, perhaps because of the comradery, the lightning fast notifications from other users, or to police the nefarious parts of the site, but all reasons point back to the existence of a robust comment section.

A large portion of the continued engagement on this site stems from Nintendo's inability or unwillingness to manage consumer expectations and commiserate stock levels. Perhaps they were unaware that the perfect nostalgia machine they created in the NES Classic would be so sought after or perhaps they were using techniques of false scarcity to maintain interest in their brands through their current flagship console, the Nintendo Switch that was released at the tail end of the NES Classic production cycle.[1] Regardless of the reason, the form of encouraged nostalgia fomented by the imbalance in supply and demand, along with retailer mishandlings of preorders, resulted in forum engagement that took on equal undertones of paranoia and fervent dedication. Taking on the roles of historian of previous mishaps, such as the Urban Outfitters Instagram/Twitter mixup that led to users of the site missing out on potential NES Classics, and of harbinger of inevitable future problems with orders, users preached an ever vigilant attitude that did not stop until, as one user noted, "that console is in your hands" (Nowinstock 2017). This proved sage advice for my experience, as I was able to secure a Walmart preorder of the SNES Classic in July of 2017, but received an email a few days later stating "due to a technical glitch, the Super Nintendo Classic Edition was mistakenly made available last Friday evening ahead of the official release date" and that my order was cancelled. Luckily, as an encouraged perpetual forum participant beyond what appeared to be my successful preorder, I continued to monitor and converse with the forum and secured an Amazon preorder of the UK version of the console in the interim. Coaxed dedication came in the form of hyperbole, with one user admonishing another that during a day a preorder was rumored to open "Don't go out and do anything man … you don't 'have' to do anything" with another user chiming in that anyone who would consider leaving to be a "Coward." Extremely low stock with the NES Classic, combined with retailer preorder problems, as well as the proven successful model of dedicated monitoring of Nowinstock.net led to a perfect storm of continued user engagement, and support, until consoles were in hand. My own track record includes two NES Classics, one from a launch day Gamestop overnight camp out and the other from Amazon releasing stock to support their Prime Now service, and four SNES Classics, two Amazon preorders and walk ins to Walmart and Gamestop. None of these would have been possible without the dedicated information and engagement of the Nowinstock user base.

Playing the Systems (and A "Bonus Level")

The differences in encouraged nostalgia fully carry over into the experiences of playing the Pi Cart versus the Classic Editions. When playing each console, I kept in mind Giddings concept of the microethnography and made sure to focus on myself, the player, the games, and the social context they were born from in analyzing my experiences. With the Pi Cart I felt encouraged to, or at least pulled towards a need to, compare the original reception of these vintage video games to their current situatedness within video game evolution and cultural history. With the Nintendo Classic Editions there were real no choices to be made, just polished and curated titles in perfect working order with new features that idealized a previously sometimes problematic playing experience. I did not have to blow air into the bottom of my Pi Cart, a common urban legend remedy for ailing NES cartridges in the 1980s and 1990s, but there were still technological challenges akin to original reception. Whereas the Classic Editions gave me everything I could have ever asked for as a vintage gamer, and much more.

Pi Cart

First and perhaps foremost in the differences between playing each system was the ability to add a seemingly unlimited catalog of vintage games onto the Pi Cart, with the wheat and the chaff together, encouraging users to not forget all of the poorly made games of any particular era. Theodore Adorno notes that certain "hits," to which he was referring to music, are "evergreen" media artifacts "that seem to defy aging and to outlast all fashions" (1976, 35). For Adorno, it was worthwhile to explore whether media are deemed classic or evergreen because the culture industry engineered them that way or whether they contained "traits that set them apart for certain periods, at least, from ephemeral products" (1976, 35). For the purposes of this analysis of emulated vintage games, it is more important to look at whether a given form of nostalgic gaming encourages an engagement with the original historical context or simply provides the evergreens. DIY emulation most certainly does not just include the classics. In fact, when perusing the grey market of vintage gaming ROMs, most sites provide a single download link for "all" of the games from a given system, which in terms of path of least resistance is appealing to anyone looking to quickly get their Pi Cart built and playable. As an alternative, I chose to one-by-one curate my game list so that the system did not get overloaded and because it seemed easier than having to sort through a massive library every time I loaded up the RetroPie interface. In either case, full library or curated collection, the encouraged form of nostalgic longing is one that retains more of the original context of reception, as classics from a given era are juxtaposed against titles that are regarded more poorly. As an example, I added all of the games that were announced for the NES Classic Edition, all of which Nintendo meticulously picked as "classics," but I also added games like *Back to the Future* (1989) and *Skate or Die* (1987). I chose the former because it was the cartridge I hollowed out for the Pi Cart and the latter because I remembered loving the game as a child, but in each case I was reminded that time is not kind to all and that some things are better left lost. Playing bad games alongside the classics, even to the point of just having them listed side-by-side in a menu, is an important factor as to whether the user will be allowed to forget the original historical context, a key feature of erasing a radical past.

The technological disadvantages in DIY emulation, fully present in the late 1990s but still lingering in the Pi Cart, serve as another reminder that what is being played today can never fully be a recreation of the past experience. The encouraged desire to place all of the components into the shell of an NES cartridge, approximating the feeling of the palm-sized NES Classic Edition, led to the necessity to use the Raspberry Pi Zero, which while more than capable of running NES era games was significantly taxed when playing resource-intensive games from the SNES era like *Super Mario World 2: Yoshi's Island* (1995). This experience was made even more salient as a comparison once the SNES Classic Edition game list revealed it would include this particular classic game, but being forced to sit through frame rate slow downs while playing *Yoshi's Island* on the Pi Cart was a consistent reminder of both the times in which this type of glitch would happen when originally playing these games as well as the inability of DIY emulation to fully recreate any gaming experience. The type of nostalgia encouraged is mourning in nature because it never lets the user forget what has been lost or the original context in which the games were played.

Nintendo Classic Editions

Playing the NES Classic Edition, and even more so the SNES Classic Edition, is to experience a form of encouraged nostalgia that seeks to recreate and simultaneously idealize a user's memories of vintage video games. Everything about these consoles, from the meticulously created, though miniaturized, housings that copy the original form to the menu interfaces that play retro-sounding music is designed to transport players back to their childhood gaming days. Even the paratextual elements like the boxart and the marketing materials seek to evoke a feeling of recapturing the past. Nintendo's NES Classic Edition accompanying marketing website does not equivocate in the manner they think gamers should be satiating the very nostalgia they themselves have encouraged, telling them to "PLAY THE SYSTEM THAT STARTED IT ALL" and to "[p]lay NES games the way they're meant to be played—with a full-size 'original' controller" (2016b). Nintendo is locked in a battle against emulators, ROMs, and their enthusiasts past and present, so the language used here with its all caps and unequivocal proper way to play nostalgically seems aimed directly at those who would stray from this commodified path.

The gameplay itself is pure melancholic recreation and idealization, as the Classic Edition systems simultaneously seeks to recapture exactly what it was like to play in the 1980s and 1990s as well as improve upon the experience. Players can choose menu options like CRT filter, which makes the screen output look as if it is being displayed on an older tube television. This digital approximation of vintage elements is what Tim van der Heijden calls "technostalgia" or the "re-staging or simulation of 'authentic' analogue elements such as film grain, scratches, flickering lights, torn borders, and degraded colours" (2015, 104). Important for this exploration of mini-consoles, van der Heijden describes how technostalgia can work to introduce the "materiality of media technologies" into memories and longing, which are "often understood as a (subjective) representation of the past" (2015, 105). On the other side of the technological spectrum, the Classic Editions also provide the option to apply a "pixel perfect" filter, which makes games look so crisp it is as if they were developed for the modern era. Providing this option serves two functions for Nintendo's goal of perpetuating their series, characters, and brands. First, the idealization of vintage games brings them in line with modern standards, paying a disservice to any notion of a radical or alien past. Second, idealizing past iterations of a series could potentially skew the perception of their historical significance, as the case for their evergreen status is retroactively strengthened as a way to justify series continuation.

The resulting perception is that only the most important and classic games are chosen for these systems, despite the obvious ability to put as many games as they wanted considering modern storage capabilities. Nintendo also prioritizes games and series that are currently popular, and mostly those that fall under the umbrella of their "first party" properties, those that they created and retain full rights to. Not only is this a strategy to perpetuate their current brands and characters, but also makes securing the rights to these games included in the Classic Editions a non-issue.[2] Playing a Nintendo Classic Edition console means never having to stumble upon a terrible game; the landscape is one of idealized nostalgic bliss. Actually playing the games has improved from their original context as well, with new features like save states (actually made popular by emulators), and a "rewind" feature introduced for the SNES Classic where any particularly difficult section of a game can be repeated until successfully completed. Anyone who has ever tried to beat Mr. Dream (originally Mike Tyson) in *Punch Out!!* (1990) or tried to survive *Super Ghouls and Ghosts* (1991) knows that a little digital help would constitute an idealized version of gameplay compared to their original reception. I have previously argued that the inclusion of the Mr. Dream version of *Punch Out!!* (1990) represents a combination of concern for the corporate brand and an idealization of the past that encourages an obfuscation of its original mediated context, the Classic Edition systems simply take this combination to its logical next step (Lizardi 2017).

Bonus Level: Sega Genesis Classics

A late entry into the classic gaming fray, Sega released their own compilation of past hits in May of 2018. Entitled *Sega Classics Collection* (2018), the fifty-three included vintage games came in the form of a disc or download for the Playstation 4 and the Xbox One. Sega does not directly manufacture consoles anymore, so it makes sense that having previously licensed their gaming library out to third parties to develop retro consoles that they would now forgo the console altogether in lieu of a compilation disc/download. Because of this difference, there is obviously no comparison to made about the experience gaining access to *Sega Classics Collection*, as it was as simple as clicking download on my Xbox One console and waiting a few minutes for the collection to be playable. There is also no comparison in terms of external aesthetics, as there are no similar replica Sega Genesis-era controllers or mini-consoles to hold in my hand. However, what *Sega Classics Collection* lacks in tangible tactile encouraged nostalgia it more than makes up for in its interface presentation.

When players load up *Sega Classics Collection* they enter into a virtual menu interface designed to tap directly into players' feelings of nostalgic longing to re-experience their vintage gaming pasts. The games library, settings, credits, multiplayer options, and a mini-thumbnail sized replication of where the games play all appear as if they are contained within a virtual bedroom. A CRT television sits at the center of the bedroom showing the current game "loaded" into the vintage Sega Genesis on the shelf below. The background of the bedroom is adorned with posters of Sega games like *Shinobi* (1987) and *Streets of Rage* (1991), as well as props from games like *Golden Axe* (1989). When players push right on their controllers, they "move" through the bedroom to the shelf that contains the game library, which mimics the look of original Sega Genesis black boxes and box art. After selecting a game to load and play an animation is shown that looks as if the original cartridge is being inserted into the top of the bedroom Sega Genesis as the CRT above goes from static to the menu of the game that was loaded. Much like Nintendo's Classic Editions, once gameplay takes over *Sega Classics Collection* uses a frame around the gaming experience to work around aspect ratio and resolution differences between current televisions and vintage games. *Sega Classics Collection*'s frame looks like a 1990s rendered virtual reality space, and attempts to extend gamers' nostalgic experience to the edges of their 4k televisions. The actual gaming experience is similar to other versions of retro gaming discussed here, with the exception of an enhanced "rewind" feature that allows students to replay the entirety of any gaming session, as opposed to the SNES Classic Edition that limits the rewind time by game. The effect is one of pure idealization of the original played experience, as one could conceivably play "one" time with infinite ability to rewrite what transpired and recreate a lost nostalgia-fueled experience.

Two Kinds of Nostalgic Experiences

It is understandable that Nintendo would not encourage DIY emulation of their catalog of vintage games, not just because it would in theory take away from Classic Edition system sales/interest but also because they explicitly describe the practices as illegal. Nintendo's goals are to perpetuate the brands, characters, and series they want to continue to monetize; ones that encourage a particular form of melancholic longing that does not allow for a comparative view of the past. I have previously argued that this type of nostalgic encouragement has the potential to impact how multiple generations connect with their pasts and their own memories (Lizardi 2017), and have also looked to develop the concept of the "perpetual commodification of the video game" through downloadable content (Lizardi 2012, 33). The Classic Edition consoles are part and parcel of Nintendo's long-term strategies for continued success. The original players of series like *Super Mario Bros.* (1985-present) and *The Legend of Zelda* (1986), myself included, are perpetually encouraged to reconnect and recreate our experiences with these games at the expense of comparative alternatives. As an appropriate extension of this form of perpetual commodification, Nintendo announced during their September 2018 "Nintendo Direct" presentation the launching of their "Nintendo Switch Online" service, which allows subscribers to play against one another online and provides access to "growing library of NES games" that can be played "anytime, anywhere" (Nintendo 2018). Retro looking "joy-con" controllers were also announced that look exactly like classic NES controllers, but are only available to purchase by those who subscribe to the four dollar a month service. What was once a free, DIY practice became a way to sell retro consoles, and has now become a perpetual payment plan to access your gaming memories. Nintendo's successes in this retro commodity arena has influenced nearly the entire industry, not only with the aforementioned *Sega Genesis Classics* but also with Sony's announcement that nostalgic gamers would soon get to "[r]elive the moments that changed gaming forever, with the iconic PlayStation Classic—featuring 20 of the best games from the original PlayStation console" (Sony 2018). Upping the price to $99, Sony is literally banking on the idea that commodifying dormant back catalogs is a viable economic strategy now and into the future.

Perhaps the most telling anecdote about the differences in subjective nostalgic experience when playing these two (three) vintage interactive consoles is the amount of time I have spent playing them since their release. After building the Pi Cart, testing it out, and diving into the playing experience it provided, I quickly grew tired of it and began plugging it in less and less. All told, I probably have played my Pi Cart in excess of ten hours, but no more than twenty. However, I have consistently played Nintendo's Classic Editions for countless more hours, especially once you add both systems together, which seems like an unfair comparison until you factor in that my Pi Cart contains all of the games from both Classic Editions. So why would I feel compelled to play through the entirety of *The Legend of Zelda:*

A Link to the Past (1991) on the Super Nintendo Classic Edition when I had access to the same ROM on the Pi Cart for ten months before Nintendo's console release? Perhaps I am just a sucker for slick marketing and flawless packaging, but I think it points more to the different encouraged forms of nostalgia involved in the similar, yet disparate, systems. My Pi Cart encourages me to compare the good and the bad vintage gaming side-by-side, and in true mourning fashion I remember the past and choose to release it as an object of desire. My Classic Editions smooth out all the rough edges of gaming past and even add new technological wrinkles like its Rewind Feature, encouraging my nostalgic desire to melancholically perpetuate. The split in the subjective experiences with the consoles (and the disc-based Genesis version) speaks directly to the differences between an encouraged feeling of nostalgic longing that has a goal of perpetuating idealized connections to the past and one that has the goal of comparison and potential release of the object of desire.

Notes

1. As proof of the manufactured nature of the NES Classic Edition scarcity, Nintendo re-released the mini-console in the summer of 2018 and it is still widely available.
2. As a side note, it remains to be seen whether Nintendo will produce an N64 Classic Edition given the vast array of classic titles on this system that were produced by third party developers, such as Rare who made titles like *GoldenEye 007* (1997) and *Perfect Dark* (2000).

References

Adorno, Theodor W. 1976. *Introduction to the Sociology of Music*. New York: The Seabury Press.

Anderson, Leon. 2006. "Analytic Autoethnography." *Journal of Contemporary Ethnography*, 35.4, 372–395.

Benjamin, Walter. 1968. *Illuminations*. Vol. 241. No. 2. New York: Random House, Inc.

Chang, Heewon. 2008. *Autoethnography as Method*. Walnut Creek, CA: Left Coast Press.

Coontz, Stephanie. 1992. *The Way We Never Were: American Families and the Nostalgia Trap*. New York: Basic.

Dickinson, Hilary, and Erben, Michael. 2006. "Nostalgia and Autobiography: The Past in the Present." *Autobiography*, 14.3, 223–244.

Giddings, Seth. 2009. "Events and Collusions: A Glossary for the Microethnography of Video Game Play." *Games and Culture*, 4.2, 144–157.

Gordon, Ian. 2017. *Superman: The Persistence of an American Icon*. New Brunswick, NJ: University of Rutgers Press.

Guttenbrunner, Mark, Christoph Becker, and Andreas Rauber. 2010. "Keeping the Game Alive: Evaluating Strategies for the Preservation of Console Video Games." *International Journal of Digital Curation,* 5.1, 64–90.

Jameson, Fredric. 1991. *Postmodernism, or, the Cultural Logic of Late Capitalism.* Durham, NC: Duke University Press.

Levine, Zach. 2016. "Pi Cart: A Raspberry Pi Retro Gaming Rig in an NES Cartridge." *HowChoo.* Accessed May 17, 2018. https://howchoo.com/g/mti0oge5nzk/pi-cart-a-raspberry-pi-retro-gaming-rig-in-an-nes-cartridge.

Lewis Galoob Toys, Inc. V. Nintendo of America, Inc. 780 F.Supp. 1991. Accessed February 28, 2016. https://scholar.google.com/scholar_case?case=14167398686354689030&hl=en&as_sdt=2&as_vis=1&oi=scholarr.

Lizardi, Ryan. 2012. "DLC: Perpetual Commodification of the Video Game." *Democratic Communiqué,* 25.1, 33–45.

Lizardi, Ryan. 2014. *Mediated Nostalgia: Individual Memory and Contemporary Mass Media.* Lanham, MD: Lexington Books.

Lizardi, Ryan. 2017. *Nostalgic Generations and Media: Perception of Time and Available Meaning.* Lanham, MD: Lexington Books.

Newman, James. 2012a. *Best Before: Videogames, Supersession and Obsolescence.* New York: Routledge.

Newman, James. 2012b. "Illegal deposit: Game Preservation and/as Software Piracy." *Convergence,* 19.1, 45–61.

Nintendo. 2016a. "Legal Information (Copyrights, Emulators, ROMs, etc.)." *Nintendo.* Accessed February 28, 2016. https://www.nintendo.com/corp/legal.jsp.

Nintendo. 2016b. "NES Classic Edition." *Nintendo.* Accessed July 28, 2016. https://www.nintendo.com/nes-classic.

Nintendo. 2018. "Nintendo Direct 9.13.2018." *Nintendo.* Accessed September 18, 2018. https://www.nintendo.com/nintendo-direct/09-13-2018/.

Nowinstock. 2017. "Nintendo SNES Classic Edition Tracker." *Nowinstock.net.* Accessed October 30, 2017. http://www.nowinstock.net/videogaming/consoles/nintendossnesclassicedition/.

Strasser, Susan. 2003. "The Alien Past: Consumer Culture in Historical Perspective." *Journal of Consumer Policy,* 26.4, 375–393.

van der Heijden, Tim. 2015. "Technostalgia of the Present: From Technologies of Memory to a Memory of Technologies." *European Journal of Media Studies,* 4.2, 103–121.

Vavrick, Justin. 2017. (owner/founder, Nowinstock.net), in discussion with the author, October 18.

Whalen, Zach, and Laurie N. Taylor. 2008. *Playing the Past: History and Nostalgia in Video Games.* Nashville, TN: Vanderbilt University Press.

Section 2

Digitally Nostalgic

5. *An Anthem for Outcasts: The Nostalgia of Friendship in* Stranger Things

RAYMOND BLANTON

Strange Things Are Happening

Given the many varied experiences of nostalgic longing, from the socio-cultural consternation of Stephanie Coontz's "nostalgic trap" (Coontz 2001) to the "hypochondria of the heart" (Boym 2001) in Svetlana Boym, our understanding of what it means to long for the past continues to be mercurial. As the call for nostalgic impulse is intensified by a seemingly unrelenting media mandate to make our past eternally relevant, our experiences and our approaches to understanding this phenomenon propel us as consumers and researchers to adequately account for the variations in our subjective experiences of longing for the past. Moreover, given this volume's aims to interrogate the significance of nostalgia through an interdisciplinary understanding of its multifaceted forms and functions, this chapter offers a rhetorically conscious criticism of interactive nostalgia in the Netflix series *Stranger Things*. Broadly, my analysis will draw upon my auto-ethnographic experiences with and reflections on the series bounded by a cultural and critical analysis to determine how the meaning making practice of nostalgic longing functions rhetorically. Put differently, this chapter offers an auto-ethnographic assessment of nostalgic longing with a particular focus on the rhetorical significance of a specific kind of longing, friendship.

To this end, I explore various themes of nostalgic longing that relate to our specific subjective experiences with nostalgia—all drawn from various performative elements within *Stranger Things*. Centrally, I am motivated by the question of what nostalgia does to/for us, and subsequently, what we can do with it. In other words, what specifically makes the nostalgia of

Stranger Things so rhetorically significant? To answer these questions, I begin by delineating the interdisciplinary and theoretical lenses through which my auto-ethnographic experience has been and continues to be shaped. Then, I critically explore some of the cultural meaning around nostalgia in the series using nostalgic song titles from 1980s tunes featured in *Stranger Things.* In short, I argue that friendship and community in the series functions rhetorically as an anthem for outcasts.

A Hazy Shade of Winter

In this section, my aims are to substantiate some of the critical lenses through which I consider nostalgia as both an individual and communal experience. In a sense, nostalgia is a meditation on time. Consider the tune "A Hazy Shade of Winter" for distinction: "Time, time, time. See what's become of me while I looked around for my possibilities" (Simon 1987). Put differently, I contend that our longing for the past, what we deem nostalgia, has two particular proclivities: time and possibilities. In between time and possibility, multiple identities are constructed, developed, traumatized, intensified, and reconstructed. Meaning is fashioned and re/formed over and again. For instance, when one thinks of "A Hazy Shade of Winter," while one person might think of the folk rock hit from the 1960s sung by Simon & Garfunkel, others will think of the 1980s rock song cover by the Bangles. And with each song comes an organic and intricately intertwined system of memories and longings.

Recall a nostalgic song and trace the varied memories and longings associated with it. That song in the here-and-now is inextricably bound to the memories of a specific place and time in the past—a romantic breakup, an accomplishment, or a road trip. In that moment, the reflections of our mind's eye, gazing upon the horizon between then and now, contributes to the formation of thoughts and memories that make up the urges of our nostalgic longing. In a similar manner, the nostalgia of *Stranger Things* tells a similar story. It also confronts time and possibilities. It has multiple identities. As such, and in the spirit of this volume, I progress along three theoretical lines of thinking that are independent and yet interrelated. I want their interrelations to tell a particular story about the substance of our nostalgic longing—friendship.

First, I consider C. Wright Mills' emphasis on the importance of experience in our critical work—thus the auto-ethnographic dimensions of this chapter. Second, I focus on Clay Routledge's adept insights on the sociocultural and psychological realms of nostalgic experience. Third, and finally, I consider the rhetorical construct of Kenneth Burke's identification as a means through which to understand the complex interplay of multiple identities. Put differently, our nostalgic experience and longings are a foundation; the social and psychological interplay of our relationships, then and now, make for a home; and identification is the heart. Home is where the heart is. Collectively, then, in this, I use the civic theorist Kenneth Burke, specifically his new rhetoric of identification and his understanding of the revolutionary symbolism of mythos as an equipment for living to explore *Stranger Things* as a representative anecdote from which we can consider the rhetorical dimensions of friendship as nostalgic longing.

Experience

All critical work should build on the past for the purposes of the future with the present in mind—all experience lies therein.

> [...] You must learn to use your life experience in your intellectual work: continually to examine and interpret it. In this sense craftsmanship is the center of yourself and you are personally involved in every intellectual product upon which you may work. To say that you can "have experience," means, for one thing, that your past plays into and affects your present, and that it defines your capacity for future experience ... You have to control this rather elaborate interplay, to capture what you experience and sort it out; only in this way can you hope to use it to guide and test your reflections, and in the process shape yourself as an intellectual craftsman. (Mills 1959, 196)

I lay the foundation with C. Wright Mills' charge. Specifically, I use *Stranger Things* as a means of capturing elements of nostalgic experience. But how do we go about accomplishing this? Mills argues that we need to be willing to capture "fringe thoughts" and snippets of overheard conversation. In other words, "The reason we treasure our smallest experiences is because in the entirety of our life it is a source of original intellectual work. To be able to trust yet to be skeptical of your own experience is a mark of a mature workman ... this ambiguous confidence is indispensable to originality in any intellectual pursuit that develops our self-reflective habits," enabling us to learn to keep our inner world awake (Mills). To situate this in the framework of *Stranger Things*, I invite you to consider *Beyond Stranger Things*, where host Jim Rash argues that experience is fundamental to the essence of the story, "That type of life experience is what feeds into your writing, which feeds into the characters, which feeds into them giving that birth and finding new things" (Rash 2017). And so, we begin with experience, that reliable, and at other times unreliable, means of meaning making.

Nostalgic Experience

In this chapter, for the sake of clarity and distinction, I stay close to this definition of nostalgia: "Nostalgia is about revisiting personally valued experiences shared with close ones … a bittersweet emotion, but more sweet than bitter … a redemptive sequence in which negative events or feelings [give] way to an emotionally positive conclusion" (Routledge 2016, 17). In other words, for better or worse, I heed this definition because it aligns with many of my experiences with nostalgia and can be substantiated critically through a close analysis of *Stranger Things*. The question remains, what validity shall come from it? That is to be determined. As for me, in my research and writing, I have come to understand nostalgic experience as a deep and committed (see the aforementioned charge of C. Wright Mills) reflection on the distance between then and now along with a subsequent reflection on the why and the how of the occurrences therein.

Specifically, I contend there are four interrelated aspects at work: inspiration, identification, imitation, and iteration. That is to say, nostalgic experience inspires, leading to an identification, be it with a sound or sight or smell, which in turn leads to imitation, either in a quip of dialogue or sporting a vintage tee, and ultimately, to iteration or repeated behavior that reinforces the initial inspiration. The more the cycle repeats, the stronger the nostalgic bond.

For an adept and nuanced perspective on nostalgia, particularly its psychological and sociological dimensions, I explore Routledge's *Nostalgia*. For my purposes, I want to highlight several important thoughts. First, "People want to mentally time travel to the past" (Routledge 2016, 7). One particular helpful insight with regards to how we conceptualize nostalgia, for instance, is that of the thirty-five distinct categories that broadly capture nostalgic themes, specifically, social relationships, memories, the past, and happiness play quite prominently (Routledge 2016, 9). In essence, I could argue that the creators of *Stranger Things* are interested, if not obsessed, with memories, the past, social relationships, and happiness—in that order.

As to how people experience nostalgia, I argue the most prominent theme of nostalgia centers on relationships: "Whether people were writing about objects, events or people, relationships were often prominently featured in the memory" (Routledge 2016, 15). With regards to what precisely makes people nostalgic or why people, regardless of age, "regularly take trips down memory lane," nostalgia is further prompted by our vast sensory experience through sight, sound and smell, taste and touch, revealing that "nostalgia may be an important component of healthy living," (Routledge 2016, 25). For example, among the many triggers, including negative emotions, loneliness, existential void manifest as feelings of meaninglessness and boredom, and self-discontinuity—the overarching revelation is that "distress causes nostalgia," (Routledge 2016, 37) with the subsequent insight that when in anguish, we travel back in time in search for some semblance of close relationships, be it family or friends.

An array of research affirms this sentiment. For instance, the distinction between the past and its relationship to friends is affirmed by Boym (2001): "Nostalgia is not only a longing for a lost time and lost home but also for friends who once inhabited it and who are now dispersed all over the world" (ix). Moreover, Bonnett (2010) denotes this process as seeking out a community of people who have found a way of being at home and finding friendship while pinned against an "alienating landscape" (156) or a "backdrop of noise, flux and dissociation" (165). Cross (2015) contends that we find identity in the past and find friends in these shared passions, at times even resolving lingering wounds (19). These desires are not dispassionate either. In the words of Bohn (2007), nostalgia is indicative of a "lustful revival" of the past—a relation of pain and longing for the past that is directed towards objects that can evoke the past (144). Altogether, Niemeyer (2014) notes: "At its core, nostalgia operates as the search for continuity of specific values and meanings from the past," or that which responds to an experience of discontinuity in the present. And by returning to that lost past and its people and or places, the nostalgic longing seeks to reconnect us with that sense of continuity—best understand not as an emotion or a sense but as a "rhetorical practice in which discontinuity is as central to its position as any assertion of continuity" (141).

Equipment for Living

Collectively, then, I contend *Stranger Things* is fundamentally a story about belonging—friendship in particular. To that end, I further argue that identification is central to belonging. And finally, that belonging is inherently rhetorical (Burke 1969b, 28). This is the first of four Burkean steps I want to make. According to Kenneth Burke, rhetoric is a means of identification in which we can persuade others insofar as we can talk their language by "speech, gesture, tonality, order, image, attitude, idea, identifying" our ways with theirs (Burke 1969b, 55). As it pertains to me, my nostalgia experience with *Stranger Things*, I find myself identifying with various realms within the series. In its style and characterization, it offers me variations of speech and tone, image and attitude, gestures and ideas. In short, *Stranger Things*, personified, thinks and talks like me. And for someone like me—an only child with no father, living transiently away from home for much of my life—reminders of bygone days when home was most salient in my innocent adolescent mind, it is not hard to imagine how and why nostalgic longings emerge.

The second Burkean step I want to make is that mythos or essential stories are fundamental to identification. The quintessential essence of humanity is to tell stories. We are storytelling animals. Returning to Burke, "And often we must think of rhetoric not in terms of some one particular address, but as a general body of identifications that owe their convincingness much more to trivial repetition and dull daily reinforcement than to exceptional rhetorical skill" (Burke 1969b, 26). In this sense, Stranger Things, through its retro aesthetic style and re/appropriation of a body of identifications in music, film, television, advertising, video games, toys, board games, décor and beyond, makes for a fascinating and fantastic representative anecdote to consider nostalgic longing.

To elaborate, in "Revolutionary Symbolism in America," Burke (1989, 267) outlines his philosophy of myth as a social tool and psychological bridge for working together with others to promote social justice. As Coupe notes, Burke was interested in the subtle attitudes and emotions inherent to a particular unifying principle around which people cooperate.

> Myths may be wrong, or they may be used to bad ends, but they cannot be dispensed with [...] they are our basic psychological tools for working together. A hammer is a carpenter's tool; a wrench is a mechanic's tool; and a "myth" is the social tool for welding the sense of interrelationships by which the carpenter and the mechanic, though differently occupied, can work together for common social ends. In this sense a myth that works well is as real as food, tools, and shelter are ... they are not "illusions", since they perform a very real and necessary social function in the organizing of the mind. (Burke 1989, 267–8)

In other words, *Stranger Things*, I contend, is a social tool and psychological bridge that tells us an essential story about friendship.

The third Burkean step confronts the essential purpose of identification and stories—they are equipment for living. This is why I referred to Burke as a civic theorist, for I would argue that the entirety of his poetry, fiction, letters, and criticism remain focused on living. And this is what *Stranger Things* does—more than a means of identification and story, it equips us for living in the face of bullying and being identified by others as outcasts. In this sense, it is reminiscent of Cervantes' famous gentleman Don Quixote of La Mancha, who became so "absorbed in his books, spending his nights from sunset to sunrise, and his days from dawn to dark, poring over them, that he lost his wits and the fancy of his enchantments so possessed his mind that to him no history in the world had more reality in it" (Cervantes 1952, 2). This feels a lot like what is at play in nostalgic longing and *Stranger Things* in particular.

Building on the other three steps, the fourth and final progression is to explore these curiosities and questions pertaining to nostalgia by examining *Stranger Things* as a representative anecdote. To be clear, in an essay titled "Literature as Equipment for Living," Kenneth Burke refers to the representative anecdote as a pattern of experience that is representative of the social (Burke 1973, 300). In this particular essay, Burke, writing in the midst of the Great Depression, is seeking to apply the comforts of proverbial wisdom to all of literature. Furthering this idea, in his essay, "Burke's Representative Anecdote as a Method in Media Criticism," Barry Brummett refers to the representative anecdote as a "trained awareness" toward types of dramatic form. In other words, it enables us to extract some semblance of order from the cultural chaos while also helping us decipher what a culture "most deeply fears and hopes" (Brummett 1984, 174).

Both Burke and Brummett give us a method for confronting not just our living, but in particular, that living in relation with others. To that end, in *A Grammar of Motives*, Burke contends, "One should seek to select as representative anecdote, something sufficiently demarcated in character to make analysis possible, yet sufficiently complex in character" (Burke 1969, 324). For an anecdote to be representative, then, it must have scope but possess simplicity, wherein "human relations grandly converge" (Burke 1969a, 329). With a representative anecdote, we can decipher patterns of experience from the confusing signals of cultural coding. In this case, I use the cultural dimensions of *Stranger Things* to ascertain insights on nostalgic longing.

Welcome to Hawkins

As I take my initial steps into Hawkins, it is necessary to self-identify as a fan of *Stranger Things*. Though some of the tone of this volume is intended to look critically at our subjectivities, this chapter chooses first to confront subjectivity by understanding the varied dimensions at play. To that end, I have binged on the series several times. Each time, it continues to evoke the same tenacious chills and childhood thrills with each new viewing. For months, an assortment of friends from all directions would ask me—have you seen *Stranger Things* yet? And though I was late to this particular nostalgic playground, I did indeed find my way. Since then, I have spent countless hours in the upside down (literally) dimensions of its nostalgic wonder. Its merry-go rounding of adolescent angst and adventurousness has dizzied me with an array of memories. It is a seesaw of sociological and psychological complexity, which moves adeptly to and fro the realms of identity embedded in our relationships with friends, family, and work, stimulating an array of curiosities and pursuits. Its eclectic visual and cultural style, like a circuitous slide, has ushered me toward a perfect balance of elation and fear. Even after multiple views, certain scenes still make the hairs on my body stand at attention. For instance, when Will first encounters the Demogorgon, it is exhilarating both at the level of suspenseful story and nostalgia. When Will runs through a wide-angle shot of the night fog, it transports me back in time to when Elliot first encounters E. T.

As a child of the 1980s, *Stranger Things,* and the various cultural dialects therein, speaks my language(s). So when I watch films like *E. T.* or *The Goonies,* there is a powerful nostalgic longing that comes over me. I'm intrigued with the why of these urges, and not just for myself but for my children, students, and countless others. I want to understand and respond accordingly to the ways in which nostalgia might enhance the quality of our life. And yes, this also means being mindful of the ways in which it may also hurt or hinder our inner and outer worlds. Interestingly, although *Stranger Things* is a product of the present, it seems rather adept at re/capturing the past in the present. And one compelling cultural byproduct of this is that the highly stylized identifications of my 1980s past are being formed in someone's 2010s now. The nostalgic past in the present is re/appropriating itself for a yet to be determined future. What will the students who are currently in middle and high school or college make of their memories then that are based on now? How, if at all, might *Stranger Things* make for substantive formation of meaning both here and now as well as then and there?

Firestarter

There is a handcrafted quality to *Stranger Things,* the tone of which is inspired by the likes of pairing John Carpenter music with vintage cinematic sequences from *E.T* (Sternbergh 2017). For instance, in the opening sequence of the series, we open in the astral sky over Hawkins National Laboratory and the U.S. Department of Energy. It is November 6, 1983 in Hawkins, Indiana. From the night sky, we transition into what appears to be a basement as we draw close to a rounded steel door shrouded in a dim strobe of light. Then, the door bursts open. A man is running. An alarm is resounding. And after some elevator button intrigue, we find ourselves anticipating the demise of the now breathless man as we eagerly wait for either the elevator doors to close or some mysterious something to round the corner and satisfy our curiosity. From the opening sequence to the final frame, *Stranger Things,* like all good stories of suspense, guides us through the process of learning to expect the unexpected. And this perpetual intrigue keeps us steadily interested and invested.

The proprietors of this realm are Matt and Ross Duffer—or, the Duffer brothers. *Stranger Things* takes many of its thematic and aesthetic cues from the cultural dialects of Steven Spielberg, Stephen King and John Carpenter, "but it's also an entirely original story that stands on its own visual inventiveness and tremendous young cast" (Fienberg 2016). Focusing on a particular dimension of the nostalgic aura of the series, the title sequence font, Ross Duffer notes:

> I don't know what it is, but it obviously brings you back. It's weird, because the font was one of the first things. When we sold the show to Netflix, and when we were pitching it around to companies, we made a little look book. In the front cover, we made it look like an old Stephen King book, and we had a very similar font in the red and the outline and there was a bike that was just on the ground that was lost … we literally took the Firestarter paperback and pasted a picture of a bike on top of it and changed the font to our font … we wanted it to be like, "This is what it felt like when we were in middle school or high school reading those paperbacks." (Fienberg 2016)

This statement, "This is what it felt like when …" aptly captures the essence of nostalgia—how it works. It is an unrelenting effort to recapture feelings that reach into some distant past. In fact, "One of the big draws of the series is, of course, its knack for channeling a certain kind of nostalgia—all BMX bikes, skinny T-shirts and 80s board games—and one of the great pleasures of watching it is trying to spot the references, from *The Goonies* to *Poltergeist* to *Stand By Me*" (Nicholson 2017).

Just Another Day

As a child of the 1980s, born in the late 1970s, there is something substantive in my nostalgic longing that I have yet to fully grasp, though there are glimpses. In reality, that is why this chapter exists. Though I am confident I know why *Stranger Things* evokes such nostalgic longing in my mind and memories, I am continually drawn to understanding how and why this is the way it is. One particular insight, which will guide the substantive focus of this chapter, comes from The Harvard Study of Adult Development. "Most of what we know about human life we know from asking people to remember the past … the clearest message we get from this 75 year study is this: good relationships keep us happier and healthier, period. Moreover, speaking directly to the lessons learned about relationships, … we've learned three big lessons about relationships … social connections are really good for us and loneliness kills … it's the quality of your close relationships that matters … good relationships don't just protect our bodies, they protect our brains" (Waldinger 2016). As such, I argue that the interactive nostalgic realms of *Stranger Things* are an anthem for outcasts that are centrally concerned with the bonds of friendship.

Stranger Things certainly isn't a parody of resilient '80s pop culture like John Carpenter and Spielberg, and it's not even really an homage. It's more like a genetic recombination; less a show that's nostalgic for '80s pop culture than a show that is a nostalgic reimagining of '80s pop culture. *Happy Days*, by contrast, was a 1970s show born of nostalgia for the '50s, but it didn't try to replicate the experience of watching a show in the 1950s. The canny advance of *Stranger Things* lies in how it acknowledges the ways that, in the age of the Internet, different eras collide, even as it recombines iconic sounds, images, and visual references to create a modernized version of a cultural experience that is all but lost. And all of it is thanks to two twin brothers who spent the '80s and '90s glued to their VCR, watching and re-watching their favorite movies, who are now committed to re-creating that feeling for you (Sternbergh 2017).

Recreating the feeling for us. Yet, in a criticism of Netflix's nostalgia strategy, particularly the 1990s nostalgia show *Everything Sucks!*, one Guardian critic refers to the dangers of uninterrogated nostalgia. In doing so, however, a telling insight is offered on the appeal of *Stranger Things*:

> It is a far cry from *Stranger Things*, where the nostalgia came from an understanding and appreciation of the references it was valorising, its retro aesthetic a tribute to stories that cared about the anxieties and vulnerabilities of young people, its many Easter eggs and callbacks speaking to its characters' escape into esoteric popular culture, over-parsing complicated adult emotions. (Williams 2018)

There are three specific aspects that are of note. The first is the recognition that *Stranger* nostalgia embodies both an understanding and appreciation for its cultural re/appropriations. The second is that its aesthetic is purposeful—a tribute to stories that actually care about anxious and vulnerable experiences of adolescence. And the third is the preeminence of its characters experiences with said culture as being a direct response or reaction to the domestic situations, something that is of central thematic importance. In sum, the banner that billows over this series, and this chapter, is that friendship propels nostalgic longing. It is, for all intensive purposes, the Duffer's channeling their days of adolescent angst as outcasts, held back in kindergarten because of their apparent social ineptitudes, coalescing with the adventurousness of their youth manifest in their favorite stories in films, board and video games, music, and otherwise.

Should I Stay or Should I Go

In my reading of the literature on nostalgia, the Clash song "Should I Stay Or Should I Go" (Headon 1982) poses a basic but important question for nostalgia. Should it stay or should it go? Briefly, I want to recognize some of the critical sentiments in the literature. These are ideas that I acknowledge and respect but they are not my focus. For instance, Janelle L. Wilson's notion of nostalgia as a "sanctuary of meaning" (Wilson 2014). I value Cassin's critical query regarding our sentiments regarding home and the particular insight on nostalgia as both rootedness and wandering (Cassin 2016, 24). Furthermore, I also value Coontz's critical evaluation of nostalgia as both the "way we never were" (Coontz 2000) and the "way we really are" (Coontz 1997) with the understanding that her focus centers on family and social misconceptions and the misgivings therein. Boym was particularly helpful for me regarding an understanding of the prejudice against nostalgia as a bad word, the kitsch of memory, "an abdication of personal responsibility, a guilt free homecoming, an ethical and aesthetic failure" (Boym 2001, xiv). In a telling title focused on nostalgia and retro, "Don't Look Back" (sorry, already did), Reynolds is interesting for its play with boundaries, as when the distinction is made between the plausible emotion of the original nostalgia in contrast to the impossible emotion of the modern nostalgia, that is incurable (Reynolds 2011, xxv–xxvi). Steiner's insight on the "deep-seated nostalgia for the absolute" left by the decline of religion is interesting (Steiner 1997, 5). And given my specific focus on identification, Davis is of particular interest, which is intriguing given that its consideration of nostalgia, identity, and the current nostalgia wave was published in the fall of 1977 (Davis 1977, 414). All of these and others have their own nostalgic focal points.

Sunglasses at Night (Heart 1984)

In this section, I am centrally concerned with the style of *Stranger Things*, specifically, how it works to mediate nostalgic longings through an intricately interrelated realm of stories in film, comics, gaming, props and products, music, characterization, and other adventures. To be clear, though I do focus on the distinct elements of style in the series, I believe the interrelation of these entities, or rather, their multilayered complexity or how each element works in symphony with the nostalgic voices in and around it, is what makes the series so rhetorically compelling. Put differently, given the theoretical foundation of experience, which supports the home of nostalgic longing, the brick and mortar become the body of identifications. This is its rhetorical function. My focus here is on Burke's notion of the rhetorical as a body of identifications rather than any one singular idea.

Briefly, to set the tone, I want to consider the teaser trailer for season two, which has nearly 14 million views since its debut. Executive producer and director Shawn Levy remarks, "There was a recognition that anything linked to *Stranger Things* tends to get some cultural topspin as a result … the show has achieved this phenom status around the world so I think I was able to articulate the value of this, beyond money. There is a cultural currency to *Stranger Things* that is separate from dollars" (Goodin 2017). In it, Levy teases out all of the intricate possibilities of the new season with a body of identifications, of which I will highlight two important ones. The first is the symbolic and thematic alignment of season two, which is set in 1984, with perhaps the most popular film of that same year, *Ghostbusters.* Moreover, the film also builds naturally upon all of the prominent themes of the series in ways that borrows and builds simultaneously. Second, though it almost never happened, Levy was able to negotiate what was originally thought to be an untouchable song, Michael Jackson's iconic "Thriller" (Temperton 1984), which was apparently stratospheric in price. Consistent with *Ghostbusters*, the song was not released as a single until, that's right, 1984. Furthermore, both nostalgic tropes play with horror themed elements of suspense. As a fan, and having experienced the second season, it is an absolutely brilliant rendering that is strengthened collectively through the use of finely crafted elements of film, music, and other entities. In short, it is rarely if ever one source of identification. When nostalgic longing is active, we should be considering the symphonic dimensions of that longing working together.

Film

Though *Stranger Things* is technically considered television, it is both inspired by and reminiscent of the cinematic. In particular, it walks the lines of science fiction, horror, adventure, and suspense. Throughout, particular films feature prominently on walls and in attire, theme, and tropes. *The Thing. Jaws. Halloween. Poltergeist. The Evil Dead. Dark Crystal. E. T. Stand By Me. All the Right Moves. Goonies. Star Wars. Ghostbusters. Firestarter. Risky Business. Indiana Jones and the Temple of Doom.* For instance, the plot for Stephen King's (who is one of the preeminent inspirations for much of the stories dark, suspenseful, and youth oriented themes) *Firestarter* also features a "young girl/woman who can move things with her mind; some bad men have lied to said girl and want to use her for nefarious purposes; and a monster has been awakened because the men tampered with her mind" (Abad-Santos 2016).

For the Duffer brothers, they were trying to capture the feel of the movies without specifically trying to reference them. "It's fun, because people are doing 'Spot the reference stuff,' and obviously some of it is absolutely true, and then some of it is so funny because I'm like, 'I've never even seen D.A.R.Y.L. I don't even know what that is'" (Nobil 2017). In other words, rather than trying to be clever, the Duffer's love of film, and specifically 1980s films, is one of their primary languages. Similar to my own experience with my father, when asked about how their affinity for film was shaped, the brothers, who were born the month *Footloose* was released, credit their father and the VCR. "Our dad is a big movie buff ... we would just go wander around the video store" (Rubin 2017).

Gaming

Gaming is another part of the body of identifications. It is rather central, actually. For instance, season one is thematically oriented around the role playing game *Dungeons & Dragons* (D&D). We are introduced to the story from the perspective of the boys playing D&D. The arch of the story uses the language and characters of D&D. Before young kids passed the hours playing video games on their electronic devices, they planned campaigns of D&D and played throughout the weekend. Moreover, season two transitions from basement role-playing to public arcade and is thematically oriented around two specific games with some continued story elements from D&D (though we never actually see them playing as in season one). The first is *Dragon's Lair*, which is featured in the aforementioned teaser trailer and tells the tale of a love triangle in the pursuit of Princess Daphne, foreshadowing the relationship between Lucas, Dustin, and Mad Max. The second is the classic arcade game *Dig-Dug*, which provides the substantive and symbolic cue for much of the plot and meaning developed in season two.

Comics

In the pilot episode, a friendly game of race-you leads to a significant insight on the essence of the series. The bet, winner gets a comic from the collection of the other—any comic. Will gets a good jump. Sensing the danger of what is about to happen, Dustin desperately tries to catch Will, but to no avail. Will races across the mark with his comic of choice, "I'll take your X-Men 134" (Schnapp 2016). In this particular case, though it might seem minor or irrelevant, the reference actually gives us our first glimpse into the cultural multiverse of *Stranger Things*. *Uncanny X-Men* No. 134 contains the first appearance of The Dark Phoenix, one of the most destructive forces in the X-Men universe. And viewed through the lens of *Stranger Things*, it's both a taste of what's to come on the show and an homage to the X-Men character known as Jean Grey. "Hear me, X-Men! No longer am I the woman you knew! I am fire! And life incarnate! Now and forever—I am Phoenix" (Claremont and Byrne 1980). Just as Jean Grey mentally snaps and inadvertently unleashes the Dark Phoenix, a cosmic force far beyond her control, Eleven must learn to master her own destructive powers.

Prop and Product

Another important part of the body of identifications is its props and products. When I was a boy, I watched *E. T.* while eating Reece's Pieces. For some, they can watch *Stranger Things* and eat Three Musketeers. Behind all of the props and products, Lynda Reiss noted, "I don't want to do a nostalgia-tinged product … I want it to be the '80s. I don't want it to be what everyone just thinks is the '80s. Our baseline was the reality of the Midwest in 1983" (Moynihan 2016). Though some of these items might seem obscure, a lot of time and attention was devoted to accurately capturing and rendering the 1980s. These include the Pentax MX SLR, Panasonic RX-5090 Boombox and Memorex MRX 1 60-Minute Cassette, Fisher MC-4550, Western Electric 554 Yellow Wall Phone, Realistic TRC-214 walkie-talkies, along with various retro bikes, Hunt's Snack Pack Chocolate Pudding in a can and other varied toys and items. For further instance, Coke is the featured soda in *Stranger Things.* And what is interesting about this, is that two of the more prominent films that Stranger Things features in season two, *Ghostbusters* and *Stand By Me*, were released when Coca-Cola, who acquired Columbia Pictures in June of 1982, were at the helm. Moreover, to maintain the connection to the body of identifications, film in particular, Reiss also notes that she was inspired after reading the scripts. "It took me back to watching every single one of the reference movies you see in the show, from E. T. and the Stephen King movies, the Steven Spielberg movies, the movies that made me want to make movies" (Canadian Broadcasting Company 2016). Like the films, the props transport you back in time.

Characters

The characters in *Stranger Things* are part of what give the story its authenticity. Though I would thoroughly enjoy eliciting reflections on all of the *Stranger Things* characters, I will focus only briefly on Dustin and Jim. In line with the anthem for outcasts thematic, Dustin was actually the first child actor cast in the series in large part due to a rare health condition known as cleidocranial dysplasia that has affected the growth of his teeth and led to bullying. In a sense, it could be argued the entire show is an anti-bullying campaign. In this sense, note the Duffer's, just like his character, Dustin is not a normal kid. "He didn't fit in very well with the other kids. It's something we felt, for other reasons, when we were kids growing up. We wanted to make a show about outsiders, about kids who didn't fit in, and who were bullied and made fun of. So I think Gaten was really able to tap into all of that" (Duffer 2017b). Then there's Jim Hopper, Hawkins Chief of Police. In a brief but telling example of how a body of identifications works, we meet Hopper as the camera pans away from a close up of a child's crayon portrait of a family to a kitchen table littered with an assortment of items that includes an unfinished sandwich near a bottle of prescription pills surrounded by empty cans of Schlitz beer and cigarette ends. But the telling insight is the copy of Ernest Hemingway's *The Old Man and the Sea*, which tells the story of an experienced but aging fisherman battling a marlin—offering a telling glimpse, of which there are many in the series, into the soul of Jim Hopper and the *Stranger Things* cosmos.

She Blinded Me With Science

In *Stranger Things*, the AV Club and Mr. Clarke's Heathkit Ham Shack radio, form the basis of the Party—the boys' self-government. "It's poetry in motion. She turned her tender eyes to me. As deep as any ocean. As sweet as any harmony [...] she blinded me with science" (Dolby 1982). Lastly, and perhaps a bit of an unconventional theme, is science, particularly given the focus on nerds and outcasts as central figures, albeit a stereotype but also an effective trope. For instance, when the boys ask Mr. Clarke, Earth and Biology teacher at Hawkins Middle School, reminiscent of many classic 1980s John Hughes teachers, about Carl Sagan's *Cosmos* he redirects them to Hugh Everett's Many-Worlds Interpretation. It is basically the notion of parallel universes—"Just like our world, but just infinite variations of it. Which means there's a world out there where none of this tragic stuff ever happened" (Havens 2017).

Friendship: Time After Time (Lauper and Hyman 1984)

Given the aforementioned theoretical lines of thought, and in the light of the body of identifications I have underlined in the story, the heart and soul of the rhetorical analysis centers on the nostalgic longings for meaningful relationships. While the parental figures trudge through the domestic dangers of divorce, the ruts of loveless marriage, government abuse and corruption, and grief, the kids thrive on the principles of unfettered friendship. They define friendship as someone you would be willing to do anything for, someone who never breaks a promise. When spit is involved, I'm there. They tell each other things that even parents don't know. They defend each other against bullies, or mouth breathers as they refer to them. And they don't lie. In the longitudinal study on adult development at Harvard, "Close relationships, more than money or fame, are what keep people happy throughout their lives … [they] protect people from life's discontents, help to delay mental and physical decline, and are better predictors of long and happy lives than social class, IQ, or even genes. That finding proved true across the board among both the Harvard men and the inner-city participants" (Mineo 2017).

Bloodstone Pass

For the kids of *Stranger Things*, loyalty to one another is ultimate. We find an indication of their philosophy of friendship in Dustin's mediation of the conflict between Mike and Lucas in "The Monster," episode six of the first season: "Do you even remember what happened on the Bloodstone Pass? We couldn't agree on what path to take, so we split up the party and those trolls took us out one-by-one. And it all went to shit. And we were all disabled! So we stick together, no matter what!" This is such a simple and yet compelling vision for friendship. We stick together, no matter what. Perhaps the adult response is an expected eye-roll and a brief but assertive lecture about that is not how it actually works. But perhaps it should be. Perhaps it could be. In short, we are drawn to stories that feature this sort of deep and committed friendship, complete with flaws. In the first episode from season two, "MADMAX," for instance, when Will is describing his visions of the Nether or the Upside Down, he asks Mike to keep it between them. Mike reciprocates with his feelings about El and the confession, "sometimes I feel like I'm going crazy," to which Will resounds, "Me too," before the essence of the show manifests once again, "Hey, well, if we're both going crazy, then we'll go crazy together, right?" (Wolfhard and Schnapp 2017). Crazy together, yet another terse but effective encapsulation of Stranger Things.

Home: Love Is a Battlefield

When Jim Hopper brings El to his granddad's cabin, he takes great fatherly pride in declaring, "This is your new home." And every true sentiment within that word compels El to turn toward Jim, and with a coy and joyous smile, repeat the word, "Home," as if she is satisfying some deep sense of longing. It is buttressed by the Jim Croce tune, "You Don't Mess Around With Jim." Ironically, the story tells us much of what we need to know about Jim Hopper. "When the bad folks all get together at night, you know they all call Big Jim boss … because you don't tug on Superman's cape. You don't spit into the wind. You don't pull the mask off that old lone ranger. And you don't mess around with Jim" (Croce 1972). It is such an endearing and sweeping moment. His jubilation at the prospect of becoming a father again—having lost his own daughter. Her sense of wonder (and wander) and curious awe, that this dancing Jim might very well be her Big Jim boss.

For further perspective, we find further support for this when Jim reads a book to El. But it is not just any book. It is *Anne of Green Gables*, a story about an orphan girl. He reads to her:

> I would feel so sad if I was a disappointment to her—because she didn't live very long after that, you see. She died of a fever when I was just three months old. I do wish she'd lived long enough for me to remember calling her mother. I think it would be so sweet to say "mother," don't you? And father died four days afterwards from fever too. That left me an orphan and folks were at their wits' end, so Mrs. Thomas said, what to do with me. You see, nobody wanted me even then. It seems to be my fate. (Montgomery 1908, 56)

It is the same book that Hopper reads to his daughter in the hospital while she is getting cancer treatment. Moreover, throughout the series, Hopper wears a blue ribbon on his wrist. This is his daughter's hair ribbon. In the final episode of season two, we find that blue ribbon on the wrist of El while she is dancing with Mike at the Snow Ball.

Conclusion

Stranger Things is a thoughtful and intelligent series. For instance, the musical dimension illuminates one of the most interesting and complex aspects of the story—the Upside Down. Oingo Boingo offers the glimpse: "There's life underground … I feel it all around. I feel it in my bones. My life is on the line. When I'm away from home. When I step out the door the jungle is alive. I do not trust my ears. I don't believe my eyes … It's just another day. There's murder in the air. It drags me when I walk. I smell it everywhere. It's just another day. Where people cling to light to drive away the fear that comes with every night" (Elfman 1985).

As someone who has experienced bullying and shaming, and as a father to elementary, middle, and high school kids, I have deep stores of sympathy and empathy for what it takes to survive and endure those days of angst and tumultuous wonder about what the next day will bring. Will they like me? Will they say something about me behind my back? I see it everyday. And I recall my own moments and long to assuage some of that debilitating angst. The great thing, in my estimation, about *Stranger Things*, is that it seems to have been done in an adept manner. "Nostalgia programming is a tricky thing. Done well, it can revive treasured memories. Done poorly, it can feel like an ill-conceived attempt at pandering, resulting in a rejection of the show and possibly the outlet responsible for its existence" (Schwindt 2016). Put differently, Routledge claims, that, "In times of uncertainty or distress or they're not sure where they're going, nostalgia is a stabilizing force, it grounds us" (Schwindt 2016).

It grounds us by reminding us of what is most important. In sum, I have often referred to *Stranger Things* as an anthem for the outcasts. And this is because the show's executive producer, Shawn Levy, basically says as much, noting, everybody in the show is a little bit broken, on the margins, and self-doubting. And the ultimate aim of the story is to raise everyone up as if to shout, "You're all going to be okay" (Levy 2017). This is an important message. For instance, in the final scene of the final episode of season two, at the Snow Ball dance, we watch as Dustin is confronted with rejection after rejection. In an endearing scene, Nancy Wheeler swoops in and gives Dustin a dance and a pep talk. Recalling his own Nancy moment with his cousin Joanna, Matt Duffer recalls:

> Everyone has that anxiety when you are growing up of feeling like you're going to be left behind. Or you're being left behind in certain areas, certainly. Especially socially, I was always behind. In fact, we were held back in kindergarten for this very reason … I think it's hard. Everyone struggles with that. You're freaked out. Are other people getting ahead of you? And figuring this stuff out. And why is this taking me so long to figure out how to deal with people? (Duffer 2017a)

An additional example is found in episode one from season two, "MADMAX," when Will Byers vulnerably shares with his brother Jonathan about the "Zombie boy" taunts he has been the victim of. So, as a defense, Will refers to himself as a freak. Using some good old-fashioned reverse psychology, Jonathan agrees. "You know what? You're right. You are a freak. No, I'm serious. You're a freak. But what? Do you wanna be normal? Do you wane be just like everyone else? Being a freak is the best. I'm a freak … and I would rather be best friends with Zombie Boy than with a boring nobody. You know what I mean … the thing is, nobody normal ever accomplished anything meaningful in this world. You got it?" (Heaton 2017). Crazy, together.

References

Abad-Santos, Alex. 2016. "Stranger Things Is a Love Letter to the X-Men's Jean Grey." In *Vox*, August 5, 2016, https://www.vox.com/2016/8/5/12375808/stranger-things-xmen-134-jean-grey

Bohn, Andreas. 2007. "Nostalgia of the Media/in the Media." In *Self-Reference in the Media,* ed. Winfried Noth and Nina Bishara. New York, NY: Mouton de Gruyter, pp. 143–153.

Bonnett, Alastair. 2010. *Left in the Past: Radicalism and the Politics of Nostalgia.* New York, NY: Continuum.

Boym, Svetlana. 2001. *The Future of Nostalgia.* New York, NY: Basic Books.

Brummett, Barry. 1984. "Burke's Representative Anecdote as a Method in Media Criticism." In *Critical Studies in Mass Communication* 1, 174.

Burke, Kenneth. 1969a. *A Grammar of Motives.* Berkeley, CA: University of California Press.

Burke, Kenneth. 1969b. *A Rhetoric of Motives.* Berkeley, CA: University of California Press.

Burke, Kenneth. 1973. *The Philosophy of Literary Form.* Berkeley, CA: University of California Press.

Burke, Kenneth. 1989. "Revolutionary Symbolism in America." In *The Legacy of Kenneth Burke*, ed. Herbert W. Simons and Trevor Melia. Madison, WI: University of Wisconsin Press.

Canadian Broadcasting Company. 2016. "The Prop Master Who Helped Stranger Things Recreate the 1980s." In Day 6, Episode 296, July 26, 2016.

Cassin, Barbara. 2016. *Nostalgia: When Are We Ever at Home?* New York, NY: Fordham University Press.

Cervantes, Miguel. 1952. *The History of Don Quixote de la Mancha.* Chicago: William Benton.

Claremont, Chris and John Byrne. 1980. "Too Late, the Heroes!" In *X-Men*, Volume 1, #134, digital.

Coontz, Stephanie. 1997. *The Way We Really Are: Coming to Terms with America's Changing Families.* New York, NY: Basic Books.

Coontz, Stephanie. 2000. *The Way We Never Were: American Families and the Nostalgia Trap.* New York, NY: Basic Books.

Croce, Jim. 1972. "You Don't Mess Around with Jim." In *You Don't Mess Around with Jim*, ABC, digital.

Cross, Gary. 2015. *Consumed Nostalgia: Memory in the Age of Fast Capitalism.* New York, NY: Columbia University Press.

Davis, Fred. 1977. "Nostalgia, Identity and the Current Nostalgia Wave." In *The Journal of Popular Culture*, 11(2), 414–424.

Dolby, Thomas and Jo Kerr. 1982. "She Blinded Me with Science." In *Blinded by Science*, Capitol Records, digital.

Duffer, Matt. 2017a. "The Duffer Brothers on How the 'Stranger Things' Kids Have Evolved." In *Nylon*, October 25, 2017, https://nylon.com/articles/duffer-brothers-stranger-things-season-two-interview

Duffer, Matt. 2017b. "Unlikely Allies." In *Beyond Stranger Things*, directed by Michael Dempsey, Los Angeles, Embassy Row, digital.

Elfman, Danny. 1985. "Just Another Day." In *Dead Man's Party*, MCA Records, digital.

Fienberg, Daniel. 2016. "The Duffer Brothers Talk 'Stranger Things' Influences, 'It' Dreams and Netflix Phase 2." In *The Hollywood Reporter*, August 1, 2016, https://www.hollywoodreporter.com/fien-print/duffer-brothers-talk-strangerthings-916180

Goodin, Jesse. 2017. "Stranger Things Producer Says Cost of 'Thriller' Was Stratospheric, But Worth It." In *Canadian Broadcasting Company*, August 21, 2017, http://www.cbc.ca/radio/q/stranger-things-producer-says-cost-of-thriller-was-stratospheric-but-worth-it-1.4253424

Hart, Corey. 1984. "Sunglasses at Night." In *First Offense*, EMI, digital.

Havens, Randy. 2017. "Chapter Five: The Flea and the Acrobat." In *Stranger Things*, directed by Matt and Ross Duffer, Los Angeles: 21 Laps Entertainment, digital.

Headon, Topper and others (The Clash). 1982. "Should I Stay Or Should I Go." In *Combat Rock*, Epic, digital.

Heaton, Charlie. 2017. "Chapter One: MADMAX." In *Stranger Things*, directed by Matt and Ross Duffer, Los Angeles: 21 Laps Entertainment, digital.

Lauper, Cyndi and Roby Hyman. 1984. "Time After Time." In *She's So Unusual*, Epic, digital.

Levy, Shawn. 2017. "Unlikely Allies." In *Beyond Stranger Things*, directed by Michael Dempsey, Los Angeles, Embassy Row, digital.

Mills, C. Wright. 2000. "On Intellectual Craftsmanship." In *The Sociological Imagination*, New York, NY: Oxford University Press.

Mineo, Liz. 2017. "Good Genes Are Nice, But Joy Is Better." In *The Harvard Gazette*, April 11, 2017, https://news.harvard.edu/gazette/story/2017/04/over-nearly-80-years-harvard-study-has-been-showing-how-to-live-a-healthy-and-happy-life/

Montgomery, Lucy Maud. 1908. *Anne of Green Gables*. New York, NY: Grosset & Dunlap.

Moynihan, Tim. 2016. "The Stories Behind Stranger Things' Retro '80s Props." In *Wired*, July 27, 2016, https://www.wired.com/2016/07/stories-behind-stranger-things-retro-80s-props/

Nicholson, Rebecca. 2017. "The Duffer Brothers: Could We Do What Spielberg Did in the 80s and Elevate It Like He Did." In *The Guardian*, October 14, 2017, https://www.theguardian.com/tv-and-radio/ng-interactive/2017/oct/14/dufferbrothers-spielberg-80s-stranger-things

Niemeyer, Katharina. 2014. *Media and Nostalgia: Yearning for the Past, Present and Future*. New York, NY: Springer.

Nobil, Taryn. 2017. "Duffer Brothers on 'Stranger Things' 2 and What Scares Them." In *Variety*, November 23, 2017, https://variety.com/2017/tv/features/duffer-brothers-stranger-things-1202621133/

Rash, Jim. 2017. "Unlikely Allies." In *Beyond Stranger Things*, directed by Michael Dempsey, Los Angeles, Embassy Row, digital.

Reynolds, Simon. 2011. *Retromania: Pop Culture's Addiction to Its Own Past*. New York, NY: Faber and Faber.

Routledge, Clay. 2016. *Nostalgia: A Psychological Resource*. New York, NY: Routledge.

Rubin, Peter. 2017. "'Stranger Things' Creators on Season 2, Binge TV, and Foul-mouthed Kids." In *Wired*, October 20, 2017, https://www.wired.com/story/stranger-thingsseason-2-duffer-brothers-interview/

Schnapp, Noah. 2016. "Chapter One: The Vanishing of Will Byers." In *Stranger Things*, directed by Matt and Ross Duffer, Los Angeles: 21 Laps Entertainment, digital.

Schwindt, Oriana. 2016. "'Stranger Things' Tests Limits of Netflix's Nostalgia Strategy." In *Variety*, July 25, 2016, https://variety.com/2016/tv/news/stranger-things-netflixfuller-house-nostalgia-strategy-1201822075/

Simon, Paul (The Bangles cover). 1987. "Hazy Shade of Winter." In *Less Than Zero*, Def Jam, digital.

Steiner, George. 1997. *Nostalgia for the Absolute*. Toronto, ON: Anansi Press.

Sternbergh, Adam. 2017. "Turned Upside Down." In *Vulture*, August 20, 2017, http://www.vulture.com/2017/08/the-duffer-brothers-upside-down-journey-tostranger-things.html

Temperton, Rod. 1984. "Thriller." In *Thriller*, Epic, digital.

Waldinger, Robert. 2016. "What Makes A Good Life?" In *Ted*, January 25, 2016, digital.

Williams, Lara. 2018. "Nostalgia Sucks! Why TV Needs to Stop Living in the Past." In *The Guardian*, February 19, 2018, https://www.theguardian.com/tv-andradio/2018/feb/19/everything-sucks-nostalgia-tv-gilmore-girls-full-house-netflixfriends-mad-men

Wilson, Janelle L. 2014. *Nostalgia: Sanctuary of Meaning*. Minneapolis, MN: University of Minnesota Duluth.

Wolfhard, Finn and Noah Schnapp. 2017. "Chapter One: MADMAX." In *Stranger Things*, directed by Matt and Ross Duffer, Los Angeles: 21 Laps Entertainment, digital.

6. *Click for Dixie: Virtual Plantation Tours' Use of White Nostalgia and Directed Narrative Experience*

Alexandra Lippert and Carson S. Kay

Picture flower beds poised like bright candies on emerald lawns leading to a wall of tall, sun-tanned fescue. Spanish moss ever so slightly swings from the boughs of broad oak trees lining the long driveway. White pillars emphasize the grandeur of the statuesque estate. Once one enters the gates, time seems to stand still. Oh, to return to the simpler days of yesteryear! Oh, to return to the American plantation. Such representations of past culture might seem delightfully charming upon first glance, especially for couples seeking breathtaking wedding venues. After all, southern plantations seem to be the epitomes of picturesque. However, reflecting upon the nostalgic diction and imagery reveals significant oversights in the locations' narratives. Namely, by dwelling upon the beauty of the past, plantation narratives construct a space in which only the white mnemonic experience is welcome. One could deem this longing to be simple nostalgia, but in the case of southern American plantations, one is really experiencing *white* nostalgia when one wishes to return to Tara once more.

The white nostalgia to which we refer is Ewa A. Adamkiewicz's (2016) re-contextualized conceptualization, a perspective that grounds the concept in historical context and temporal significance (16–17). Although fellow scholars tie white nostalgia to racism in film stereotypes (Winch 2013, 117), the feminist movement (Breines 2002, 1122), and neighborhoods (Maly, Dalmage, and Michaels 2012, 765), little research situates white nostalgia within the plantation heritage museum context. As "nostalgic discourses and practices are foundations underlying the fields of heritage and tourism" (Berliner 2012, 770), these plantations are ideal landscapes for scholars to examine the intersections of culture, memory, heritage, and nostalgia. Adamkiewicz (2016) addresses this overlooked context by presenting white nostalgia "as a mode of remembrance celebrating *a specific time and place* in history" (17, emphasis added). Rather than white nostalgia simply occurring *in* certain locations, it occurs *because* of these locations.

If not acknowledged, the white nostalgic narrative reconfigures public recollection of the past to the point that marginalized communities are virtually nonexistent. Current scholarship emphasizes the social harm stemming from historical white-washing, like that surrounding antebellum culture, and underlines the presence of whitewashing in written texts, visual imagery, and spoken discourse within and about southern plantation spaces (e.g., Adamkiewicz 2016; Anderson 2005, 2017; Bright and Butler 2015; Butler 2001; Buzinde and Osagie 2011; Commander 2018; Giovannetti 2009; Litvin and Brewer 2008; Mason 2011; Modlin 2008; Modlin, Alderman, and Gentry 2011; Shields 2017a, 2017b). Scholars recognize the deleterious potentials of social constructions that privilege the white race alone, especially constructions that misconstrue the past to form justification for a homogenous sociocultural existence (Bright and Carter 2018, 27). By posing that the past is devoid of abuse, the present racial tension is erased or framed as a problematic threat. The subjective representations of the threat—the presence of non-white people—allow certain experiences and voices to be heard while others remain silent and invisible. The tale of mutual master-slave existence, for instance, overpowers the reality of the damaging power differential (Commander 2018, 28–29). Consequently, visitors begin to see the marginalized population as content with inequality, reflecting a potential allowance, if not acceptance, of post-racism. After all, cultural representations arise from larger power structures that further bifurcate social relationships (Alderman and Modlin 2013, 7). Thus, heritage narratives that glorify an era of social dominance inherently perpetuate racial marginalization of the African American experience in the antebellum South.

It is this problematic heritage narrative that we seek to dissect. However, instead of further examining face-to-face tours of plantation museums (see Bright and Carter 2018; Buzinde and Osagie 2011; Giovannetti 2009; Litvin and Brewer 2008; Mason 2011; Modlin 2008; Modlin, Alderman, and Gentry 2011; Shields 2017b), the prose penned and pop culture presentations about the seemingly glorious days of white yesteryear (see Anderson 2005, 2017; Bernstein 1996; Commander 2018; Glazer and Key 1996; Hatt 2001; Kelting 2016; Ritterhouse 2003; Robison 2009; Turner 2008), or promotional plantation websites (see Adamkiewicz 2016; Alderman and Modlin 2008), we are intrigued by the narrative arising at the intersection of public memory, white nostalgia, and *computer-mediated* representation. Specifically, we wish to examine how the white nostalgic narrative of the Old South is reinforced through *virtual* plantation tours found *on* plantation websites. Although the virtual tours could be perceived as innocent previews of the plantation space, the tours reflect the value the sites place on sharing the American slavery story. While historic home tours have improved their (re)presentation of on-site slavery (Litvin and Brewer 2008, 80), plantation tours continue to minimize, if not silence, the marginalized realities of the Africans and African Americans forced to labor on the sites (see Adamkiewicz 2016, 15, 28; Butler 2001, 170; Buzinde and Osagie 2011, 41, 49; Eichstedt and Small 2002; Litvin and Brewer 2008, 81; Mason 2011, 3; Modlin 2008, 266; Modlin, Alderman, and Gentry 2011, 15; Shields 2017b, 10–14, 18). By portraying the slave experience as amicable—or by refusing to acknowledge its existence entirely—plantations misconstrue African and African American antebellum realities, contribute to historical white-washing, and feed contemporary white yearning for a past that never existed.

Despite the rise in social justice research, heritage narratives, and computer-mediated communication, few studies have examined how plantations' online framing of history contributes to the marginalization of suppressed voices (Adamkiewicz 2016, 13–31). In our study, we extend Adamkiewicz's analysis of plantation websites by narrowing in on one specific rhetorical tool on these sites: virtual tours. More specifically, we examine the ways in which interactive virtual tours create a directed experience that privileges white narratives and underskirts black experience. To reveal how the virtual tours create subjective, directed experiences of the Old South, we critically investigate eight virtual plantation tours for the representation of slavery and presence of white nostalgic voice in the visual and textual aspects present. We argue that the white nostalgic narrative of the Old South is reinforced through virtual plantation tours and that immersive media storytelling can direct public memory and maintain social orders that contribute to a sanitized construct of history. In the next section, we outline existing literature on areas of significance to our inquiry, including the history of southern U.S. plantations, public memory, and (white) nostalgia in our analysis. Immediately following, our attention turns to an examination of the virtual tours found on the eight plantation websites, leading us to a discussion critiquing the choices that further white nostalgic sentiment over accurate historical representation of black subjugation. The final section of the paper offers potential implications and future studies for dissecting why certain virtual tours privilege white nostalgia, while others reverently reveal the black struggles of slavery.

Public Memory

The ways in which the citizenry recollect the Old South may be described through the concept of public memory. Public—or collective—memory is a social construction of history, of the events, people, and places of the past (Coker 2017, 240, 245). These memories "are instantiated beyond the individual by and for the collective" (Zelizer 1995, 214). They are formed and dictated by the broader social existence. Through "discourses, events, objects, and practices" of memory (Blair, Dickinson, and Ott 2010, 4), social sense-making mechanisms situate the people to historical symbols and occurrences (see Halbwachs 1992). In other words, public memory tells the population what to think about their culture's past triumphs, tribulations, and treachery. Due to its directive nature, public memory is intrinsically linked to critical inquiry. After all, with public memory, "power is always in question" (Bodnar 1993, 15). Namely, "because cultural understanding is always grounded in the material structure of society itself" (Bodnar 1993, 15), public memory exists in a tense battle between historical fact, institutional intentionality, and public contemplation. Often, all do not coexist in reflective harmony. Due to the discursive interplay surrounding and infiltrating collective memory, it is no surprise that public memory is political; in shifting past remembrance, memories construct a collective identity and suggest justification of comparable, contemporary actions (Blair, Dickinson, and Ott 2010, 6). As Derek H. Alderman notes, "The politics of remembering/forgetting through commemoration is certainly controlled by those in power" and in shaping how the public perceive the past, those in power can dictate how the public perceives the present (Alderman 2010, 90).

However, public memory is more than a blank canvas onto which the powerful seek to dominate with strategically selected color. As public memory directs the people to a singular interpretation of historical truth, memory simultaneously constructs and confirms the collective or public identities to which members of the public belong (Blair, Dickinson, and Ott 2010, 15–17). Collective recollection can admittedly dictate the national narrative through the twisting and choking of minority truths, but even memories wrought with conceit can bind individuals in meaningful, shared coalitions (Coker 2017, 243). For example, those who write about the post-antebellum Reconstruction reminisce over the shared loss of not only a white lifestyle, but of the very culture the Old South represented (Anderson 2005, 110). Through the shared sense of stripped cultural identity and remembrance of the glorious days past, individuals find comfort in company, shared solace in mourning a memory. Regardless of the memory's historical accuracy and nuanced exhaustiveness, memories marry members of humankind.

One predominant way in which memories mold identity communities of the South is through the intricate experiencing of material objects. The notion of object-as-memory is not novel; for example, many memorial museums use objects as the bricks of historical narrative (see Williams 2007). As Carole Blair, Greg Dickinson, and Brian L. Ott (2010) note, "publics emerge in relationship to discourses, events, *objects*, and practices" (15, emphasis added). Furthermore, when placed within the context in which they were historically used, objects take on a new level of memorialization. This material culture has been defined as "the material manifestations of the social realities understood to be relevant and powerful" (Leeds-Hurwitz 1993, 77–78). Objects contain "signs that may take on a range of signification" that grant participants a stronger understanding of their immediate social surroundings (Blair, Dickinson, and Ott 2010, 3). For example, plantations and historical homes create specific representations of antebellum culture through objects; text can merely complement physicality. The "influence of objects 'beyond text', the role played by material culture in composing memory" (Mackay and Pittock 2012, 191), fortifies the meaning within the grand, white narrative of the Old South. It could be said that place, memory, and identity formation are linked (see Booth 2008; Dienstag 1997). As objects are "both things that are acted upon and things that act upon us," they hold the potential to influence how we perceive our social world (Lindlof and Taylor 2011, 219). Through objectified memorialization, items become embodied sources of cultural meaning and memory construction that guide tourists' engagement in immersive experiences of once-occupied homes, plantations, and white lives.

Nostalgia

During these experiences, tourists may feel a sense of nostalgia amid remembrance. Fred Davis (1977) explains that nostalgia stems from two Greek words, "*nostos*, to return home, and *algai*, a painful condition," meaning "a painful yearning to return home" (414). However, "to remember the places of our youth is not the same as to feel nostalgic over them; nor does even active reminiscence ... necessarily capture the subjective state we associate with nostalgic feeling" (Davis 1979/2011, 448). Rather, "nostalgia is an imaginative experience in which the past is altered to fit an idealized recollection, an 'operation of fantasy'" (Hook 2012, 17). Through both material agents—like photographs (Sontag 1977, 71) and religious symbols—and spatial agents—like graveyards, monuments, and buildings—tourists develop nostalgic reminiscence. Turner (1987) argues that the paradigm of this nostalgia contains four major dimensions: a sense of historical decline, a sense of absence or loss of fulfillment and clear moral norms, a sense of losing one's personal autonomy as social relationships fade and disappear, and the notion that simplicity and personal authenticity has been lost (150–151). Susceptibility to this nostalgic paradigm is largely culture-specific; intellectual groups, those who feel as though they have lost their "motherland" (Turner 1987, 154), and social classes stripped of former imperial power are more prone to experiencing nostalgia. Through its conscious forgetfulness, nostalgia evokes personal and political implications regarding selective memory of choice narratives.

Through the conscious, decision-making process of nostalgia, particular narratives become attached to objects and spaces. As Adamkiewicz (2016) describes, narratives can dictate meaning (16). Walking through a historically preserved home on a tour, a tourist might learn that a closet was the setting for beautiful dressmaking and a placeholder for luxurious ball gowns. However, this narrative ignores the possible story of a slave who slept nightly away from her husband and children in the tiny, windowless closet (Adamkiewicz 2016, 19). A story is presented in that space, but too often the story privileges pleasantry over reality. Through the material vessel of objects and spaces, nostalgia sells *positive* emotions.

White Nostalgia

White nostalgia downplays or eliminates race issues by ignoring or minimizing the realities of slavery. While nostalgia is "a longing for a home that no longer exists or has never existed" and "a romantic captivation with one's own fiction of an ideal home" (Drobnick 2006, 352), white nostalgia specifically yearns for the ideals of Caucasian life. This construction of a subgroup desire can occur due to nostalgia's ability to bring people together. Boym (2001) claims nostalgia is a particular mode of remembering and longing that is often experienced by groups of people (16). Through joint remembrance, groups construct ambiguous, shared spaces. For white people desiring antebellum norms in the post-antebellum era, thus experiencing white nostalgia, the history of southern spaces becomes distorted and devoid of racism. Memory becomes a means to perform a white-washed representation separate from the emotional legacy of slavery. In these white-washed constructions of white nostalgic narratives, individuals and groups opt for a painless past rather than confront a painful present (Anderson 2005, 131). Words have power, especially when they affect public memories of oppression. In interpreting southern monuments,

Alderman (2010) believes "the politics of remembering slavery be examined in terms of surrogation, the search for a suitable commemorative stand in for the enslaved, and textual politics, the recognition that the words used to represent slavery are at the heart of the struggle to remember (or forget) the trauma of enslavement" (90). Popular culture has often times romanticized the black person's role in antebellum society. Instead of acknowledging the realistic roles of black lives in white antebellum culture, like the role black women played in rearing and serving white southern women, movies and novels mythologize the past. From *Gone with the Wind* to *Song of the South*, white nostalgic narratives portray slaves and planters as existing in harmony (see Bernstein 1996; Mitchell 1936). Meanwhile, the realistic stories of the enslaved remain ignored; in fact, many southern plantations, heritage museums, and texts sell narratives that silence slavery.

Some estates incorporate slave narratives to educate white audiences; while others incorporate the trials of black folk for capitalistic gain. Plantations may market tours of former slave churches and houses; sell products traditionally made by slaves, such as corn husk dolls; or hire reenactors to show the roles slaves might have performed on farms and plantations for educational field trips. While slavery is addressed, the goal of these profit-driven narratives is to perpetuate a dominant hegemonic discourse of history (Fabos 2014, 223), a narrative hinting at white nostalgia.

In the midst of lifestyle loss following the Civil War in the South, white socialites yearned to recall the South as a vanished oasis rather than a place of suppression. To cope, white affluent southerners knew "the new south would require a new past" (Anderson 2005, 126). Through white nostalgic constructions, regaining control becomes feasible. Memories can be picked up, dusted off, restored, and embellished, while others are left behind to rot. The memories that survive often provide an "aesthetically complete and satisfying recollection of the Old South" (Anderson 2005, 140), even if those nostalgic recollections omit key elements of the greater historical story.

Adamkiewicz's (2016) analysis of plantation websites reveals that white nostalgia continues to infect the representations within and about southern spaces (25–27). She explains that most plantations silence—or at least muffle—the history of slavery on their websites, redirecting the audience's focus away from the site's racial injustices (Adamkiewicz 2016, 26–27). To accomplish this directed narrative experience, plantation websites evoke white nostalgic sentiment, which can be seen in five ways. Namely, the website (a) downplays the implications of racism, (b) presents history as static and stable, (c) celebrates a historical time and space, (d) constructs an unproblematic past and present, and (e) portrays an emotional, affective home. Although plantations are all directly connected to "agents of memory that impact how slavery in the United States is remembered and forgotten" (Modlin 2008, 269), these websites tend to differentiate plantations into two categories, those that deny slavery and those that attempt to create counternarratives that integrate the memories and stories of slavery (Adamkiewicz 2016). The first category attempts to simulate a history without racism. Many of these plantations either never rebuilt the slave cabins that would have historically been located on the estate. Other plantations have been found to rebuild slave cabins to use as guest rooms. Here visitors participate in appropriation and domination over the memories attached. The memories become white-washed. In the second category, plantations may attempt to address slavery by merely mentioning the number of slaves who lived and works on the plantation or the jobs the slaves performed; however, this is a minimizing way of recalling the history of slavery (Adamkiewicz 2016). It eliminates the live experience of slaves at the hands of white elite (Adamkiewicz 2016). Despite the deep connection between southern history and slavery, plantation tourism sites tend to celebrate personal narratives depicting the antebellum South as a time and place of union and gaiety.

Plantation Virtual Tours

Within online spheres of discourse, however, are specific components that warrant individual consideration. As Adamkiewicz illustrated, websites can perpetuate white nostalgic sentiment (see Adamkiewicz 2016). We further argue that websites incorporate white nostalgia through their virtual tours of the plantations. Heritage tourism has skyrocketed in popularity and the majority of travelers are planning vacations around their genealogy (Lippe-McGraw 2017). In addition, the majority of families are using technology, surfing the web and exploring destination websites to determine their vacation locations (Bearne 2016). These changes in travel have created a greater need for locations to up their virtual tour game to entice potential guests. Before investing in traveling costs, however, individuals can have a replicated experience of southern spaces by examining the virtual tours on the plantations' websites. Whether accessed through a computer or a smartphone, virtual tour technologies "allow interaction of previously separate domains of experience: desire, identity, tourism, memory, and marketing" (Garau and Ilardi 2014, 79). The tours function as access keys that can take the user into other cultural and temporal domains. With a quick click or tap, tourists can navigate plantations through interactive floor plans, images, videos, and textual descriptions. Heaven is but a click away, a click that reveals a narrative from which sociocultural anxieties emerge. We argue that southern plantations exploit white nostalgia on virtual tours through their use of visual and textual imagery, the elimination of the black bodies, the missing narratives of slaves, and their attempts to create a fixed perception of history as unproblematic.

Methods

Our close textual analysis examines the ways in which white nostalgia emerges in the virtual tours of southeastern American plantations. Although our analytical process partially resembled the work of grounded theorists (e.g., Charmaz 1983; Glaser and Strauss 1967; Strauss 1987; Strauss and Corbin 1990) by initially searching the tours for emergent themes, we ultimately chose to frame our findings based on the pre-existing scholarship of Adamkiewicz. As previously mentioned, the Internet has become a space in which the rhetoric of racial injustice simmers (e.g., Bristor, Lee, and Hunt 1995; Campelo, Aitken, and Gnoth 2011). Simultaneously, the online medium has become a multi-billion-dollar advertising space in contemporary culture (Miller 2011) due to its accessibility to diverse publics. One of the modes of plantation heritage advertising is through interactive virtual tours, giving the tourist an opportunity to explore constructed spaces through strategically focused lenses. Through the marriage of textual, visual, and auditory symbols, a representation of white existence creates a marketable brand of the Old South.

The virtual tours selected for our analysis met three criteria. The tours (1) identify on websites as virtual tours, (2) focus explicitly on a plantation, and (3) examine sites located in the southern United States. Based on the U.S. Census Bureau's (n.d.) definition of the southern states, we conducted online searches for plantations in Texas, Oklahoma, Arkansas, Louisiana, Mississippi, Alabama, Tennessee, Kentucky, Georgia, Florida, South Carolina, North Carolina, West Virginia, Virginia, Maryland, and Delaware. Furthermore, the virtual tours varied in format. While all existed on an online platform, the extent of textual description, narration, photography, videography, and interactivity differed from site to site. Thus, the tours in our sample exhibited diverse content and structure. Our initial search yielded 12 plantations with online tourism features. However, we removed four plantations from our sample for failing to explicitly identify a virtual tour feature (i.e., Oak Alley Plantation), for focusing on multiple plantations simultaneously (i.e., Cajun Encounters Tour Company), for no longer primarily identifying as a plantation (i.e., Pebble Hill Plantation), and for existing primarily as a wedding venue rather than a historical landmark (i.e., Southern Oaks Plantation). Consequently, our final sample consisted of eight plantation's virtual tours (see Table 6.1).

Table 6.1: Plantations of interest.

Preliminary Sample	Final Sample
Cajun Endeavors Tour Company	Destrehan Plantation
Destrehan Plantation	Evergreen Plantation
Evergreen Plantation	Lakeport Plantation
Lakeport Plantation	Long Branch Plantation
Long Branch Plantation	Mansfield Plantation
Mansfield Plantation	Mount Vernon Plantation
Mount Vernon Plantation	Sherwood Forest Plantation
Oak Alley Plantation	Stella Plantation
Pebble Hill Plantation	
Sherwood Forest Plantation	
Southern Oaks Plantation	
Stella Plantation	

This elimination process followed our preliminary analyses of the virtual tours posted on the plantations' websites. To ensure we did not influence each other's analytical perspectives, we each randomly selected half of the total sample to analyze individually for symbolic and representational themes. During our solo analyses, we flagged plantations we felt violated our selection criteria. Upon compiling our preliminary findings and discussing our concerns, we collaboratively removed questionable sites from our final sample. Our final selection process did not take the specific audience nor specific location promoted (e.g., city) into consideration. Only virtual identity, plantation emphasis, and regional location contributed to our decision. Our openness to examining virtual tours of regional sites reflects our interest in documenting and critiquing the ways in which plantations direct the white narrative experience of the Old South while cloaking the bleak realities of the black slaves who literally and symbolically maintained the white antebellum culture. Furthermore, we did not take the date in which the tours were constructed into consideration; only the websites' copyright records were available, so we had no way to identify the year in which each tour came into being.

After compiling our final sample, we examined each virtual tour for indications of white nostalgia per Adamkiewicz's conceptualization. Namely, we looked for ways in which the virtual tours downplay the implications of racism; present history as fixed, static, and stable; celebrate historical times and spaces; construct an unproblematic past and present; create an emotional, affective home; and connect tourists to objects for material remembrance. We examined the visual (i.e., photographs, videos, sketches), textual (i.e., descriptions and captions), and auditory (i.e., music, narration) aspects of each tour for the process by which white nostalgia was silencing black narratives. Numerous findings stem from our analysis, which we will now condense and detail.

White Nostalgic Voice in Virtual Plantation Tours

While slaves labored on each of the plantations in our sample, the representation of those slaves in virtual tours is often one-dimensional and devoid of the daily hardships slavery created for black individuals across the South. Ultimately, the tours incorporate a white nostalgic narrative by (a) downplaying racism, (b) presenting history as static, (c) celebrating historical times and spaces, (d) framing of past and present as unproblematic, and (e) constructing an emotional, affective home.

Downplaying of Racism

Virtual tours may incorporate white nostalgic voice by downplaying the implications of racism and slavery. This downplaying occurs through unacknowledgement of race, disregarding of slave tribulations, and rhetorical softening. First, many of the plantations' virtual tours poorly acknowledge race. Lakeport, Long Branch, Sherwood Forest, and Destrehan do not mention the race of the slaves in their virtual tour narratives. In some cases, websites, like that of Destrehan, devote separate pages for discussions of slavery (see Destrehan n.d., "Our History"). Nevertheless, while this particular site acknowledges slavery, the tour remains silent, devoting itself to the grandeur of the home and landscaping instead through non-narrated, drone-filmed video footage (se Destrehan n.d., "Virtual Tour"). Despite Destrehan's reputation for acknowledging the slave narrative—and its considerable description of the black slave experience elsewhere on its website—the plantation's virtual tour lacks recognition of racial suppression.

Only one virtual tour in our sample admits that American slavery was racially determined. Evergreen Plantation (2003) notes the deep and tragic connection between blackness and enslavement, explicitly stating that "African slaves provided the labor" (slide 9). Nevertheless, Evergreen's virtual tour still downplays the implications of racism by textually framing slaves as picturesque contributors. While the virtual tour acknowledges race in its textual descriptions, it skirts the horrific realities of discrimination. Race is noted, but *racism* is kept at arm's length. For instance, on one slide about slavery, Evergreen (2003) frames slaves not as victims of an inhumane economic and social system, but as individuals who improved southern culture (see slide 9). The tour states that "before and after emancipation, African-Americans contributed many elements of their traditional lifestyles to the rich and varied cultural tapestry of Southern Louisiana" (Evergreen Plantation 2003, slide 9). In framing slaves as cultural contributors, the tour appears to give credit to the African and African American population. However, the tour ultimately perpetuates the idea that slaves must give something to white folk for their narrative to warrant consideration. They enter the conversation only when serving the white population. White's impact on black voices and bodies remains hidden in silence.

Unfortunately, racism is not the only silenced reality in virtual plantation tours. Just as unacknowledged are the trials and tribulations of black slaves. At Mansfield Plantation, the virtual tour reduces the history of slavery to a few simple words, claiming, "Generations of African American families spent their entire lifetimes on these grounds. The entire village stands, unchanged, as a tribute to their place in American History" (Mansfield Plantation 2004, "Mighty Mansfield Interactive Map"). While Evergreen's virtual tour does acknowledge race in its textual descriptions, the tour fails to address the horrific realities stemming from discrimination. This observation is not localized to Evergreen alone. For example, the virtual tour of George Washington's Mount Vernon Plantation submerges the hardships faced by the site's black slaves (Mount Vernon 2018, "Virtual Tour"). Although virtual visitors can tour the slave cabins and read and hear about slaves in the virtual tour's embedded videos, the narratives focus solely on minute processes—like the slaves' button currency system—and the records of the plantation's slaves (Mount Vernon 2018, "Virtual Tour"). Race and trials of being a slave are eliminated from the conversation.

This strategic elimination of select words is what we call rhetorical softening, which can manifest either through the relabeling of the black slave or through admittance of owner guilt. For instance, in Mount Vernon's tour, African slaves are simply "enslaved laborers" (Mount Vernon 2018, "Virtual Tour"). At Sherwood Forest Plantation, they are "field hands" and "house servants" (Sherwood Forest 2002, "Dependencies"). One could argue that Evergreen provides the most honest representation, but its tour still only mentions race as a descriptive feature, not as a critique of suppression. Essentially, these alternative terms rhetorically soften the blow that American citizens forced Africans to work for them without compensation. Similarly, two of the plantations smooth over the realities of president-as-slave-owners by mentioning the ethical dilemma the planters felt. Several times, Mount Vernon's virtual tour mentions Washington's ethical questions regarding slavery (Mount Vernon 2018, "Virtual Tour"). Sherwood Forest also notes Tyler's grappling elsewhere on the site, but not explicitly in the virtual tour itself.

While the rhetorical choice to include internal battles humanizes the planters, it ultimately pads the raw reality of the pain and suffering black slaves experienced at the hands of white men.

Presentation of Static History

While white nostalgic voice appears by downplaying racism through the unacknowledgement of race, disregarding of slave tribulations, and rhetorical softening, white nostalgia also manifests through portrayals of history as fixed, static, and stable. Many of the virtual plantation tours construct such portrayals by employing passive voice. By only offering still imagery and a predominantly passive descriptive voice, virtual plantation tours erase black bodies. After reading Long Branch Plantation's virtual tour descriptions, one might notice how the sentence construction itself minimizes the presence of black slaves. The tour repeatedly states that tasks were done in a specific fashion, rather than placing black agency in the text to state that slaves did the tasks. Consequently, the tour both removes black bodies from the narrative and implies that the blackless account is accurate and unchangeable. In contrast, the white bodies in Long Branch's tour receive agency through active voice. Virtual visitors read that white "visitors, guests and family entered Long Branch" and "the Nelson's entertained and impressed" (Long Branch 2018, "House Tour"). The only case in which the tour mentions the slaves in active voice is to reference labor, tasks, or objects, such as "slaves prepared and cleared that space … domestic slaves who catered to the family's needs" (Long Branch 2018, "House Tour"). Through the simple (dis)allowance of agency through passive or active voice, virtual tours can quite literally remove black bodies from the narrative. Saying a task *was done* hides the most critical reality of *who* was laboring.

Celebration of Historical Times and Spaces

With the white nostalgic portrayal of a past static and devoid of blackness comes the celebration of the historical era through aesthetic glorification and florally diction. The tours tend to distance the plantations from their historical context by structurally glorifying the site's aesthetic rather than its full story. Long Branch Plantation's virtual tour, for instance, avoids discussing the ugliness that occurred under its tall, white pillars by instead referencing the physical beauty of the buildings. In its textual descriptions, the Long Branch virtual tour gushes over the "19th century dining room … flanked by a striking mahogany sideboard and ornate stove" instead of describing who prepared the food that would cover said sideboard and stove (Long Branch

2018, "House Tour"). Just as praised, however, is structural simplicity. For example, Long Branch's tour applauds a sparse space with "a few chairs, pine tables and chests" that was likely "used as a simple sitting space" (Long Branch 2018, "House Tour"). The reverence granted to such a simplistic space reflects the uncomplicated lifestyle sentiment of white nostalgia, the yearning for a time in which white Americans could enjoy their surroundings without distraction. Text in the form of florally diction adds to the ways in which history is celebrated. The virtual tour and text ask audiences to envision a fairytale setting using poetic language, both sanitizing history and causing it to be stationary. History is something to be celebrated and savored, not critiqued. Stella Plantation invites guests to experience the life of what was a "true Southern belle," describing the rooms and gardens as romantic and elegant (Stella Plantation 2016, "About Us") as it walks tourists through stunning views of its grounds (Stella Plantation 2016, "Explore the Grounds"). These descriptions depict a historic life of glamour and propriety, but lack a critical reflection on the lives of white elites who owned plantations.

Framing of Unproblematic Past and Present

Just as virtual plantation tours downplay racism, (re)present a static history, and revel in antebellum times and spaces, the tours also tend to frame both past and present culture as racially unproblematic. Adamkiewicz notes in her analysis that "in both the nostalgic narratives of the post-Civil War period and the plantation websites, the construction of an 'unproblematic' past reveals an attempt to construct an 'unproblematic' present" (Adamkiewicz 2016, 18). After all, if the past is devoid of racial insensitivity and subjugation, how could one possibly fathom racial injustice *continuing* today? Through the stifling and/or silencing of African and African American slave narratives, virtual tours subtly insist that nothing was, nor is wrong between the races in American culture. This construction of unproblematic past and present occurs through three tour techniques: portrayal of simplistic life, dehumanization in description, and teamwork tones.

The first way in which virtual plantation tours construct an unproblematic past and present is through the simple portrayal of antebellum life. While the ethics surrounding racial suppression clearly indicate slavery as inhumane, the social constructs allowing racial atrocities to occur are often much more complicated. By suggesting life in the Old South was carefree, virtual tours fallaciously imply that the sociocultural complexity of racism could not possibly have been at play. One way this arises is through photographs and sketches that offer seemingly straightforward views of southern spaces. Lakeport

Plantation, for example, advertises a virtual tour of the facility (see Lakeport Plantation n.d., "Virtual Tour"). However, the tour itself is merely comprised of a rotating, panoramic photograph of the kitchen and a computerized sketch of the main house's exterior. With text only present for identification purposes, the virtual tour is devoid of any interpretive framing. One could argue that this grants the virtual tourist greater agency in translating the meaning within the photograph and sketch. However, the simple presentation also leaves the viewer feeling as if there is nothing more to the imagery, that there are no deeper narratives hiding under the floorboards or around the corner of the front porch. From the virtual tour alone, there is no way to know the logic behind this overly simplistic presentation, but even if Lakeport Plantation was attempting to avoid rhetorically dictating the images' meanings, it unfortunately *contributes* to the conception that plantations offered life without socio cultural qualms. From Lakeport's virtual tour, one perceives life on the plantation to be nothing more than a majestic house with a homey kitchen.

Unlike Lakeport, many of the virtual tours we examined provide rich textual and visual descriptions of the plantations. Nevertheless, alongside this detailing arose an intriguing visual style. Namely, while Lakeport omits historical complexity through simplistic touring, Long Branch and Destrehan portray plantation life through dehumanized imagery. Now, we refer to dehumanized description not in terms of alienation nor scorn, but rather in regards to the erasure of living bodies in the representation. In Long Branch's virtual tour, pictures are a predominant vessel of information and shared meaning-making with online tourists. However, in the 10 photographs imbedded on the virtual tour page, not one person appears. Although Destrehan utilizes video rather than photographs, it also solely focuses on architecture and landscape, rather than the white and black souls living on the estate. Due to the absence of life, there is a particular stillness to the imagery, even when that imagery is moving, which could appeal to the tourist of the non-stop technological era. In these images, a person could simply exist without the constraining stressors typical of everyday life. All that appears to be missing in these spaces is the tourist. After all, there are no indicators of human difference to prevent present folk from engaging in past simplicity. By removing representations of past bodies from the plantation spaces, though, Long Branch's and Destrehan's virtual tours visually oversimplify the past, framing plantation life as synonymous with raceless existence. By not representing all of the lives that walked through—and worked in—those rooms, the virtual tour offers a sterile, dehumanized portrait that cuts out the narratives just outside of the photograph's edge.

Nevertheless, other plantations deviate from dehumanized description, offering instead a tone of collaboration on estate grounds. Like Lakeport's and Long Branch's virtual tours, Sherwood Forest avoids showing live bodies. However, through textual explanation, Sherwood Forest's tour radiates with a sense of planter-slave teamwork. The virtual tour boasts that the Tyler family still resides at Sherwood Forest and maintains its interior and exterior. It states, "President Tyler's grandson, Harrison Ruffin Tyler, currently lives here with his family. For over 150 years, Tyler descendants have continually occupied and privately maintained Sherwood Forest. It is the only presidential home in America with this distinction" (Sherwood Forest 2002, "Front Porch"). By underlining the family's role as a continued process, the tour subtly suggests that the Tyler family was just as instrumental in maintaining the grounds during the antebellum era and, in doing so, minimizes the role of President Tyler's slaves in conducting the work. Indeed, the portrayal of slaves in the tour furthers the collaborative aura. One excerpt, in particular, summarizes the tour's treatment of slaves.

> Visitors to Sherwood Forest are always asked to consider the season in which they are visiting and how the current weather might have affected the daily activities and operations of the plantation, especially for the field hands and house servants. There was much work to be done. And without that hard work, the working plantation of the mid-19th century, preserved here today, would have been vastly different. (Sherwood Forest Plantation 2002, "Dependencies")

Through this framing, slaves become field hands and servants who worked with the Tyler family to maintain the estate's physical and functional integrity. By describing the master-slave relationship as collaborative, the virtual tour furthers the notion that white and black folk did—and continue to—work together amicably. It subtly attempts to undermine past narratives of racial oppression to construct a rosier past and suggest a continuation of a rosy present.

This collaborative framing technique, along with the portrayal of simplicity and dehumanized description, create a historical, one-dimensional narrative that sweeps over the layers existing beneath the immediate visual and textual surface. In disregarding the historical depth of the locations, virtual plantation tours more easily airbrush the past's transgressions and pose the present as the continuing chapter in the Old South's tale. If the past is emptied of racial suppression, disregarding contemporary insensitivity becomes much more feasible.

Construction of Emotional, Affective Home

Deeply intertwined with the construction of an unproblematic past/present is the inter-tour creation of an affective home. Christine Buzinde (2007) explains the "unproblematic construction of 'home' and its selected traditions invoked as an affective response describing feelings of common experiences, unity, purity, identity, and comfort" (243). These everyday, ordinary affects, Kathleen Stewart would argue, "are public feelings that begin and end in broad circulation, but they're also the stuff that seemingly intimate lives are made of … Their significance lies in the intensities they build and in what thoughts and feelings they make possible" (Stewart 2007, 2–3). Considering the deep connection between people and home, it is not surprising that "anxieties about the loss of home so cloud the horizon of the modern world, as to make our experience of home qualitatively and quantitatively distinctive" (Bonnett 2016, 142). Home is universal, yet subjectively constructed. Adamkiewicz (2016) notes that a multiplicity of scholars have connected plantation tours with a longing for home (e.g., Boym 2001, xiii; Buzinde 2007, 243; Drobnick 2006, 352), an emotional connection from which plantations may profit (19). Ryan Lizardi (2017) notes that the media industry "sees financial gain in making reimagined content available" (4). Like the media industry, virtual plantation tours construct an affective home as a means of commodifying emotional connection to familial affects. This construction primarily occurs through material positioning, description of familial-spatial interaction, and pathos-laden diction.

Virtual tours tend to emphasize spaces and objects over human presence. Nevertheless, this presence is implied by capturing imagery with realistically posed items. For instance, in both the Lakeport and Evergreen Plantation virtual tours, the kitchen is staged as if still in use (see Evergreen Plantation 2003, slides 6–7; Lakeport Plantation n.d., "Virtual Tour"). When scrolling through the panoramic image of Lakeport's kitchen, the tourist experiences the illusion of continued use. Jars and jugs line the wooden shelves within reach, while a kettle sits patiently on the stovetop and an emptied sack of fine granulated sugar peeks from a cupboard drawer (see Lakeport Plantation n.d., "Virtual Tour"). Similarly, pots hang from hooks on the wall of Evergreen and fresh flowers fill the vases placed amongst the platters waiting to be filled (see Lakeport Plantation n.d., "Virtual Tour"). Were tourists not to know the spaces were merely for show, they might conclude that the cook had simply stepped out momentarily and would return any moment to continue the tasks seemingly at hand. Food and kitchen spaces hold nostalgic sentiment, especially in southern domains (see Anderson 2017; Kelting 2016). Thus, staging the kitchen as if in use furthers the sentimental feeling that the tourists have *returned* home when they peer through the doors and imagine stepping onto the weathered hardwood floor, even if they have never experienced the space before.

However, the emphasis on hominess is not limited to the space alone. In fact, virtual plantation tours also incorporate the narratives of the families who once lived in those spaces, even if no re-enactors are present. As previously mentioned, Long Branch's virtual tour is devoid of human bodies. Nevertheless, the tour documents the past family's activities in the rooms. For example, the tour's textual description notes, "This is Long Branch's 19th century dining room. Flanked by a striking mahogany sideboard and ornate stove, this room was where the Nelson's entertained and impressed" and "socializing, music, drinking, and meetings—they all occurred here in Long Branch's parlor" (Long Branch 2018, "House Tour"). By describing the actions that once occurred in these empty spaces, the virtual tours give the spaces homey life. Nevertheless, by focusing on the family, these narratives simultaneously brush over the additional realities which took place in these spaces. Immediately following both examples are brief statements alluding to, yet minimizing the presence of slaves. Some statements are subtle, such as "A set of stairs behind the closed door led to the winter kitchen downstairs" (Long Branch 2018, "House Tour"), implying the door and stairs allowed slaves to make brief appearances to serve the family, then quickly disappear from the white gaze. Others offer more explicit, yet silencing explanations. "The pocket doors are original to that period," the description of the parlor reads, "and were originally faux-grained mahogany. They allowed this room to be shut off from the dining room while slaves prepared and cleared that space. Prior to the Civil War the Nelson family who owned Long Branch had several domestic slaves who catered to the family's needs" (Long Branch 2018, "House Tour"). While the tour acknowledges that slaves existed among the family on the *site*, they are referenced in terms of the ways they were hidden from *sight* so that the white family narrative could continue uninterrupted. Thus, while the *spaces of home* are maintained by black bodies, these bodies are not welcomed in the *narrative of home*.

What are welcomed, however, are appeals to the emotions of white nostalgia. One way in which virtual tours achieve emotional connection is through pathos-heavy diction. Tours that rely heavily on textual description tend to incorporate words that evoke sentimentalism. Evergreen Plantation's (2003) virtual tour is a prime example. Throughout its visual experience, the tour includes rich, active description of the surrounding environment. "As the sun rises over Southern Louisiana," the tourist reads, "the morning mist fades away to reveal the South's most intact plantation" (slide 1). Furthermore, the tourist views "The French Parterre, buildings all around: laid out with precision and symmetry. Proof of order in an otherwise chaotic world" (Evergreen Plantation 2003, slide 2). The presence of nostalgic continuity rhetoric is especially evident in Evergreen's descriptions, constructing the plantation as a thread allowing time to touch lives, regardless of year. The tour instructs the viewer, "Looking out over the sugar cane fields; you understand that on these fields, the very life of Evergreen depends, past, present, and future" (Evergreen Plantation 2003, slide 11). Thanks to the continued participation in and support of the estate, "As the sun sets over Evergreen plantation, its survival is assured" (Evergreen Plantation 2003, slide 12). Through select diction, the virtual plantation tours interweave emotion and time to create a nostalgic experience of the white antebellum lifestyle that previous families experienced.

Conclusion

Southern plantations are a place to learn about our past and our present. When virtual plantation tours minimize the atrocities of the past, they minimize the damage those moments still play in America's present. White nostalgia guides and perpetuates dangerous understandings of the Old South, erasing the horrific memories of slavery. The absence of slavery, race, and black bodies along with the fixed portrayal of history through eight virtual plantation tours need to be examined critically regarding the memories they create of the antebellum South's history. While several of the tours mention slavery or enslaved people, the terror faced in the everyday lived experiences of slaves remains silenced and in turn forgotten. Plantations and their virtual tours could share important narratives that could not only shape memories of history, but the actions of individuals in the future.

References

Adamkiewicz, Ewa A. "White Nostalgia: The Absence of Slavery and the Commodification of White Plantation Nostalgia." *Aspeers* 9 (2016): 13–31. https://www.aspeers.com.

Alderman, Derek H. "Surrogation and the Politics of Remembering Slavery in Savannah, Georgia (USA)." *Journal of Historical Geography* 36 (2010): 90–101. doi:10.1016/j.jhg.2009.08.001.

Alderman, Derek H., and E. Arnold Modlin, Jr. "(In)visibility of the Enslaved within Online Plantation Tourism Marketing: A Textual Analysis of North Carolina Websites." *Journal of Travel & Tourism Marketing* 25, no. 3–4 (2008): 265–281. doi:10.1080/10548400802508333.

Alderman, Derek H. and E. Arnold Modlin, Jr. "Southern Hospitality and the Politics of African American Belonging: An Analysis of North Carolina Tourism Brochure Photographs." *Journal of Cultural Geography* 30, no. 1 (2013): 6–31. doi:10.1080/08873631.2012.745978.

Anderson, David. "Down Memory Lane: Nostalgia for the Old South in Post-Civil War Plantation Reminiscences." *The Journal of Southern History* 71, no. 1 (2005): 105–136. http://www.jstor.org/stable/27648653.

Anderson, David. "Consuming Memories: Food and Childhood in Postbellum Plantation Memoirs and Reminiscences." *Food, Culture, & Society* 20, no. 3 (2017): 443–461. doi:10.1080/15528014.2017.1288800.

Bearne, Suzanne. "How Technology has Transformed the Travel Industry." *The Guardian*, February 29, 2016. https://www.theguardian.com/media-network/2016/feb/29/technology-internet-transformed-travel-industry-airbnb.

Berliner, David. "Multiple Nostalgias: The Fabric of Heritage in Luang Prabang (Lao PDR)." *Journal of the Royal Anthropological Institute* 18 (2012): 769–786. https://doi.org/10.1111/j.1467-9655.2012.01791.x.

Bernstein, Matthew. "Nostalgia, Ambivalence, Irony: Song of the South and Race Relations in 1946 Atlanta." *Film History* 8 (1996): 219–236. http://www.jstor.org/stable/3815336.

Blair, Carole, Greg Dickinson, and Brian L. Ott. "Introduction: Rhetoric/Memory/Place." In *Places of Public Memory: The Rhetoric of Museums and Memorials*, edited by Greg Dickinson, Carole Blair, and Brian L. Ott, 1–56. Tuscaloosa, AL: University of Alabama Press, 2010.

Bodnar, John E. *Remaking America: Public Memory, Commemoration, and Patriotism in the Twentieth Century*. Princeton, NJ: Princeton University Press, 1993.

Bonnett, Alastair. *The Geography of Nostalgia: Global and Local Perspectives on Modernity and Loss*. London: Routledge, 2016.

Booth, W. James. "The Work of Memory: Time, Identity, and Justice." *Social Research* 75 (2008): 237–262. http://www.jstor.org/stable/40972059.

Boym, Svetlana. *The Future of Nostalgia*. New York: Basic, 2001.

Breines, Wini. "What's Love Got to Do with It? White Women, Black Women, and Feminism in the Movement Years." *Signs* 27, no. 4 (2002): 1095–1133. doi:10.1086/339634.

Bright, Candace Forbes, and David L. Butler. "Webwashing the Tourism Plantation: Using Historic Websites to View Changes in the Representation of Slavery at Tourism Plantations." In *Social Memory and Heritage Tourism Methodologies,* edited by Stephen P. Hanna, Amy E. Potter, E. Arnold Modlin, Jr., Perry Carter, and David L. Butler, 31–47. London: Routledge, 2015.

Bright, Candace Forbes, and Perry Carter. "Social Representational Communities and the Imagined Antebellum South." *Sociological Spectrum* 38, no. 1 (2018): 24–38. doi:10.1080/02732173.2017.1396944.

Bristor, Julia M., Renée Gravois Lee, and Michelle R. Hunt. "Race and Ideology: African American Images in Television Advertising." *Journal of Public Policy & Marketing* 14 (1995): 1–24. http://www.jstor.org/stable/30000378.

Butler, David L. "Whitewashing Plantations: The Commodification of a Slave-Free Antebellum South." *International Journal of Hospitality & Tourism Administration* 2, no. 3/4 (2001): 163–175. doi:10.1300/J149v02n03_07.

Buzinde, Christine N. “Representational Politics of Plantation Heritage Tourism: The Contemporary Plantation as a Social Imaginary.” In *Globalizing Cultural Studies: Ethnographic Interventions in Theory, Method, and Policy*, edited by Cameron McCarthy, Aisha S. Durham, Laura C. Engel, Alice A. Filmer, Michael D. Giardina, and Miguel A. Malagreca, 229–252. New York: Peter Lang, 2007.

Buzinde, Christine N., and Iyunolu F. Osagie. “Slavery Heritage Representations, Cultural Citizenship, and Judicial Politics in America.” *Historical Geography* 39 (2011): 41–64. https://ejournals.unm.edu/index.php/historicalgeography/index.

Campelo, Adriana, Robert Aitken, and Juergen Gnoth. “Visual Rhetoric and Ethics in Marketing Destinations.” *Journal of Travel Research* 50 (2011): 3–14. doi: 10.1177/0047287510362777.

Charmaz, Kathy. “The Grounded Theory Method: An Explication and Interpretation.” In *Contemporary Field Research*, edited by Robert M. Emerson, 109–126. Boston: Little, Brown, and Company, 1983.

Coker, Calvin R. “Harriet Tubman, Women on 20s, and Intersectionality: Public Memory and the Redesign of U.S. Currency.” *Southern Communication Journal* 82, no. 4 (2017): 239–249. doi:10.1080/1041794X.2017.1332091.

Commander, Michelle D. “Plantation Counternarratives: Disrupting Master Accounts in Contemporary Cultural Production.” *Journal of American Culture* 41, no. 1 (2018): 28–44. doi:10.1111/jacc.12838.

Davis, Fred. “Nostalgia, Identity and the Current Nostalgia Wave.” *The Journal of Popular Culture* 11, no. 2 (1977): 414–424. https://doi.org/10.1111/j.0022-3840.1977.00414.x.

Davis, Fred. “Yearning for Yesteryear: A Sociology of Nostalgia.” In *The Collective Memory Reader*, edited by Jeffrey K. Olick, Vered Vinitzsky-Seroussi, and Daniel Levy, 446–451. New York, NY: Oxford University Press, 2011.

Destrehan Plantation. “Our History.” N.d. http://www.destrehanplantation.org/history.html.

Destrehan Plantation. “Virtual Tour.” Last updated 2015. http://www.destrehanplantation.org/.

Dienstag, Joshua Foa. *Dancing in Chains: Narrative and Memory in Political Theory.* Palo Alto, CA: Stanford University Press, 1997.

Drobnick, Jim. “Eating Nothing: Cooking Aromas in Art and Culture.” In *The Smell Culture Reader*, edited by Jim Drobnick, 342–356. Oxford: Berg, 2006.

Eichstedt, Jennifer L., and Stephen Small. *Representations of Slavery.* Washington, DC: Smithsonian Institution Press, 2002.

Evergreen Plantation. “Home.” Last updated 2018. http://evergreenplantation.org/.

Evergreen Plantation. “Virtual Tour.” Last updated 2003. http://evergreenplantation.org/past/tour/t3.htm.

Fabos, Bettina. “The Trouble with Iconic Images: Historical Timelines and Public Memory.” *Visual Communication Quarterly* 21 (2014): 223–235. doi:10.1080/15551393.2014.987282.

Garau, Chiara, and Emiliano Ilardi. "The 'Non-Places' Meet the 'Places:' Virtual Tours on Smartphones for the Enhancement of Cultural Heritage." *Journal of Urban Technology* 21, no. 1 (2014): 79–91. doi:10.1080/10630732.2014.884384.

Giovannetti, Jorge L. "Subverting the Master's Narrative: Public Histories of Slavery in Plantation America." *International Labor & Working Class History* 76 (2009): 105–126. doi:10.1017/S0147547909990111.

Glaser, Barney G., and Anselm L. Strauss. *The Discovery of Grounded Theory: Strategies for Qualitative Research.* Chicago: Aldine, 1967.

Glazer, Lee, and Susan Key. "Carry Me Back: Nostalgia for the Old South in Nineteenth-Century Popular Culture." *Journal of American Studies* 30, no. 1 (1996): 1–24. doi:10.1017/S0021875800024294.

Halbwachs, Maurice. *On Collective Memory.* Edited and translated by Lewis A. Coser. Chicago, IL: University of Chicago Press, 1992.

Hatt, Michael. "Sculpting and Lynching: The Making and Unmaking of the Black Citizen in Late Nineteeth-Century America." *Oxford Art Journal* 24, no. 1 (2001): 1–22. http://www.jstor.org/stable/3600376.

Hook, Derek. "Screened History: Nostalgia as Defense Formative." *Peace and Conflict: Journal of Peace Psychology* 18, no. 3 (2012): 225–39. doi:10.1037/a0029071.

Kelting, Lily. "The Entanglement of Nostalgia and Utopia in Contemporary Southern Food Cookbooks." *Food, Culture, & Society* 19, no. 2 (2016): 361–387. doi:10.1080/15528014.2016.1178549.

Lakeport Plantation. "Virtual Tour." N.d. http://lakeport.astate.edu/virtual-tour-2/.

Leeds-Hurwitz, Wendy. *Semiotics and Communication: Signs, Codes, Cultures.* Hillsdale, NJ: Lawrence Erlbaum, 1993.

Lindlof, Thomas R., and Bryan C. Taylor. "Producing Data III: Analyzing Material Culture and Documents." In *Qualitative Communication Research Methods,* 217–240. Thousand Oaks, CA: Sage, 2011.

Lippe-McGraw, Jordi. "Why Heritage Tourism is More Popular Than Ever." *Condé Nast Traveler*, May 11, 2017. https://www.cntraveler.com/story/why-heritage-tourism-is-more-popular-than-ever.

Litvin, Stephen W., and Joshua David Brewer. "Charleston, South Carolina Tourism and the Presentation of Urban Slavery in an Historic Southern City." *International Journal of Hospitality & Tourism Administration* 9, no. 1 (2008): 71–84. doi:10.1080/15256480801910541.

Lizardi, Ryan. *Nostalgic Generations and Media: Perception of Time and Available Meaning.* Lanham, MD: Lexington Books, 2017.

Long Branch. "House Tour." Last updated 2018. https://www.visitlongbranch.org/virtual-tour/.

Mackay, Pauline, and Murray Pittock. "Highland Mary: Objects and Memories." *Romanticism* 18, no. 2 (2012): 191–203. doi:10.3366/rom.2012.0084.

Maly, Michael, Heather Dalmage, and Nancy Michaels. "The End of an Idyllic World: Nostalgia Narratives, Race, and the Construction of White Powerlessness." *Critical Sociology* 39, no. 5 (2012): 757–779. doi:10.1177/0896920512448941.

Mansfield Plantation. "Mighty Mansfield's Interactive Map." Last updated 2004. http://www.mansfieldplantation.com/history_01.html.

Mason, Sara F. "The Plantation Tour: Constructing History on the Ground." Presentation at the American Sociological Association Annual Meeting, Las Vegas, NV, August 20–23, 2011.

Miller, Miranda. "Google Now Owns 44% of Global Advertising Market." *Search Engine Watch*, last updated December 7, 2011. https://searchenginewatch.com/sew/study/2130985/google-owns-44-global-advertising-market.

Mitchell, Margaret. *Gone with the Wind*. New York, NY: Macmillan, 1936.

Modlin, E. Arnold, Jr. "Tales Told on the Tour: Mythic Representations of Slavery by Docents at North Carolina Plantations Museums." *Southeastern Geographer* 48, no. 3 (2008): 265–287. doi:10.1353/sgo.0.0025.

Modlin E. Arnold, Jr., Derek H. Alderman, and Glenn W. Gentry. "Tour Guides as Creators of Empathy: The Role of Affective Inequality in Marginalizing the Enslaved at Plantation House Museums." *Tourist Studies* 11, no. 1 (2011): 3–19. doi:10.1177/1468797611412007.

Mount Vernon. "Virtual Tour." Last updated 2018. http://www.mountvernon.org/the-estate-gardens/.

Ritterhouse, Jennifer. "Reading, Intimacy, and the Role of Uncle Remus in White Southern Social Memory." *The Journal of Southern History* 69, no. 3 (2003): 585–622. doi:10.2307/30040011.

Robison, Lori. "Bodies, Southern Nostalgia, and the Construction of Whiteness in *Divine Secrets of the Ya-Ya Sisterhood*." *The Journal of Popular Culture* 42, no. 6 (2009): 1115–1133. doi:10.1111/j.1540-5931.2009.00725.x.

Sherwood Forest Plantation. "Dependencies." Last updated 2002. http://www.sherwoodforest.org/VR/depend_new.html.

Sherwood Forest Plantation. "Front Porch." Last updated 2002. http://www.sherwoodforest.org/VR/front_new.html.

Sherwood Forest Plantation. "Virtual Tour." Last updated 2002. http://sherwoodforest.org/VRtour_new.html.

Shields, Tanya. "Correction to: Magnolia Longing: The Plantation Tour as Palimpsest." *Souls: A Critical Journal of Black Politics, Culture & Society* 19, no. 3 (2017a): 397. doi:10.1080/10999949.2017.1324686.

Shields, Tanya. "Magnolia Longing: The Plantation Tour as Palimpsest." *Souls: A Critical Journal of Black Politics, Culture & Society* 19, no. 1 (2017b): 6–23. doi:10.1080/10999949.2017.1268517.

Sontag, Susan. *On Photography*. London: Penguin Books, 1977.

Stella Plantation. "About Us." Last updated 2016. https://www.stellaplantation.com/about-us.

Stella Plantation. "Explore the Grounds." https://www.stellaplantation.com/explore-the-grounds.

Stewart, Kathleen. *Ordinary Affects*. Durham, NC: Duke University Press, 2007.

Strauss, Anselm L. *Qualitative Analysis for Social Scientists.* Cambridge: Cambridge University Press, 1987.

Strauss, Anselm L., and Juliet Corbin. *Basics of Qualitative Research.* Newbury Park, CA: Sage, 1990.

Turner, Bryan. "A Note on Nostalgia." *Theory, Culture, & Society* 4 (1987): 147–156. doi:10.1177/026327687004001008.

Turner, Daniel Cross. "Restoration, Metanostalgia, and Critical Memory: Forms of Nostalgia in Contemporary Southern Poetry." *Southern Literary Journal* 40, no. 2 (2008): 182–206. http://www.jstor.org/stable/20077914.

U.S. Census Bureau. "Geography: Regions." Last accessed May 27, 2018. https://www.census.gov/geo/reference/webatlas/regions.html.

Williams, Paul. *Memorial Museums: The Global Rush to Commemorate Atrocities.* New York, NY: Berg, 2007.

Winch, Alison. *Girlfriends and Postfeminist Sisterhood.* Hampshire: Palgrave Macmillan, 2013.

Zelizer, Barbie. "Reading the Past against the Grain: The Shape of Memory Studies." *Critical Studies in Mass Communication* 12 (1995): 214–239. doi:10.1080/15295039509366932.

7. *Subjectivities in Automated Nostalgia: Social Media and Everyday Nostalgic Longing for the Past/Present*

JEONGHYUN LEE

Introduction

About a week before Christmas every year, every Facebook user receives the notification, "This is your memory of the year." Once the user opens the Facebook account, the notification appears on their News Feed with a short video, which is composed of the selected photos and posts of the user on Facebook. This feature, called Year in Review, takes users back to the past through the automatically generated video by Facebook's algorithms. This chapter focuses on Facebook's past-oriented features that encourage us to be the nostalgic subjects who eternally engage in the past with the algorithmically suggested ways.

Since its first launch, Facebook has developed platforms and services to create, store, and evoke memories. Even though their major platform, News Feed, has emphasized the "now" of users in order to let them post their status in an almost real-time, Facebook has shown the continuous interest in creating platforms and services to make their interfaces the "sites of memory" for communities and individuals (Nora 1989, 7). On the following year of introducing their first memory-related feature, Timeline, Facebook launched the Year in Review feature. After minor and major changes in the service itself, they relocate the feature to the inside the new tool called Memories in June 2018, which is composed of four sections showing users' past posts and activities (Gheller 2015; Hod 2018). As its naming indicates, the new tool, Memories, reflects on several moments in the past that have been shared on Facebook. The Memories feature creates the automatic notifications about the posts made on this day in the previous years (On This Day), the new

Facebook friends made at the date (Friends Made On This Day and Friend-versaries), and a seasonal, monthly, or yearly summary of users' past posts (Recaps of Memories), in addition to Year in Review (Hod 2018).

With the development of their four features in Memories, Facebook has evoked not only memory practices but also nostalgic connections to the past. From their first service of Year in Review in 2012 to the new feature titled Memories in 2018, Facebook has tested several designs and algorithmic filters to shape the nostalgic subjects, suggesting nostalgia for certain types of past. Facebook's original emphasis on News Feed has encouraged users to share their time and space information, and Facebook has accumulated a huge amount of individual and social contents. In addition to developing multiple mechanisms of the storage system that can store millions of users' data without storage failure, Facebook has continuously introduced the new services that recirculate the already stored past. Even though their purpose might rely on the Capitalist logic that pushes more people to use and return to their services for Facebook's profit, these memory-evoking features in Facebook should be examined with the discussions of nostalgia and subjectivity.

This chapter explores these memory-oriented features in Facebook by focusing on the ways in which the socio-technical cultures shape the automatic desires and standardized reflections on the past. This chapter builds on a series of documents, including magazines, news articles, opinion pieces, commercials, and research around Facebook Memories feature to reveal the algorithmic organization, curation, and reanimation of the past in Facebook Memories. The major sources are documents published by Facebook, such as terms and policy, patent documents, commercials, manuals, published research and interviews from the Facebook research team and newsroom. This broad analysis aims to demonstrate how social media automate our longing for the past in everyday life and how the algorithms form the subjective experiences of nostalgia.

While I explore ways in which the automated nostalgia constructs the new nostalgic subjectivities, this chapter will contribute to understanding the medium specificity of the nostalgic practices and the subject formations by joining the relatively recent conversation on nostalgia, which emphasizes the role of different medium in evoking the longing for the past (Davidson 2011; Lange 2011; Lizardi 2014; Winkler 2011). In order to conceptualize the automated nostalgia, this chapter first reviews the scholarly discussions of nostalgia, focusing on its conceptual relations with time, memory, and subject formations. Next, I address a short history of Facebook's memory-oriented features and articulate the way the features expand and revise our understanding of nostalgia. Then, at the end of this chapter, I illustrate how the automated nostalgia shapes the nostalgic subjects who become a part of algorithmic operations in their memory practices.

Nostalgia and Temporal Experiences

Since the twentieth century, nostalgia has been pervasive in a variety of cultural context. With the cultural attention to revisiting the past and reproducing the past contents, the concept of nostalgia has been interdisciplinarily discussed.

The concept of nostalgia has primarily engaged in the affective connections to the past. The dictionary definition of nostalgia has shifted in the 1970s from a medical term of homesickness to a sentimental and obsessive yearning for the past (Becker 2018, 237). The concept is originated from Greek roots, Nostos (returning home) and Algos (pain, grief, or suffering) to refer to pathological symptoms of the Swiss Army fighting abroad (Hofer 1934). The original term has described a general sense of loss and mourning for the unattainable past because the return to the object of longing and the past is impossible (May 2017, 404). However, the recent conceptualization of nostalgia implies the pleasurable contemplation as well. Dickinson and Erben argue that the modern sense of nostalgia emphasizes more "the feature of concentrated pleasurable contemplation" than recalling "an ache of longing" (2006, 1).

Either a sense of loss or pleasure, the concept of nostalgia highlights the ambivalent temporal experiences with a desire to return to a specific time. Following Bergson (1998, 2014), the reality is a movement that continuously changes and indivisibly flows. Our visual perceptions of external objects are images of the constant transitions in the flux of perpetual becoming, and our measurements of time only give the fragmented understanding of the time. In Bergsonian reality, the time has no divisible moments, such as past, present, and future, but the durational flow. In the continuous flows of time, the nostalgic desires spatialize the time and wish to revisit time like space. In *The Past is A Foreign Country* (1985), Lowenthal argues that the past is foreign, which is distinct from the present and the future. Against the durational flow of time, nostalgic subject spatializes time and continuously longs for the past in comparison with the perception of present and future. At this point, nostalgia is different from recollection in that nostalgia involves a comparison between the past and present as distinct entities, and the comparison inspires a desire to return to a different time (Wilson 2005).

In the longing for the past, the foreignness of the past also plays an ever-changing role in shaping the present and the future. This understanding of nostalgia is related to Boym's concept of "reflective nostalgia," which emphasizes "taking time out of time" and "grasping the fleeting present" (Boym 2001, 14). Through the reflective longing, the past does not indicate the disappeared truth but becomes a potentiality that "might act and will act by inserting itself into a present sensation from which it borrows the vitality" (Bergson 1988, 240). The reflective nostalgia would not restore the past as the truth but mediate the passage of time with a potentiality of past. The past "opens up a multitude of potentialities" and enables us to understand time in non-linear and non-teleological ways (Boym 2001, 14). In these ambivalent values of nostalgia, the nostalgic desires make the past both distant and close to the present.

Based on the affective engagements and temporal experiences of nostalgia, Boym (2001, 7) defines nostalgia as a longing for the home that "no longer exists or has never existed," implying both a sentiment of loss and a romance with one's fantasy. The fantasy plays an important role to differentiate nostalgia from memory. When Coontz (1992) analyzes nostalgic ideology in the American television shows, she argues that the television shows depict the 1950s as the era of an ideal family structure to reaffirm the ideological images of the family. For Coontz, the nostalgic wish to return to 1950s family value builds on the utopian and ideal images of the past that never existed in reality (Coontz 1992, 35). Similarly, in his analysis of post-communist cities, Svetlana Boym (2001) argues that the actual past tends to be forgotten once nostalgia possesses one. The idealized version of mediated past replaces the real past. The past exists only in narrative, imagination, and fantasy. The images and narratives of the past that nostalgia reflects are not necessarily authentic, but ideological and utopian. The nostalgia creates the longing for the imagined and idealized past, which is constructed by memory and desire, not by experience (Hutcheon 2000; Jameson 1991; Stewart 1984).

In sum, I define nostalgia as an affective engagement to a certain time, an ambivalent temporal experience, and the reconstruction of the past based on fantasy and desire. The previous scholarly discourses of nostalgia have tended to focus on the formation of collective, national, and generational subjects, which are constructed by a collective sense of loss and longing for the same historical period (Bach 2002; Berdahl 1999; Boyer 2006; Hutcheon 2000; Stewart 1984). However, recent scholarly interests in social media highlight the individual nostalgic experiences in everyday life (Chopra-Gant 2016; Lizardi 2017; Takvam and Vale 2016). The next section expands the idea of individual nostalgic experiences in Facebook through my concept, the automation of nostalgia.

Nostalgia Machine: Facebook and the New Archive

Facebook has been prominent to engage in memory practices through their platform designs and services. Timeline, the Facebook service introduced in 2011, first shows Facebook's interest in memory. Combining their Profile and Wall pages, the Timeline started with the one's profile picture and information, and reverse-chronologically displayed one's post on Facebook. The Timeline provides a single space of all the posts each user has shared on Facebook. By scrolling down, users could review all photos, posts, and life events in reverse-chronological order, from the most recent post to the day each user was born. This new feature highlights one's trajectory of entire posts, rather than the most recent one.

Before the Timeline, Facebook's services focused on the connection and network with friends on Facebook. The original design of Facebook in 2006 emphasized News Feed, which is the major Facebook interface that each user can review a collection of what all friends wrote in their Wall Page. Each user had the separate Profile page that enables them to share their personal information such as job, education, the current residency, and hometown, to get acknowledged by Facebook friends.

By featuring Timeline, however, Facebook emphasizes individual practices of curating and collecting posts to manage one's life trajectory. With Timeline, each user becomes able to have a separate page showing a chronology of what one has posted. The design of the Timeline allows users to shape one's life trajectory on a single page and review their and others' past posts anytime. As an initial response to Timeline, *Wired*'s website mentioned on December 16 in 2011, that "you may be interested in curating the new interface" because "your life can be exposed for everyone to see and scrutinize." Timeline encourages the user to curate one's life trajectory and collect the best moments in one's life, highlighting the life story rather than the most recent post. All the post previously ephemeral and unorganized become organized in reverse chronological order to be reviewed anytime. Facebook becomes a storage medium or an individual digital archive, which is capable of remembering and storing the ephemeral.

This storage function of Timeline serves as a condition of memory practices in Facebook. As Kittler (1999) emphasizes with the newness of the phonograph, storage media can reverse the time-axis by storing and replaying the record later in the future. In the storage media, time does not flow linearly, but time-axis can be reversed. Kittler (1999) argues that the storage capacity of media becomes conditions of what and how we remember. Following Kittler, Facebook Timeline also becomes a storage medium, which conditionalizes what to remember and how to remember our daily life.

Facebook's further emphasis on memory has developed the individual archive in motion. In addition to the Timeline, Facebook introduced Year in Review in 2012, which recirculates one's posts archived in the Timeline. Year in Review takes users back to the summary of the past year through the algorithmically generated video, which is composed of most liked and commented events or memories. When Facebook first launched Year in Review in 2012, the service showed a montage of users' activities on Facebook, which includes the most liked posts, the user's birthday message, the Facebook pages the user liked, and the number of Facebook friends the user made during the year. In the next year, Facebook revised the service a bit by allowing users to review only the selected posts and comments. Along with the Year in Review, users were also able to create a video of the major life events, such as graduations, weddings, and vacations.

In 2014, Facebook re-introduced the new algorithm-based Year in Review. The new design of Year in Review offered a customizable slideshow of the most liked photos. The slideshow came along with the default tagline, "It's been a great year! Thanks for being a part of it." Facebook algorithms automatically selected one particularly well-engaged photo as the cover image, with the tagline of "Here's what your year looked like" followed by a series of the most liked photos displayed in chronological order (Hern 2014).

However, the automatic memory practices did not guarantee a pleasant remembrance. The new Year in Review faced complaints because the automatically selected cover page or photos often reminded an unpleasant and a painful memory to those who have been through a bad year. Despite Facebook's assumption on every user's "great" year, some users were forced to remember unwelcome memories or traumatic events through the summary of the year that Facebook algorithms suggested. For example, Eric Meyer's story has been popular. Facebook's algorithms chose Eric's six-year-old daughter's face as a cover page. Facebook asked Eric to edit or share this Year in Review, which starts from his daughter's face in an upbeat mood of background. Unfortunately, Eric lost his daughter to brain cancer in the year, and he did not want to share the difficult year with his Facebook friends. Eric wrote in his blog that this automatically created video could be the "inadvertent algorithmic cruelty," even though it is not a deliberate assault. Eric's episode and similar other cases triggered a significant change in Facebook's algorithm to decide which picture they should include and exclude.

The quantification of attention, selecting and organizing photos based on the number of "likes" received, was not able to catch the qualitative differences in the attention, resulting in suggesting the undelightful memories for some users. After the several complaints from users, including Eric's case, Facebook added new layers to filter out possibly painful memories. According to Facebook research in 2017, Facebook developed a "sophisticated algorithm" to identify which memories are "good" and "bad" (Konrad 2017). First, the new algorithm sorts out someone who is blocked, dead, or has a memorialized account on Facebook to avoid reminding the possibly painful relationships. After filtering out some users may have an unpleasant history with the user, the algorithm chooses posts based on the number of likes and comments. In addition to this quantified measurement, they add the layer that may catch qualitative values in it. For example, the new algorithm prioritizes the comments with the positive words and important people, such as family, miss, face, graduation, wedding, and love, over the negative words or less important words, such as food-related words. Then, they categorize users' post into a theme by following "Taxonomy of Memory Themes," that helps them to classify memories based on the algorithm-notifiable importance. Third, they provide options to users to customize what to appear in their video by allowing them to choose preferred people and timespans. In this way, Facebook believes that users can control their memories and the feelings about the past on Facebook.

If Timeline makes Facebook an individual archive, Year in Review allows Facebook to be an archive in motion. While Timeline encourages users to curate their life story, Year in Review algorithmically and automatically selects, organizes, and reanimates memories. The notification of Year in Review appears at the top of one's News Feed and automatically evokes the nostalgia to the past, which is algorithmically narrativized. Through this new feature, Facebook creates and facilitates nostalgia through their algorithmic operations. Remembering the algorithmically curated past becomes another daily practice besides the archiving everyday life.

At this stage, Facebook becomes a nostalgia machine that suggests affective engagements to a certain time in the past, introduces the new temporal experiences, and reconstructs the past based on fantasy, desire, and ideology. Facebook's memory-oriented services have consistently triggered the longing for the unattainable past posted and archived on Facebook. Specifically, Year in Review has been developed to evoke the pleasurable and joyful past. In the process, each user's past is reconstructed by Facebook's desire and fantasy. Facebook creates the narrative of the past through the selections and organizations of certain photos, music, background, and captions. The latest version sophisticatedly builds the idealized past that triggers only joyful engagements to the past. The algorithmically generated video is not necessarily an authentic past. The past appears ideologically utopian with upbeat music and bright background images. The video is nostalgic for the exceedingly joyful past, which is mostly constructed by the algorithmic speculation, quantification, and desire.

More importantly, all the process of nostalgic experiences become automated by the algorithmic operations. The algorithmic operations select, suggest, and, ultimately, manipulate what to remember and how to remember. The reconstructed past becomes a potentiality that continuously works on shaping one's experiences of Facebook and the subjective experiences of the past. Boym argues that "[w]ho is speaking in the name of nostalgia?" is always important to ask (2001, 17). The answer to Boym's question in this chapter is the algorithmic operations. In what follows, building on this answer, I articulate how the algorithmic media construct the nostalgic subjects who engage in algorithmic memory practices and become objects of the algorithmic observation, operation, and manipulation.

Nostalgic Subjects in Automated Nostalgia

On the surface level, Facebook's services recirculate past photos to evoke one' memories. The role of photographs in memory practices has long been discussed. The photograph captures and freezes the fleeting time. This uniqueness makes many people photograph their life events for remembrance. In addition to photography's role as recording and documenting tools, photographs are associated with the affective engagements with past. In *Camera Lucida* (1981), Roland Barthes develops the concept of "punctum" through his experience of reviewing the family photo album, which denotes the sudden and strong emotion of wounds that builds a direct relationship between the viewing subject and the object or person within the photograph. Building on Barthes's analysis, Marianne Hirsch also argues that the photograph can transfer memories from one to other by evoking affective connections between the viewing subjects and the photographs (2008, 115).

Likewise, the image itself can have the capacity to address the viewer's bodily memory by letting viewers not only to see the events but also to feel the past "through a process of affective contagion" (Bennett 2005, 36). However, this photographic method is not the only way to evoke memories in the Facebook. Through Timeline and Year in Review, Facebook becomes an archive in motion that categorizes the inaccessible amount of records stored in their archive and reorganizes them in the standardized orders. Facebook as an archive provides "templates for imagining such new forms of subjectivation" (Packer 2010, 102). In the reorganization and recirculation of the past, the archiving subject turns into the nostalgic subject who consumes the standardized past and ideologically joyful memories suggested by the algorithmic operations. This section articulates the formations of the nostalgic subject in the socio-technical memory practices of the automated nostalgia.

When Bush prophesizes a new machine, the Memex, in *As We May Think* (1945), Bush dreams of the machine that can free us from remembering. A Memex is an analog machine for selecting and preserving data, which is frequently cited as a precursor of a hyperlink and World Wide Web (Chun 2008, 75). In needs of aids to store and consult the massive amount of scientific data, Bush designs the machine that not only stores documents permanently but also manages a prodigious amount of record effectively.

A Memex is a desk-like machine that has two projectors: one is for enabling users to create associative trails and personal annotations on in documents, and the other is to recall these trails at will. If individuals want, the documents are compressed and stored as microfilm and dropped into the machine. Individuals could add or remove microfilm reels if necessary. In addition to this storage capacity, the Memex has associative trails, the distinguished indexing system of the machine. An associative trail is a way to create a new order of stored microfilm frames along with personal comments in order to manage records for the future uses. The Memex's indexing creates the association of related documents with personal comments, enabling easy access for the future. The Memex envisions not only how we can store the explosive amount of records, but also how we manage them for future access and retrieval.

By designing the machine of storing, organizing, and retrieving a huge amount of records, Bush envisions that humans are liberated from any practices of remembering, by relying on the machine. The mechanism of Memex, the synthesized system of storage and indexing, sounds very similar to the overall logic of the Facebook interface. Facebook becomes a machine that has a system to store and manage individual data. The way Facebook organizes the massive amount of data in Timeline turns the stored data to memories. Then, Year in Review arranges the memories to be nostalgic. All activities on Facebook, such as pushing a "Like" button, leaving comments, posting photos, become associative trails and annotations on the data to recall it later in specific ways. The mechanism of Facebook has liberated users from the voluntary remembering of the past by notifying and suggesting what and how we should remember.

The algorithmic operations of Facebook automate nostalgia. Facebook regularly recirculates the past and actively engages in our memory practices. The algorithmic selections and organizations manipulate what should be remembered and standardize our affective engagements to the past. In the socio-technical memory practices of the automatic selection, organization, and reanimation, users become the nostalgic subjects who maintain a specific affection to the idealized past and the present, the soon-to-be past.

The relationships between memory practices and the subject formations have frequently discussed. The process of recording, reviewing, and remembering has constructed the self. Humphreys (2018) argues that writing and sharing everyday life details are not new phenomena of social media. People have written and shared the diary since the eighteenth and nineteenth centuries. People who travel or young women who get married have documented mundane life events and activities in their diary. The diary has been reviewed by themselves as well as sent to their family to share their everyday life and feeling (Humphreys 2018, 2). Documenting daily and special experiences has been a reflexive practice that reveals one's characteristics and certain aspects of lived events. Historically, the practices of recording, sharing, and reviewing have been the practices to understand and make sense of the self, and the ideas resonate with Michel Foucault's technologies of the self.

Michel Foucault (2000) theorizes a subject as a product of relational forces between discourses. The subject is constituted at the intersection between external forces of the social structure and the internal practices of understanding the self. In the dynamics of two forces, a subject has never been an absolute position. While Foucault's early works have focused on the external forces of the power systems that discipline the subject, such as government, science, and prison, the later works of Foucault have theorized the way individuals govern and know themselves, which he called "technologies of the self."

The concept, technologies of the self, indicates the subject's performance on their own bodies, thoughts, souls, and ways of being "to transform themselves in order to attain a certain state of happiness, purity, wisdom, perfection, or immortality" (Foucault 2000, 225). It is "the procedures [...] suggested or prescribed to individuals [to] determine, maintain, and transform their identity through relations of self-mastery or self-knowledge" (Foucault 2000, 86). For Foucault, technologies of the self are always cultural and historical.

In his essay, *Technologies of the self* ([1984] 2000), Foucault traces self-caring techniques to determine, maintain, and transform one's identity and state in the Stoic and Christianity. In the Stoic, for example, students wrote a letter about one's daily life to disclose the conscientious and independent self. Christian confession or the religious diary writing encourages people to examine one's life by reflecting on "what one has done and what one has had to do" (Foucault 2000, 238). Historically, different techniques of looking back one's everyday life have been engaged in attaining a certain state of affect and shaping one's behaviors. People recall the principles of actions and reflect on one's mode of living, existence, and subjectivity to govern one's life. The permanent self-examination constructs the self in a certain way.

In the contemporary society, social media practices become technologies of the self, which are techniques to examine oneself and discipline oneself toward the socially normative and ideal self. As Hunter (1992) argues that diary-writing has been an internalized discipline, Facebook-archiving and reviewing can be ways of being to transform and maintain the self in a specific way. The automated nostalgia in Facebook shapes, influences, and persuades one's mode of action and subjectivity.

As of the diary-writing, users document what one has done and what one has felt by leaving posts and photos as records and reflections. Then, the self looks back media traces of whom we used to be, what we have done, and what we have experienced. Humphreys argues that social media posts show the strategic representations and performances of the self, constructing the "qualified self" (2018, 11). Users select and document the parts of daily life in Facebook Timeline and review one's mode of actions and livings later. Like the Stoic diary and the Christian confession, Facebook Timeline becomes the technique of examining the self that determines, maintains, and transforms one's subjective experiences.

The self-examination through Facebook is, however, socio-technical that the algorithmic operations become an element of the self-examination. Instead of being passive storage media, Facebook animates the individual digital archives of everyday life and remediates one's memories to shape the nostalgic subject. When people can understand and govern the self in the process of reviewing whom we used to be, what we have done, what we have felt, and what we have experienced, the algorithmic operations of Facebook select, determine, and manipulate one's mode of being and the state of happiness.

The algorithms select the most memorable moments based on quantification of attention and analyze one's linguistic and non-linguistic expressions to sort out painful memories. Even though users might strategically select the photos and posts on Facebook, they review them through the algorithmic operations. The subject reviews the algorithmic organizations of "what one has done and what one has had to do" that evoke the state of happiness, joy, and nostalgia (Foucault 2000, 238). In the algorithmic operations of automating nostalgia, individual experience becomes once memory, then, the object of algorithmic observation and analysis creating a standardized longing for the past.

Conclusion

Memory practice becomes socio-technical, which is a mixture of social practices and technological operations. While we believe that memory solely belongs to a human subject, we become more connected with media to remember in a certain way without specific knowledge of how they gather, analyze, select, organize, reanimate, and distribute our memories. We are habitually engaging with media to be connected with the past, but we do not recognize or cannot perceive the logic of automation and datafication associated with our memory practices and subjectivations.

This chapter problematizes these essential knowledge imbalances in the automation of nostalgia and demonstrates how the subjectivity can be constructed in the algorithmic operations of automating nostalgia. In the algorithmic selections and organizations, the real past is less important than the algorithmic anticipation about individual actions and desires in the future. The delightful summary of the past is not simply associated with the experiences in the past but also oriented to users' further engagements with the services in the present and the future. By building joyful relationships with one's past and Facebook, Facebook anticipates enhancing user engagement with the site for the present and future.

The algorithmic operations of selecting, organizing, and reanimating memories idealize and fantasize the past and construct the nostalgic subjects that become objects of the algorithmic assumption and speculation. In the algorithmic process, programming and coding authorize the speculation of the memorable past and the prediction of the future memory practices. As Adrian MacKenzie argues, we move from the society of statistics, which emphasizes population and normality, to the society of machine learning, which builds on a generic set of prediction and speculation to the individual (MacKenzie 2013, 402). The automated nostalgia predicts and speculates individual engagements with the past/present and, ultimately, the future of/in/for Facebook.

Even though this chapter focuses on Facebook, the recirculation of the past posts and the automation of nostalgia have been popular sociotechnical cultures across various social network sites. Before Facebook's On This Day feature, which reminds past posts on a specific day, the similar service has been carried by the web service, Timehop in 2011. Timehop connects users to social network sites, such as Facebook, Twitter, Instagram, and Foursquare, and uncovers what they posted on these social network sites on the same day in previous years. Along with Facebook, in iOS 10, Apple often provides a notification, saying that "You have a new memory." The notification leads one to open the photo album and a slideshow of photos in it, which is composed of photos that the user has taken in past months. In the same name, Memories, Apple algorithms automatically organize and reanimate stored photos into a short film-like slideshow. Similarly, the Google Photos Assistant automatically organizes a collage of photos with a certain design and music based on time, space, people and mood of the photos. Under the user's permission, the algorithm periodically shows and reanimates the memories through their platform. Before and after Facebook, the past has been recirculated through the various algorithmic media.

The automation of nostalgia is pervasive in the twentieth-first century media and becomes the socio-technical culture of remembering. In this new vibe of the automated nostalgia, individuals are once the subjects of memory, then, become the objects of the archive in motion that categorizes the inaccessible amounts of digital memories stored in the archive and reanimates them in the idealized portrayal of the past. When Facebook becomes an archive in motion, it distinguishes the past from the present, determines the memorable and the forgettable, and standardizes how we remember. Automation of nostalgia is a socio-technical technique of shaping the subject that suggests or prescribes the way of being joyful nostalgic subjects.

References

Bach, Jonathan. "The taste remains: Consumption, (N)ostalgia, and the production of East Germany." *Public Culture* 14, no. 3 (2002): 545–556.

Barthes, Roland. *Camera Lucida: Reflection on Photography*, translated by R. Howard. New York: Hill and Wang, 1981.

Becker, Tobias. "1. The meanings of nostalgia: Genealogy and critique." *History and Theory* 57, no. 2 (2018): 234–250.

Bennett, Jill. *Empathic Vision: Affect, Trauma, and Contemporary Art.* Stanford: Stanford University Press, 2005.

Berdahl, Daphne. "'(N)Ostalgie' for the present: Memory, longing, and East German things." *Ethnos* 64, no. 2 (1999): 192–211.

Bergson, Henri. *Creative Evolution.* translated by A. Mitchell, New York: Dover Publications, 1998.

Bergson, Henri. *Matter and Memory*, translated by N. M. Paul, W. S. Palmer. Kent: Solis Press, 2014.

Boyer, Dominic. "Ostalgie and the politics of the future in Eastern Germany." *Public Culture* 18, no. 2 (2006): 361–381.

Boym, Svetlana. *The Future of Nostalgia.* New York: Basic Books, 2001.

Bush, Vernard. "As we may think." *The Atlantic Monthly*, 176, no. 1 (1945): 101–108.

Chopra-Gant, Mike. "Pictures or it didn't happen: Photo-nostalgia, iPhoneography and the representation of everyday life." *Photography and Culture* 9, no. 2 (2016): 121–133.

Chun, Wendy Hui Kyong. "The enduring ephemeral, or the future is a memory." *Critical Inquiry* 35, no. 1 (2008): 148–171.

Coontz, Stephanie. *The Way We Never Were: American Families and the Nostalgia Trap.* New York: Basic Books, 1992.

Davidson, Tonya. "Nostalgia and post-memories of a lost place: Actualizing my virtual homeland." In *Ecologies of Affects: Placing Nostalgia, Desire, and Hope*, edited by T. K. Davidson, O. Park, and R. Shields, 19–42. Waterloo: Wilfrid Laurier University Press, 2011.

Davidson, Tonya K., Ondine Park, and Rob Shields, eds. *Ecologies of Affect: Placing Nostalgia, Desire, and Hope.* Waterloo: Wilfrid Laurier University Press, 2013.

Dickinson, Hilary, and Michael Erben. "Nostalgia and autobiography: The past in the present." *Auto/Biography* 14, no. 3 (2006): 223.

Foucault, Michel. *Ethics: Essential Works of Foucault 1954–1984.* London: Penguin, 2000.

Gheller, Jonathan. "Introducing On This Day: A new way to look back at photos and memories on Facebook." Facebook Newsroom, March 24, 2015.

Hern, Alex. "Facebook apologies over 'cruel' year in review clips." *The Guardian.* December 29, 2014.

Hirsch, Marianne. "The generation of postmemory." *Poetics Today* 29, no. 1 (2008): 103–128.

Hod, Oren. "All of your Facebook memories are now in one place." *Facebook Newsroom*, June 11, 2018

Hofer, Johannes. "Medical dissertation on nostalgia." *Bulletin of the History of Medicine* 2 (1934): 376–391.

Humphreys, Lee. *The qualified self: Social media and the accounting of everyday life.* Cambridge: The MIT Press, 2018.

Hunter, Jane. "Inscribing the self in the heart of the family: Diaries and girlhood in late-Victorian America." *American Quarterly* 44, no. 1 (1992): 52.

Hutcheon, Linda. "Irony, nostalgia, and the postmodern." In *Methods for the Study of Literature as Cultural Memory*, edited by R. Vervliet and A. Estor, 189–207. Amsterdam: Rodopi, 2000.

Jameson, Fredric. *Postmodernism, or, The Cultural Logic of Late Capitalism.* Durham, NC: Duke University Press, 1991.

Kittler, Friedrich. *Gramophone, Film, Typewriter*, translated by G. Winthrop-Young and M. Wutz. Stanford: Stanford University Press, 1999.

Konrad, Artie. "Facebook memories: The research behind the products that connect you with your past." *Facebook Research*, September 6, 2017.

Lange, Patricia. "Video-mediated nostalgia and the aesthetics of technical competencies." *Visual Communication* 10, no. 1 (2011): 25–44.

Lizardi, Ryan. *Mediated Nostalgia: Individual Memory and Contemporary Mass Media.* Lanham: Lexington Books, 2014.

Lizardi, Ryan. *Nostalgic generations and media: Perception of time and available meaning.* Lanham: Lexington Books, 2017.

Lowenthal, David. *The Past is a Foreign Country-Revisited.* Cambridge: Cambridge University Press, 2015.

Mackenzie, Adrian. "Programming subjects in the regime of anticipation: Software studies and subjectivity." *Subjectivity* 6, no. 4 (2013): 391–405.

May, Vanessa. "Belonging from afar: Nostalgia, time and memory." *The Sociological Review* 65, no. 2 (2017): 401–415.

Nora, Pierre. "Between memory and history: Les lieux de mémoire." *Representations*, no. 26 (1989): 7–24.

Packer, Jeremy. "What is an archive?: An apparatus model for communications and media history." *The Communication Review* 13 (2010): 88–104.

Stewart, Susan. *On Longing: Narratives of the Miniature, the Gigantic, the Souvenir, the Collection*. Raleigh, NC: Duke University Press, 1984.

Takvam, Monica, and Vale, Sam. "Introduction to nostalgias: Visualising longing special issue." *Photography & Culture* 9, no. 2 (2016): 99–102.

Wilson, Janelle L. *Nostalgia: Sanctuary of Meaning*. Bucknell University Press, 2005.

Winkler, Anne. "Not everything was good, but many things were better: Nostalgia for East Germany and its politics." In *Ecologies of Affects: Placing Nostalgia, Desire, and Hope*, edited by Tonya K. Davidson, Ondine Park, and Rob Shields, 19–42. Waterloo: Wilfrid Laurier University Press, 2011.

8. *Representations of the Communist Period in Romanian Digital Communities: A Quest for Online "Displaced Nostalgia"*

ALEXANDRA BARDAN AND NATALIA VASILENDIUC

The 20th anniversary of the fall of the communist regime in Romania prompted a new and animated approach of the communist period, prolonged in public debates that were extended beyond 2009. Several lines of discussion can be identified, calling for a broader context, where nostalgia appears as a key theme associated with the process of coming to terms with the communist past.

Opinion polls carried out starting with 2009 (Pew Research Center 2009; IRES–IRESOP 2010; IICCMR–CSOP 2010, 2011; Adevărul–INSCOP Research 2013, 2014; CURS 2018) became the subject of a specific media coverage fueling polemics. Mainstream media outlets framed the polls' results with titles such as "Communist Nostalgia Haunts Eastern Europe" (Evenimentul Zilei 2009), "Poll: 83% of Romanians, Nostalgic for the Communist Period" (Ştirile ProTV 2010), "Communism Remains a Good Idea for most Romanians" (Evenimentul Zilei 2011), "Poll: Half of the Romanians Yearn for Communism" (Adevărul 2013), "Nostalgia for the Golden Era: 40% of Romanians consider the Communist Period was the best in the History of Modern Romania" (B1 2018), setting an alarmist tone for the understanding of nostalgia mostly as a longing for communism. A more nuanced perspective can be observed in examples concerning commodification, advertising and consumption practices related to the past, as most narratives were inspired by the social and cultural aspects of life in communism, drawing on a selective and positive memory of this bygone era (Iacob 2010; Marin 2013). Both semantic instances of the post-communist nostalgia were shortly put under scrutiny, while they were also adopted and adapted within several layers of the public discourse. First, the growing trend of polls' results related to the nostalgia for the communist past were commented and placed in the context of the 2008 global economic crisis (Cioflânca 2010; Vassilev 2011). Further analysis called for a wider social and political chronological framework: Luminiţa Murgescu (2012) took into account the generational change as an important variable for explaining the polls and the idealized recollection of the communist past, while Manuela Marin (2016) put in perspective the emergence of post-communist nostalgia, retracing the steps of the slow and challenging institutional process of coming to terms with the country's communist legacy. Thus, in December 2006 the report of the Presidential Commission for the Analysis of the Communist Dictatorship in Romania (known as the "Tismăneanu Report") was issued, representing "the first clear and public condemnation of communism by a Romanian head of state" (King 2007, 718). The extensive report (663 pages) was also charged with a high symbolic value, as it was meant to foster "a national debate about long-denied and occulted moments of the past" (Tismăneanu 2011, 175), yet it was met with vehement critiques, and generated heated debates and political turmoil "in a time and culture (…) increasingly prone to nostalgia for Communism" (Hogea 2010, 28).

Subsequent studies display the multiple dimensions of the fractured view on the remembrance processes at work in the Romanian society. These may take the form of a competition advancing a wide variety of images of the communist period mediated by products of the popular culture, as noted by Vasile Dâncu commenting the IRES poll of 2010 (Dâncu 2015), or a competition of narratives identified by Caterina Preda, who examined how the counter-memories created by artists were prompting an alternative view over the nostalgia expressed in polls (Preda 2015). Contradictory, even conflicting positions are related to the mainstream representations of the past that disqualify alternative memory practices, in view of the latter as "misinterpretations of 'true' history" (Asavei 2016, 27). Moreover, Mihai Rusu underlined a "latent conflict" and a "mnemonic battle" within the collective memory regarding the communist past, with an official narrative of communism, codified in the "Tismăneanu Report," opposed to vernacular cultures of remembrance (Rusu 2013, 2015).

Our aim in this chapter is to reflect upon the issue of post-communist nostalgia within Romanian generations born before and after 1989, along with an empirical analysis, as we identified several online Facebook[1] communities gathering hundreds, even thousands of members that collect and share visuals and narratives about the communist period. The concept of "post-communist nostalgia" is explored here as a subjective form of engagement with the communist past, while we attempt to questions whether the membership in an online "community of the longing" (Jeziński and Wojtkowski 2016) may be related to a specific representation of the past. The present study is part of an ongoing extensive research on post-communist nostalgia, aiming to examine local grassroots alternative memory practices, in the line of studies documenting the nature and the functions of these remembrance processes (Georgescu 2010; Asavei 2016; Bardan 2018).

Post-Communist Generations and a "Displaced Nostalgia"

Some of the aforementioned polls revealed a peculiar trend of positive representations of the communist past, as favorable opinions were recorded not only among elderly respondents, but also among youngsters. Another survey carried out earlier in 2010, titled "Civic and Political Implication of the Youth," focused on the analysis of how adolescents relate to communism in absence of direct experiences. It showed unexpected results as well, with more than a third of the respondents opting for the assertion that "the Communist period was better than the current one" (Gheorghiță 2010, 65). Gheorghiță correlated the results with variables concerning lower socioeconomic status and education, but also with a lack of relevant instruction about the communist past provided in high-school.

On one hand, this trend was further associated with various forms of mediation of the past. According to Luminița Murgescu, the opinion polls were a sign that "for a large part of the population, the Communist regime no longer signifies a trauma, and the regime is not passed on to the young generation as a traumatic experience" (Murgescu 2012), while Vasile Dâncu advanced the hypothesis of an intense identity crisis emerging in a flawed sociopolitical context as factors that may explain why the youngsters chose a positive valorization of the past (Dâncu 2015). On the other hand, Romania seems to be no exception if compared with other post-communist states in the area, as Maria Todorova considered that post-communist nostalgia reveals a new phenomenon within Eastern European countries, namely, "the tentative but growing curiosity among the younger generation" (Todorova 2010).

Translated as a field of research, this phenomenon falls within a sociological and anthropological conceptual framework, designating an "imagined" or "armchair nostalgia" (Appadurai 1996) that is not based on direct experience, a "displaced nostalgia" (Wilson 2005) as one for times not known firsthand, or an "exo-nostalgia" (Berliner 2014) as a posture towards bygone worlds. Our study draws mainly from Wilson's understanding of the "displaced nostalgia" as one reflecting the feeling of displacement of a generation in a quest for identity, and in a context where the products of popular culture project a romanticized and mythologized image of the past. In this perspective, we shall narrow our research question, asking whether Romanian post-communist generations contribute in the virtual space of online mediated memory with their own idealized, yet incomplete, representations of the communist past.

Figures of the Communist Past in New Media

In the growing body of literature on nostalgia related to post-socialist contexts, the studies of digital memories appear as an emerging field where we can identify two main research trajectories concerned by our study: (1) the way in which digitally mediated post-socialist memories are shaping opposing narratives of the past and (2) the dynamics of re-appropriation and production of new symbolic meanings via the digitalization of the socialist material culture.

Maja Mikula's study (2003) on two virtual projects recalling former Yugoslavia opened the exploration of opposing mediated memories. Mikula analyzed the use of a parodic key to present alternative views of national identity and political leadership, by taking advantage of the structural features of the Internet. According to Mikula, the online narratives also correspond to a repressed collective memory embodying "the ethnic tolerance associated with former socialist Yugoslavia", as an alternative to the dominant "mobilizing ethno-nationalist rhetoric of the early post-Yugoslav regimes" (Mikula 2003, 171). Contributions bearing similar approaches are united in a collection of studies focusing on the construction of post-socialist digital memories within the countries of the former soviet bloc (Rutten, Fedor and Zvereva 2013). Reflecting on a wide variety of memories that are negotiated and shaped in national and transnational contexts, the studies share a common objective: to examine how new media provide the ground for new forms of collective memories, for political and national identity building which is "irreversibly affected by thinking about the past" (Rutten and Zvereva 2013, 2). An internationalizing approach is also used by Mārtiņš Kaprāns (2015), who decoded the online construction of transnational discourse on the past focusing on the content generated by a highly disputed Latvian documentary. Kaprāns reviewed the edit wars on Wikipedia and the conflicting hegemonic representations of the Soviet period in YouTube comments and highlighted the features of the networked environment: the representations of history are the work of an interactive core of memory agents, while the community of practices convey digital agency resulting in the emancipation of hegemonic representations. Yet, as Kalinina and Menke (2016) argue, the online collaborative and participatory (re)creation of memory has limited effects when considering the emancipation from state-propagated narratives. Their analysis of the online space of contemporary Russia showed a raising practice of the political elites aimed at controlling alternative discursive productions in social media through ownership and the use of partisan agents in communication, as well as the use of a sanitized picture of the past and of nostalgia to "popularize the official narrative, thus establishing discursive dominance" (Kalinina and Menke 2016, 71). Although the spread and impact of such practices of digital control are still to be further documented, the study conducted by Kalinina and Menke (2016) brings a top-down approach on the emergence of opposing mediated narratives, unlike previous cited research exploring mainly bottom-up strategies.

The digitalization of socialist material culture is approached in studies that cover different aspects of the growing body of content from online archives, communities and sharing platforms, where manifold strategies can be identified. Vlad Strukov (2009) questioned the editorial and mediation mechanisms supporting "The Name of Russia," a web-based contest designed to evaluate the popularity of Russian historical figures. The contest was marked by a hacking attempt of the voting system in favor of Stalin, seen as a takeover strategy revealing "the volatile structure of the Russian Internet, which appears to be prone to activists' movements" (Strukov 2009, 37). The collaborative work dedicated to preserve collective memories was analyzed by Ekaterina Kalinina (2014) in relation to the editorial control of the wiki model used for the online childhood encyclopedia "Entsiklopediia Nashego Detstva": users were not allowed to add, modify or delete the content they uploaded, while moderators and editors were in charge of the updates, seeing also that the articles would be compliant with the editorial style of the site. The articulation of opposite narratives on history has been discussed too in studies focusing on the memory work produced by digital communities on Web 2.0 platforms, yet with different angles. On one hand, Ewa Sidorenko (2014) explored how a web thread on childhood in communist urban Poland conveyed a visible nostalgia understood as a critique to contemporary concerns, contrasting with conventional narratives of the communist past. On the other hand, as noted in studies by Rajagopalan (2018) and Morenkova (2012), video-sharing and Russian 2.0 platforms are seen as communities of remembering that become a propitious ground for the expression of diverging historical visions, opposing "the 'Soviet generation'", critical on the past, and "the '*perestroika* generation'" who "chooses to escape into an entirely constructed mythological-utopian reality" (Morenkova 2012, 61), the latter recalling our study's framework of the "displaced nostalgia."

Romanian Research on the Digital Space Dedicated to the Communist Past

Migrating from offline to online debates, the collective memory of the Romanian communist past has taken various digital forms, still defined by a lack of consensus.

Nicolae Ceauşescu, the last Romanian communist party leader, was portrayed in manifold and contradictory ways. According to Caterina Preda (2013, 209), online narratives emphasizing Ceauşescu's legitimate role appeared, contrasting with the negative discourse prevailing in traditional media. Also, compared to previous offline representations, social media drew, over the years, a more composite image of Ceauşescu's persona. The slow, yet steady shift of perceptions building the public memory of the communist past was also analyzed by Cristina Petrescu (2014), who focused on the emergence of websites of memory. With the beginning of the new millennia, the Internet prompted the voice of a generation consisting of young, urban and highly educated people articulating "a new vector of memory" and overcoming the unique collective narrative on communism that "(self)censored public remembrance and marginalized any alternative versions of the past" for more than twenty years (Petrescu 2014, 596). Moreover, contrary to the hegemonic discourse on the past, websites did not challenge the dominant public representations and conveyed "a rather complementary perspective" (Petrescu 2014, 597). Drawing on Petrescu's analysis of the generational memory in post-communist Romania, Alina Pohrib (2017) explored the emergence of an online memory discourse in social media with a focus on the "latchkey generation"[2] shaped by a dual experience of transition: from the childhood lived in the communist period to the teenage years and the coming of age consumed in the new socio-political context of the 1990s. According to Pohrib, analysis of the online grassroots alternative memory practices reveals new forms of mediation of the past, as "members of Facebook communities are aestheticizing memory and creating templates that perform a semiotic and axiological re-framing of communism" (Pohrib 2017, 12). The multi-layered online memory discourse was further prolonged with an approach of the transition from a technological angle, as the advent of Internet deeply reshaped social practices and relationships (Petrescu 2017), integrating, in this respect, a broader question opened by Katharina Niemeyer (2018) when interrogating the complementarity of analogue and digital nostalgia. Alina Pohrib approached digital communities with the question of how identity is negotiated online, on how "users mediate various nostalgic modes or deflect accusations of reactionary nostalgia" (Pohrib 2017, 8), while Cristina Petrescu considered the generational identity construction as a post-communist nostalgia that is neither self-censored, nor fascinated by "the alleged communist achievements," but becomes an exercise of remembering with a "curative function" (Petrescu 2017, 213).

Methodology

The aim of this chapter is to identify specific representations of the past among Romanian Facebook users, focusing on generations born after 1989, who are also members in groups and pages targeting the communist period. A twofold methodological approach was used during April–May 2018.

For the first step, an exploratory investigation was intended to map the Facebook communities that address the communist past. We used the platform's search bar with each of the following keywords (in their Romanian version): communism, communist, Ceaușescu, Ceaușism, Socialist Romania, golden age,[3] *The Spark*,[4] nostalgia, memories, childhood, the past, old days, old music. Two types of communities were found: one of users following a specific page, and the other of users that were members in a group. A qualitative content analysis was used for the text in the communities' "About" section and results were organized according to Svetlana Boym's (2001, VIII) typology of "restorative nostalgia" and "reflective nostalgia." As such, the "restorative nostalgia" category covered communities that described themselves as rebuilders of "a lost home" by various means: promoting the traditions and values of the communist past, preserving communist artifacts, recreating online museums, supporting the "historical truth" and glorifying the past of Socialist Romania. For the "reflective nostalgia" category we considered communities that covered various aspects of the communist period by posting archive images, sharing audiovisual content such as music and clips of TV shows and series, photos of owned memorabilia, books, toys and other consumer products. In brief, the first category of virtual communities recreated the symbols of a national communist identity, while the second category reflected on social memory, on past and current impressions about the communist period. In the first category were selected four groups and 27 pages, while five groups and 13 pages entered the second one. Further exploration focused on the quantitative data, using an analysis grid with several variables such as the number of followers, the frequency of posts, the number of comments and of shares, in order to evaluate the popularity and the dynamics of the communities. A qualitative themed analysis was applied to identify subgroups.

All 49 sampled Facebook pages and groups were considered as a relevant source for the pool of respondents needed in the second step of this research: an online survey intended to question specific representations of the communist past. Community admins were contacted, via email or Facebook's messenger, with the request to post a link to the online survey on the page or on the group they were managing. This post also had a message asking the members to respond to the survey. The questionnaire we used was adapted from the "Time Machine" experimental survey conducted on a sample of college students by Wilson and Markle (1996), within their initial conceptualization of the "displaced nostalgia." The key question taken from the "Time Machine" survey was redesigned for this study as follows: "If you could step into a time machine and press any year to go to—forward or backward in time, in Romania—what year would you pick, and why?" This unframed question required no additional inquiry, and it did not compel the respondents from our targeted pool to choose and to comment on the communist past, in contrast to traditional polls that frame responses within a specified theme. Instead, sampling respondents from specific digital communities would provide only a restorative or a reflective "frame of remembrance" (Pohrib 2017). Moreover, two identical versions of the survey were created, one for each of the two categories of communities, "restorative nostalgia" and "reflective nostalgia," so that the answers could be analyzed in correlation with a specific pool of respondents.

Results from this survey may be compared with the findings of a forthcoming study, where we replicated the same "Time Machine" experiment on a group of over 500 students.[5] From this sample, 18 percent selected the communist past as a reference point for their time travel. For them, the imaginary journey into an unlived past was motivated by: (1) the desire to witness at first hand the epoch, (2) the will to change historical events for a better future, and (3) the fascination for a vintage vibe mediated by current popular culture. The online "displaced nostalgia" may well be correlated with this last type of fascinating remembrance.

The next two sections provide an overview of our exploratory investigation mapping the digital communities dedicated to memory practices that address the communist past.

Digital Communities of "Restorative Nostalgia"

Communities within a rhetoric of "restorative nostalgia" included both groups and pages. The number of selected groups is rather small, four, compared to the 27 thematic pages.

The most popular and long-established group is *Generația Ceaușescu* [Ceaușescu Generation]. Created in December 2012, it has started to gather members only in 2014. This open group has 486 active users. Its purpose is to revive an era lived by the nostalgic group members, as the admin asks newcomers requesting access: "Would you like to live in the time of the deceased [nickname of Nicolae Ceaușescu], to be again the comrades, to have the discipline and the education we have received?"[6] (Generația Ceaușescu 2012). Some posts turn to conspiracy theory to unveil the failure of nowadays Romanian democracy. Most of them are shared from other online sources such as blogs, online media, other groups or Facebook pages with similar topics. The least popular group, *România socialistă–Amintiri* [Socialist Romania–Memories], with only 82 members, was created in January 2018. Self-defined as a debating club on the Romanian communist past, its viral posts are shared content from other social networks accounts. Almost every post contains images from the communist period evoking a strong emotional reaction for an era representing a "Golden age" for the group members. In terms of posting rates, the groups do not exceed four posts per month, recording a very low engagement rate of likes, shares, and comments. The most active group is *Mișcarea comunistă* [The Communist Movement]. Set up in October 2013, it has 160 members and an activity of over 100 posts per month, gathering also a couple of likes, comments and shares per post. Content conveys an interest for historical communist subjects and topical political affairs. They are critical of Romanian royalty and the current democratic system, while they praise the achievements of the communist period. This group appears to be a rather political community, self-dubbed the "Socialist Alternative Party," established to carry on the activity of the former Romanian communist party. The only closed group in our sample is *Epoca de Aur a lui Ceaușescu!* [The Golden Age of Ceaușescu!]. Created in February 2014 and counting 398 members, it aims to reconstitute the glorious history of communist Romania. Blaming the country's present drift, it is directed against the "people who didn't love the country and the party, if they betrayed once, they will always betray" (Epoca de Aur a lui Ceaușescu 2014). The group lacks activity, as no content was posted in the first months of 2018.

Facebook pages targeting "restorative nostalgia" record a more intense activity. Out of the 27 sampled pages, three count between 10,000 and 86,000 followers. The other 24 pages gather between 100 and 4,000 followers. Among the three most popular pages are *Nicolae Ceaușescu* (85,931 followers), *România în timpul lui Nicolae Ceaușescu* [Romania under Nicolae Ceaușescu] (38,313 followers), and *În amintirea lui Ceaușescu* [In Ceaușescu's Memory] (12,073 followers). The most popular page, *Nicolae Ceaușescu,* is dedicated to the communist leader, focusing on a positive political recollection of the "Golden age" during Ceausescu's Romania. The next two most popular pages, *România în timpul lui Nicolae Ceaușescu* and *În amintirea lui Ceaușescu*, figure as self-appointed guardians of Ceaușescu's memory. These pages stand out as they document the past in a rather professional way, through specific artifacts of the period: images, historical texts, statements, footage, etc. This type of content receives an average of 200–300 likes and several dozens of shares, and the comments support the same patriotic discourse. The *România în timpul lui Nicolae Ceaușescu* page promotes Romanian identity and national values. On average, it attracts a few dozens of likes, shares and comments mainly for content related to more mundane topics such as traditional food recipes, ancient agricultural practices and household items. On the other hand, the *În amintirea lui Ceaușescu* community does not have a clear communist message, but instead it conveys a topical content framed in tabloid manner. Occasionally, pictures of Nicolae Ceaușescu are posted with mobilizing messages, such as: "Respect, comrades!" or "Ceaușescu was the president of Romania, another one will never be" (În amintirea lui Ceaușescu 2018).

The other 24 Facebook pages record followers ranging from 100 to 4,000 and provide a quasi-similar content. Among less active pages, but with a hard communist discourse, are noted: *Amintiri din communism* [Memories of Communism] (135 followers), *Orașul Stalin–Comunismul în Brașov și Țara Făgărașului* [Stalin City–Communism in Brașov and Făgăraș] (105 followers), *Republica Socialistă România–RSR* [Socialist Republic of Romania–RSR] (1,830 followers), *Muzeul "Epoca de aur"* [The "Golden Age" Museum] (174 followers), *Epoca de aur* [The Golden Age] (364 followers), *Fragmente de Comunism* [Fragments of Communism] (112 followers). All of them emphasize communist events, patriotic messages, greeting cards addressed to the users celebrating communist anniversaries, and attempts to refresh the collective memory with communist symbols and artifacts. Also, relatively active are the pages that sell various communist memorabilia, such as *Amintiri din Epoca de Aur* [Memories from the Golden Age] (290 followers). Besides the *Nicolae Ceaușescu* community gathering 85,931 followers, we identified another seven pages with the same name: five of them lacked any activity during the last year, while the other two kept alive the memory of the communist era through statements of regret and nostalgia for the past.

Digital Communities of "Reflective Nostalgia"

Communities that mediate memories concerning past experiences of life during the communist period count five groups and 13 pages.

By far, the most active and large community is *Nostalgia copilăriei noastre din Epoca de Aur* [Nostalgia of our childhood in the Golden Age], a public group created around 2018 and counting 9,428 members. It is dedicated to "those who have spent at least part of their childhood in socialist Romania, in the so-called 'Golden Age', and who feel a certain nostalgia for that period" (Nostalgia copilăriei noastre din Epoca de Aur 2012), while members are invited to post mainly childhood memories, such as "photos from celebrations, when you became pioneers, excursions, camps or any other pictures of that period". With an average of seven daily posts, the engagement rate is quite high, every post recording about 20–30 likes and at least a couple of shares. The content consists mainly of documentary images shared from other Facebook feeds, clips from movies and TV series, or archive footage. Occasionally, photos from exhibitions related to life in communism are posted. The second group, in terms of membership, is *Obiecte vechi româneşti* [Old Romanian objects], set up in 2016 and counting 4,447 members. Seen as a community "full of history and memories", it was created "in the hope of resurrecting, through images, objects that were made before the 90s (…) in Romania" (Obiecte vechi românesti 2016). Opened also for commerce, a review of May's (2018) activity shows an average of 18 posts per day, mainly selling vintage objects. Two more commerce group of souvenirs are *Obiecte de colecţie din comunism (româneşti)* [Collectibles from communism (Romanian)], created in 2016 and counting 2,873 members, and *Lucruri, jucării, discuri vinil din communism* [Stuff, toys, vinyl records from communism], with a smaller community, of 590 members. Last one in the "Reflective Nostalgia" sample is *Nostalgia Comunism* [Nostalgia Communism], created in 2017, with 338 members, dedicated to "fans of objects and goods made in Ceauşescu's era" (Nostalgia Comunism 2017). The two admins assure a pretty high frequency of posts, displaying every two-or three days images of objects from the communist period.

The sample of Facebook pages covers a wide variety of topics that can be ranged in three subgroups: childhood memories (six groups), aspects of everyday life in communist Romania (six groups) and specific places anchored in time (one group). From the first subgroup, the two most popular pages are *Generaţia cu cheia la gât* [The Latchkey Generation], created in 2011 and *Copilăria anilor '80–'90* [Childhood in the 80s–90s], created in 2012; the first counted 311,478 followers and the second one 234,489. Analyzed previously by Pohrib (2017, 4), both pages had a communication strategy featuring content that was "departing from its announced purpose", childhood experiences of communism for *Generația cu cheia la gât* and a visual recycle of communist memorabilia in the case of *Copilăria anilor '80–'90.* Our own review of these pages concurs with Pohrib's observations. Another three pages with an apparently strong community are *Amintiri din copilărie* [Childhood memories], with 22,894 followers, *La Trecut* [The past], with 5,805 followers and *Copilăria noastră* [Our childhood], with 2,631 followers. However, page analysis showed an absence of activity since May, 2015 for *La Trecut*, and a highly irregular content flow for the other two pages. The last page in this subgroup is *Epoca de aur–Amintiri din copilarie* [The Golden Age–Childhood memories], with 1,067 followers. With no apparent schedule, the posted content consists almost exclusively of photos displaying consumer goods, thoroughly organized in several albums.

The second subgroup featured three Facebook pages linked to offline projects, a virtual museum, a hobbyist page, and a culinary community of remembrance. The most popular page is *Reclame Vechi Românești 1840–1995* [Old Romanian Advertisements 1840–1995], created in 2010 and counting 127,884 followers. Approached in a professional manner, the page provides detailed information about its mission and scope, to offer "an illustrated history of advertising in Romania" based on "examples of more than 4000 scanned printed ads" (Reclame Vechi Românești 1840–1995 2010) from the personal collection of the admin. The second most popular page is *Alimentara* [Grocery Shop], with 13,123 followers, marked as "an illustrated attempt to recreate the culinary (recent) past of Romania" (Alimentara n.d.). It features also an impressive collection of scanned or shared images documenting the food industry from the communist period. The pages of the two museums, one in Timisoara, *Muzeul Consumatorului Comunist* [Museum of Communist Consumer], followed by 3,130 persons, and the other in Botosani, *Muzeul Vieții Cotidiene în Comunism–Botoșani* [Museum of Daily Life in Communism–Botoșani], with 726 followers, present mainly photos of the exhibits. A review of both timelines shows also the developments of the offline projects; the first museum stands as a new landmark of Timisoara, while for Botosani it appears to be a museum in the making. The last page in the subgroup is *Jucării din Epoca de Aur* [Toys from the Golden Age], with 315 followers, and is belonging to a hobbyist. The page fulfills a double role, to display the collection of ancient toys, and as a call for collectibles, by purchase or donations.

The page of the last subgroup featuring specific places is a community with 3,160 followers, *Vasluiul Comunist* [Communist Vaslui], dedicated to the homonymous town situated in the Nord-Est region of Romania. Started in 2013, the project is developed meticulously within an archive drive intended to "'recompose', through images, the city of Vaslui, as it appeared between 1960 and 1989" (Vasluiul Comunist 2013).

An Online "Displaced Nostalgia"?

Inspired by our previous researches, the present study focused on how, among Facebook members of digital communities of remembrance, the generations born after 1989 are representing the communist past. To this purpose, we used an experimental method, consisting of an unframed online survey on time travel, which allowed us to overrule the limitations of traditional polls. The sampling process considered a selection of Facebook pages and groups related to the communist past, which were grouped within two categories of communities ("restorative nostalgia" and "reflective nostalgia"). We planned to give an identical version of the survey to each category, in order to analyze the results separately. From the 49 communities of our sample, only two admins from the "restorative nostalgia"[7] category agreed to post a link to our survey on the page or group they managed, and for the other category only three admins complied.

Considering this first limitation, the overall response rate was much lower than we expected at the beginning of our research. The total number of responses was 84, meaning nine questionnaires were answered by respondents from the "restorative nostalgia" community and 75 by those from the "reflective nostalgia" one. Compared to the potential pool of 26,164 respondents from the communities where the survey was posted, it follows that the overall response rate was 0.32 percent.[8] As respondents were aged between 18 and 70 years old, we selected only responses coming from those who marked their year of birth starting from 1990. Out of the total of 84 responses, only 10 complied with this criterion: two coming from the "restorative nostalgia" category and eight from the other one. Furthermore, the age structure within the overall responses ranges as follows: eight respondents are born in the 1950s (8.9 percent), 16 are born in the 1960s (16.19 percent), 25 are born in the 1970s (25.3 percent), 25 are born in the 1980s (25.3 percent), and 10 respondents are born in the 1990s (10.12 percent). In this perspective, the percentage of respondents born after 1990 brings the hypothesis that a more detailed audience analysis of our target sample will show that this segment is under-represented and would probably profile a negative case analysis.

Putting aside the above methodological limitations, the results of our unframed survey are the following: one of the respondents from the restorative category selected the past (the period between 1860 and 1880), and the other picked the future (the year 2020). The first answer was motivated by a "very attractive historical period described in history textbooks" such as "*Junimea* classicism"[9] and the second by the curiosity for a not-too-distant future. The other eight respondents from the reflective nostalgia communities picked the past as a place of reference: one would visit the ancient world (year 1 BC), four would travel to the interwar period (1920s–1930s), one would return to 1990 and only two respondents would choose the communist period as a destination, in 1962 and 1968. Both motivations were quite personal, one related to a specialized professional engineering question and the other one concerning an administrative strategy of that period. In this respect, if the "displaced nostalgia" concept was not correlated to our empirical findings, what representations of the past emerged from the other respondents?

When considering the overall number of respondents from the "reflective nostalgia" community, almost half of them (36 responses) chose a year from the communist period as destination, while the preferred decade was the 1980s. Again, when focusing on the arguments for their choices, content analysis brought two new types of motivations, in addition to the three ones identified in our previous students' "Time Machine" experiment: a large majority (more than half, with 19 responses) expressed a longing or an interest for the childhood and youth years, recalling Petrescu's analysis (2017) on generational identity. The second type of motivation, gathering seven responses, was translated as a nostalgia for a better past, while critically addressing the present, displaying discursive features specific rather to the "restorative nostalgia" category.

Conclusions and Future Work

The focus of this chapter was to examine specific representations of the communist past among Romanian generations born before and after 1989, members of digital communities of remembrance sampled from Facebook pages and groups.

On one hand, framed by a series of methodological limitations related to the design and the configuration of our experimental approach, findings of this study require a revision of the sampling process, in order to achieve a representative population of our targeted post-communist group. On the other hand, the results of the survey point towards the "latchkey generation" (born in the 1970s and the 1980s) as the core audience of our investigated field, counting 50.6 percent of the respondents in the "reflective nostalgia" community. In this respect, our findings put in a larger perspective Pohrib's "Facebook *generatiography*" analysis (2017) based on only two case studies, namely the Facebook community pages *Generația cu cheia la gât* [The Latchkey Generation] and *Copilăria anilor '80–'90* [Childhood in the 80s–90s]. As such, the "latchkey generation" may be reviewed as the core audience of a much larger digital community, while the generational approach becomes a useful analytical lens when considering the collective dimension of the engagement with the communist past expressed within Facebook pages and groups. Yet, there is more to these specific online groups, for the practice of collecting and displaying childhood memorabilia transcends geographies and ideologies, calling for a parallel with what Gary Cross (2015) identifies as communities of "consumed nostalgia."

From a technological perspective, Ryan Lizardi (2017) unveils a reflection on the generational uses of social media and on its potential to encourage specific types of nostalgic mindsets. Considering the affordances of social networks, our analysis brings new insights about how digitally mediated post-socialist memories are shaping opposing narratives of the past. First, within the same category, the mnemonic engagement to the past may rely on manifold objects, ranging from products to practices, from childhood memories to colorful pioneer paraphernalia, increasing the cohesion of Facebook groups "through a shared and displayed history" (Lizardi 2017, 122). Moreover, comments articulate here on a fairly consensual line, evacuating ideological arguments, recalling the process described by Nadkarni and Shevchenko (2015, 80), where "in order to retain an aura of authenticity, nostalgia has a stake in insisting on its political neutrality". However, a dedicated content analysis of the comments may bring a few instances where narratives and nostalgia identities are negotiated (Pohrib 2017). Second, when considering both categories, content analysis showed little to no intersection between the two communities, suggesting that the binary discourse on the communist past takes here the form of a parallel communication, and figures as an exemplary case of Pariser's understanding of the "filter bubble" (2011).

Further research should question the reasons behind the quasi-absence of the targeted post-communist generations, prone to manifest a form of "displaced nostalgia" in the online communities dedicated to recover lost memories of a bygone era. Another research trajectory should reposition the experimental approach used here, placing the online "Time Machine" survey in other networked media contexts, such as YouTube and Instagram.

Notes

1. Facebook is currently the most popular social media platform in Romania, gathering roughly 9,600,000 user accounts (as of January 10th, 2017), or more than 85 percent of the Internet users in the country, at a 58 percent Internet penetration for a total

general population estimated at 21,599,736 (data compiled from www.facebrands.ro and www.internetlivestats.com).

2. In families where parents worked late hours, the children used to wear around the neck their home's latchkey attached to a string, so they wouldn't lose it when playing outdoors.
3. The *Golden Age* is the name used in the official propaganda of the '80s to glorify the leadership of Nicolae Ceausescu as General Secretary of the Romanian Communist Party, starting from 1965.
4. *Scânteia* (*The Spark*) was the official newspaper edited by the Romanian Communist Party.
5. BA undergraduate students at the Faculty of Journalism and Communication Studies, University of Bucharest.
6. "Ati vrea sa mai fie timpul raposatului, sa fim din nou tovarași și tovarașa, sa fie disciplina și educatia care am primit-o noi?" [Our translation].
7. An admin from a *Nicolae Ceaușescu* page refused to post a link to the online questionnaire, arguing that it did not fit into the group's theme, because it lacked any reference to Ceausescu.
8. Lower than the estimated 2 percent of Facebook's algorithm determining the organic reach of posts (Bernazzani 2018).
9. *Junimea* is a nineteenth century Romanian literary movement.

References

Adevărul. 2013. "SONDAJ: Jumătate dintre români suspină după comunism (Poll: Half of the Romanians Yearn for Communism)." *www.adevarul.ro*. December 10. Accessed April 15, 2018. http://adevarul.ro/news/societate/sondaj-jumatate-romani-suspina-comunism-1_52a6af42c7b855ff5696fd58/index.html.

Adevărul-INSCOP Research. 2013. *Barometrul "Adevărul despre România" (Barometer "Truth about Romania"*. Bucharest: INSCOP Research. Accessed May 20, 2018. http://www.inscop.ro/wp-content/uploads/2014/01/INSCOP-noiembrie-ISTORIE.pdf.

Adevărul-INSCOP Research. 2014. *Barometrul "Adevărul despre România" (Barometer "Truth about Romania")*. Bucharest: INSCOP Research. Accessed May 20, 2018. http://www.inscop.ro/wp-content/uploads/2014/12/INSCOP-Dec.2014-PCR-Ceausescu-presedinti-comunism-vs-democratie.pdf.

Alimentara. n.d. *@alimentara*. Accessed May 20, 2018. https://www.facebook.com/alimentara/.

Appadurai, Arjun. 1996. *Modernity Al Large: Cultural Dimensions of Globalization*. Minneapolis: University of Minnesota Press.

Asavei, Maria-Alina. 2016. "Nicolae Ceausescu: Between Vernacular Memory and Nostalgia." *Twentieth Century Communism* (Lawrence and Wishart). 11 (11): 27–42.

B1. 2018. "NOSTALGIA EPOCII DE AUR: 40% dintre români consideră că perioada comunistă a fost cea mai bună din istoria României moderne" *www.b1.ro*. Accessed March 20, 2018. https://bit.ly/2EYSaUn

Bardan, Alexandra. 2018. "Marketing Post-Communist Nostalgia in Romania: A Case Study on Contemporary Anniversary Events." *Styles of Communication.* 10 (1): 50–73.

Berliner, David. 2014. "Are Anthropologists Nostalgist?" In *Anthropology and Nostalgia*, by Olivia Angé and David Berliner, 17–34. New York and Oxford: Berghahn Books.

Bernazzani, Sophia. 2018. "The Decline of Organic Facebook Reach & How to Adjust to the Algorithm." *Hubspot/Blog.* May 4. Accessed May 10, 2018. https://blog.hubspot.com/marketing/facebook-organic-reach-declining.

Boym, Svetlana. 2001. *The Future of Nostalgia.* New York: Basic Books.

Cioflânca, Adrian. 2010. "Nostalgia pentru comunism." *www.revista22.ro.* September 9. Accessed May 15, 2018. https://www.revista22.ro/nostalgia-pentru-comunism 8962.html.

Cross, Gary. 2015. *Consumed Nostalgia: Memory in the Age of Fast Capitalism.* New York: Columbia University Press

CURS. 2018. *Perceptii asupra celei mai benefice perioade din ultimii 100 de ani (Perceptions of the most beneficial period over the past 100 years).* Bucuresti: CURS (Centrul de Sociologie Urbană şi Regională). Accessed September 25, 2018. https://www.stiripesurse.ro/sondaj-ca-i-romani-considera-ca-perioada-comunista-a-fost-cea-mai-buna-din-istoria-romaniei-cui_1244215.html.

Dâncu, Vasile. 2015. "Nimic nu este mai imprevizibil decat trecutul." *vasiledancu.blogspot.ro.* February 21. Accessed March 25, 2018. http://vasiledancu.blogspot.ro/2010/07/nimic-nu-este-mai-imprevizibil-decat.html.

Epoca de Aur a lui Ceausescu. 2014. "About." *www.facebook.com.* February. Accessed May 15, 2018. https://www.facebook.com/groups/591953344207839/.

Evenimentul Zilei. 2009. "Nostalgia comunismului bântuie Europa de Est (Communist Nostalgia Haunts Eastern Europe)." *www.evz.ro.* November 4. Accessed April 20, 2018. http://evz.ro/nostalgia-comunismului-bantuie-europa-de-est-874415.html.

Evenimentul Zilei. 2011. "Comunismul rămâne o idee bună pentru majoritatea românilor." *www.evz.ro.* May 27. Accessed April 15, 2018. http://evz.ro/comunismul-ramane-o-idee-buna-pentru-majoritatea-romanilor-931653.html.

Generaţia Ceauşescu. 2012. "Join community question." *www.facebook.com.* December. Accessed May 15, 2018. https://www.facebook.com/groups/454100891305347/.

Georgescu, Diana. 2010. "'Ceausescu Hasn't Died': Irony as Counter-Memory in Post-Socialist Romania." In *Post-Communist Nostalgia*, by Maria Todorova and Zsuzsa Gille, 155–176. New York and Oxford: Berghahn Books.

Gheorghiţă, Andrei. 2010. "Trecutul comunist în constiinta adolescentilor." In *Implicarea civica si politica a tinerilor*, by Soros Foundation, 64–71. Constanta: Editura Dobrogea.

Hogea, Alina. 2010. "Coming to Terms with the Communist Past in Romania: An Analysis of the Political and Media Discourse Concerning the Tismăneanu Report." *Studies of Transition States and Societies* 2 (2): 16–30. Accessed March 22, 2018. http://publications.tlu.ee/index.php/stss/article/view/62.

Iacob, Cristian Bogdan. 2010. "Avem nevoie de o pedagogie a memoriei colective a trecutului comunist." *www.evz.ro*. September 23. Accessed March 25, 2018. https://bit.ly/2GZhrLp.

IICCMR-CSOP. 2010. *Atitudini şi opinii despre regimul comunist din România (Attitudes and opinions about the communist regime in Romania)*. Bucharest: CSOP TNS. Accessed April 25, 2018. http://www.iiccr.ro/pdf/ro/evenimente/perceptiile_romanilor_asupra_comunismului/raport_sondaj_opinie.pdf.

IICCMR-CSOP. 2011. *Atitudini şi opinii despre regimul comunist din România (Attitudes and opinions about the communist regime in Romania)*. Bucharest: CSOP TNS. Accessed April 25, 2018. http://www.iiccr.ro/pdf/ro/raport_sondaj_opinie_publica_iiccmer_mai_2011.pdf.

În amintirea lui Ceauşescu. 2018. "Photos." *www.facebook.com*. January 26. Accessed May 15, 2018. https://www.facebook.com/%C3%8En-amintirea-lui-Ceau%C8%99escu-353400151801708/.

IRES-IRESOP. 2010. *Românii si nostalgia comunismului (Romanians and communist nostalgia)*. Cluj-Napoca: IRES (Institutul Român pentru Evaluare şi Strategie). Accessed April 25, 2018. http://www.ires.com.ro/uploads/articole/romanii_si_nostalgia_comunismului.pdf.

Jeziński, Marek, and Łukasz Wojtkowski. 2016. "Nostalgia Commodified. Towards the Marketization of the Post-Communist Past Through the New Media." Edited by Manuel Menke and Christian Schwarzenegger. *Medien & Zeit* 31 (4): 96–104.

Kalinina, Ekaterina. 2014. *Mediated Post-Soviet Nostalgia*. Huddinge: Södertörn University.

Kalinina, Ekaterina, and Manuel Menke. 2016. "Negotiating the Past in Hyperconnected Memory Cultures: Post-Soviet Nostalgia and National Identity in Russian Online Communities." *International Journal of Media & Cultural Politics* 12 (1): 59–74. doi:10.1386/macp.12.1.59_1.

Kaprāns, Mārtiņš. 2015. "Hegemonic Representations of the Past and Digital Agency: Giving Meaning to "The Soviet Story" on Social Networking Sites." *Memory Studies* 1–17. doi:10.1177/1750698015587151.

King, Charles. 2007. "Remembering Romanian Communism." *Slavic Review* 718–723.

Lizardi, Ryan. 2017. *Nostalgic Generations and Media. Perception and Time of Available Meaning*. London [et al.]: Lexington Books.

Marin, Manuela. 2013. "Between Memory and Nostalgia: The Image of Communism in Romanian Popular Culture. A Case Study of Libertatea Newspaper." *Palimpsest* (5): 4–16. Accessed April 5, 2018. www.palimpsest.socjologia.uj.edu.pl.

Marin, Manuela. 2016. "Re-assesing Post-Communist Nostalgia in Romania: Chronological Framework and Opinion Polls." *Twentieth Century Communism* (Lawrence and Wishart) (11): 10–26.

Mikula, Maja. 2003. "Virtual Landscapes of Memory.' *Information, Communication & Society* 6 (3): 169–186. doi:10.1080/1369118032000093879.

Morenkova, Elena. 2012. "(Re)creating the Soviet Past in Russian Digital Communities. Between Memory and Mythmaking." *Digital Icons: Studies in Russian, Eurasian and Central European New Media* (7): 39–66. http://www.digitalicons.org/issue07/re-creating-the-soviet-past-in-russian-digital-communities-between-memory-and-mythmaking/.

Murgescu, Mirela-Luminita. 2012. "Romanian Perceptions of Communism." *Euxeinos* (3). Accessed August 23, 2015. http://www.gce.unisg.ch/~/media/internet/content/dateien/instituteundcenters/gce/euxeinos/euxeinos%203_2012.pdf.

Nadkarni, Maya and Shevchenko, Olga. 2015. "The Politics of Nostalgia in the Aftermath of Socialism's Collapse: A Case for Comparative Analysis." In *Anthropology and Nostalgia,* by O Ange and D Berliner, 61–95. Oxford: Berghahn Books.

Niemeyer, Katharina. 2018. "Du mal du pays aux nostalgies numériques. Réflexions sur les liens entre nostalgie, nouvelles technologies et médias." *Recherches en Communication* 46: 5–16.

Nostalgia Comunism. 2017. *www.facebook.com.* Accessed May 20, 2018. https://www.facebook.com/groups/840177299492356/.

Nostalgia copilăriei noastre din Epoca de Aur. 2012. *www.facebook.com.* July 14. Accessed May 20, 2018. https://www.facebook.com/groups/19639979300/.

Obiecte vechi românesti. 2016. *www.facebook.com.* Accessed May 20, 2018. https://www.facebook.com/groups/994037643996656/.

Pariser, Eli. 2011. *The Filter Bubble: What the Internet Is Hiding from You.* New York: Penguin Press.

Petrescu, Cristina. 2014. "Websites of Memory: In Search of the Forgotten Past." In *Remembering Communism. Private and Public Recollections of Lived Experience in Southeast Europe*, by Maria Todorova, Augusta Dimou and Stefan Troebst, 595–613. Budapest: CEU Press.

Petrescu, Cristina. 2017. "Nostalgia, Identity and Self-Irony in Remembering Communism." In *Justice, Memory and Redress in Romania: New Insights*, by Lavinia Stan and Lucian Turcescu, 192–213. Newcastle upon Tyne: Cambridge Scholars Publishing.

Pew Research Center. 2009. *End of Communism Cheered But Now With More Reservations.* Washington, D.C: Pew Research Center. Accessed April 25, 2018. http://www.pewglobal.org/2009/11/02/end-of-communism-cheered-but-now-with-more-reservations/.

Pohrib, Codruţa Alina. 2017. "The Romanian 'Latchkey Generation' Writes Back: Memory Genres of Post-Communism on Facebook." *Memory Studies* 1–20. Accessed May 20, 2018. doi:org/10.1177/1750698017709869.

Preda, Caterina. 2013. "The Digital (Artistic) Memory of Nicolae Ceauşescu." In *Memory, Conflict and New Media. Web Wars in Post-Socialist States*, by Ellen Rutten, Julie Fedor and Vera Zvereva, 197–213. London: Routledge.

Preda, Caterina. 2015. "Le rôle de la nostalgie dans la mémoire artistique du passé communiste dans la Roumanie contemporaine." *Canadian Slavonic Papers* 57 (3–4): 268–283. doi:10.1080/00085006.2015.1092709.

PRO TV. 2010. "Sondaj: 83% dintre romani, nostalgici dupa perioada comunista." *stirileprotv.ro.* December 9. https://bit.ly/2qwftf8.

Rajagopalan, Sudha. 2018. "Remix Videos and the Mnemonic Imagination: Emotional Memories of Late Soviet Childhood." *International Journal of Cultural Studies* 1–28. doi:10.1177/1367877917741540.

Reclame Vechi Românești 1840–1995. 2010. *@ReclameVechiRomanesti.OldRomanianAds.* May 1. Accessed May 20, 2018. https://www.facebook.com/ReclameVechiRomanesti.OldRomanianAds/.

Rusu, Mihai. 2013. "Setting the Historical Record Straight: Judging the Romanian Communist Past against the Backdrop of Popular Nostalgic Resistance." *Analele științifice ale Universității "Al. I. Cuza" din Iași. Sociologie și Asistență Socială* 6 (2): 40–58. Accessed March 23, 208. https://bit.ly/2H0mqQc.

Rusu, Mihai. 2015. "Battling Over Romanian Red Past. The Memory of Communism Between Elitist Cultural Trauma and Popular Collective Nostalgia." *The Romanian Journal of Society and Politics.* X (I): 24–48.

Rutten, Ellen, Fedor, Julie and Zvereva, Vera. 2013. *Memory, Conflict and New Media: Web Wars in Post-Socialist States.* London: Routledge.

Rutten, Ellen, and Zvereva, Vera. 2013. "Old Conflicts, New Media: Post-Socialist Digital Memories." In *Memory, Conflict and New Media: Web Wars in Post-Socialist States*, by Ellen Rutten, Julie Fedor and Vera Zvereva, 1–18. London: Routledge.

Sidorenko, Ewa. 2014. "Playing Free in the Polish People's Republic: Making Do Without Consumerism." *Childhood in the Past* 7 (2): 95–116. doi:10.1179/1758571614Z.00000000020.

Stirile ProTV. 2010. "Sondaj: 83% dintre romani, nostalgici dupa perioada comunista." *www.stirileprotv.ro.* December 9. Accessed April 15, 2018. https://stirileprotv.ro/stiri/social/sondaj-83-dintre-romani-nostalgici-dupa-perioada-comunista.html.

Strukov, Vlad. 2009. "Possessive and Superlative: On the Simulation of Democracy and Nationhood in." *Russian Cyberspace* 1 (1): 31–39. http://www.digitalicons.org/issue01/pdf/issue1/Possessive-and-Superlative_V-Strukov.pdf.

Tismăneanu, Vladimir. 2011. "Dealing with Communist Past: The Case of Romania." *Hungarian Studies* 25 (2): 175–183. doi:10.1556/HStud.25.2011.2.1.

Todorova, Maria. 2010. "From Utopia to Propaganda and Back." In *Post-Communist Nostalgia*, by Maria Todorova and Zsuzsa Gille. New York and Oxford: Berghahn Books.

Vasluiul Comunist. 2013. *@vaslui607080.* June 15. Accessed May 15, 2018. https://www.facebook.com/vaslui607080/.

Vassilev, Rossen. 2011. "The Tragic Failure of 'Post-Communism' in Eastern Europe." *www.globalresearch.ca.* March 8. Accessed March 22, 2018. https://www.globalresearch.ca/the-tragic-failure-of-post-communism-in-eastern-europe/23616.

Wilson, Janelle L. 2005. *Nostalgia: Sanctuary of Meaning.* Lewisburg: Bucknell University Press.

Wilson, Janelle L., and Markle, Gerald E. 1996. "PAST OR FUTURE? A Re-Formulation of Ortega's Question." *ETC: A Review of General Semantics* (Institute of General Semantics) 53 (2): 152–169. http://www.jstor.org/stable/42579747.

Section 3

Rethinking Nostalgic Experiences

9. *Media-as-Things: A Nonhistorical Nostalgia Through Failure*

MANI MEHRVARZ AND MARYAM MULIAEE

Introduction

"Outbreaks of nostalgia often follow revolutions," said Svetlana Boym (2001, 9). Technology of recording memory has also been impacted by revolution, in which the emergence of nostalgia is assured. The leap from mechanical storage media like photography, phonography, and cinematography to signal transmission like radio and television and digital computer (Ernst 2016a) has brought with it new forms of nostalgia, whose implied meanings have invaluable possibilities for the world of media. As Boym said, "The history of nostalgia might allow us to look back at modern history not solely searching for newness and technological progress but for unrealized possibilities, unpredictable turns and crossroads" (2001, 16).

Scholarship on *media nostalgia* is expansive and diverse, relying mostly on the content of mass media such as film and TV shows, video games, and literature. Drawing from Fred Davis (1979) and Fredric Jameson (1991), Paul Grainge (2000) argues for an aestheticization of nostalgia in which nostalgic *modes* bring a new and dynamic engagement with the past. Andreas Böhn introduces the aspects of media's *self-reference* assigned to nostalgia on which media rely on "different historical ways of positioning themselves in relation to other media" (2007, 152). Ryan Lizardi articulates a *subjective nostalgia* for media that is perpetual and constructed on an individualized version of the past, "as opposed to a comparative, collective, or adaptive view of history" (2014, 2). Katharina Niemeyer reflects on *nostalgia boom*, and how we "nostalgize" in the context of everyday life (2014, 10). Within its diversity and remediation, nostalgia in the previous research is content-oriented, past-centered and commits to common media historical analysis and representational contexts. What if there anything remains about technical media that evades the plot of history, the linear time and the narratables? Can nostalgia be imagined potentially in excess of the supremacy of representation as well?

Media are, as Siegfried Zielinski argues, situated in *deep time* (2006). In his book *Deep Time of the Media*, he suggests that: "do not seek the old in the new, but find something new in the old" (3). Moreover, technical media, both analog and digital, operate in a temporal regime different from that of historical time (anthropocentric), as Wolfgang Ernst argues (2013b). Ernst builds on the concept of media's processuality and emphasizes that "the signals on a magnetic tape only take place in the inductive moment of the passing machine, the unwinding, when it is converted to a signal" (2016a, 21). What follows is the argument that the temporality of technical media disregards the historical time and the past in a linear conception. In Ernst's words: "… there is something at work (at the level of both the artifact and the epistemological *dispositif*) that is indifferent to the historical" (2013b, 185).

What do the above arguments imply for and impose on nostalgia? If media are studied in an epistemological level and in their own technical and non-historical laws, then, can nostalgia be re-thought likewise in a different and alternative regime? Can nostalgia be framed beyond the previous common content-oriented analyses? To examine media in their own technical mode, one needs to abandon the linear time of progress (historical time), towards a look that deploys a media-archaeological tuned perspective. In this context, Jussi Parikka clarifies that: "History is the form of narratives, while media archaeology is a non-linear engagement with devices and concrete apparatuses that physically carry the past into the present" (Hertz and Parikka 2010). The shift from the term *history* to *archaeology* is promising here, and leads to the discovery of sideways for hearing and seeing in media that remain unseen and undiscovered as triggers for nostalgia. Cherishing these hidden opportunities, Ernst emphasizes: "The media-archeological view virtually lurks, waiting for such moments of uncertainty in order to formulate them as opportunities for venturing other means of perception, for blazing other memory trails, as an alternative to the media-historical viewpoint" (2013a, 159).

In this chapter, the authors aspire to imagine a *what if* for nostalgia and to expand its meaning and application. What does nostalgia mean for media in a *nonhistorical* view and specifically when failure occurs? Borrowing the phrase nonhistorical from the media archaeologists such as Ernst, this chapter employs the framework of *media archaeology* to draw new connections between media and nostalgia. The prefix of "non-" in this speculation, importantly, does not mean "anti-" or reduce this analysis to the level of technological determinism that Kittlerian views mostly have been accused of; on the contrary, it is to emphasize on an attention to "more than", "other-than", and "different than" representational and historical analyses and to saturate the meaning of nostalgia for media in the manner that *non-representational* theory and *affect* studies have advocated for (Seigworth 2017, ii). With a focus on the role of failure in construction of nostalgia, this chapter explores the unfulfilled moments in media beyond the prevalent categorization of the old and the new, aiming to open up a new and different understanding of nostalgia for future research and art practice.

Failure and Nostalgia

The acceleration in demand for better quality and function in media (either in production industry or everyday use) is prevalent in contemporary media society. Along with this desire comes a competition for an ever-improved media apparatus that can capture extra image resolution or more advanced noise reduction techniques in production and broadcasting. However, failure in media sheds light on the sovereignty of the current capitalist market and brings attentions to the relationship between human and media apparatus that enters a new phase. In recent scholarship, error has been mainly theorized as digital failure and in the context of digital network culture (Parikka 2007; Parikka and Sampson 2009; Krapp 2011; Nunes 2011). This chapter, however, takes a different path in which the conceptual focus on failure in media is towards the formation of nostalgia.

Failure is a two-dimensional term that bears contrary meanings in different contexts; consider art versus science. Scientists seek to conduct error-free experiments and observations to prove a hypothesis correct; for the artist, however, failure becomes precedent in a work of art instead of posing any problem. In art, failure is not the opposite of perfection and success. Art enjoys this uncertainty, as Samuel Beckett said: "To be an artist is to fail as no other dare fail" (quoted in Le Feuvre 2010, 12). Taking advantage of unpredictable and accidental occurrences, art becomes unique and imbued with a certain aura. Artists' use of failure in technology revives the aura and most often imposes on the work a nostalgic quality.

Failure is rooted in modern art's emphasis on experimentation. Scholars have historically valued experimental art, for it demonstrates both discrepancies and failure "in the confrontation with the unknown, the incommensurable, the uncontrollable, i.e. reality," as suggested by Bazon Brock (2010, 178). "The Art of Failure," according to Hans-Joachim Müller, "is nothing less than an artistic practice that assumes that failure is not merely an error," but, "as a cultural technique, a manner of enlightened awareness that rehabilitates the aesthetic principle by the very act of freeing it from the duty of having to be an absolute principle at the same time" (2010, 202). Giorgio Agamben has praised artists' experimental urges for failure seeing that "they call into question Being itself, before or beyond its determination as true or false. These experiments are without truth, for truth is what is at issue in them" (2010, 83). Some artists and filmmakers have benefited significantly from the value of failure in media toward producing auratic works that simultaneously engender nostalgic experiences in their audience as well.

Across the past three decades, British documentary filmmaker Adam Curtis has been making documentaries that provoke nostalgic feelings in the audience for his use low-quality image. He mainly deploys amateur found footage recorded by soldiers, and reporters in uncomfortable situations, or amateur home video by family members, all of whom may share a videographer's lack of experience. The use of amateur footage is the filmmaker's tactic in deploying the potentiality for failure. The blurred and grainy videos, taken in accidental framing, indeed create believable scenes in Curtis' documentaries. The credibility of the scenes is ascribed to their imperfection, which generates nostalgic qualities beside the films' social and political statement. As the audience, we are encouraged to believe the self-broadcasting of a soldier because we recognize the failure: the poor quality of his helmet-mounted camera, the small-sized video, and the errors in the footage imply that the film is not an expensive studio film production. Curtis' frames do not follow common film school rules and aesthetics. Even if someone is unfamiliar with the historical context in Curtis' films, she or he experiences a nostalgic feeling. The construction of nostalgia is resulted from the purposeful use of failure that makes the films more credible for the audience, which is fundamental in Curtis' documentaries.

Failure causes technology to find an anthropomorphic quality and to take on a nostalgic tint. Boym's remarkable quote of a Roman proverb reminds us of this transformation: "To err is human" (2018, 395). While technology is based on the assumptions that our being is not perfect, it aims to reduce its own level of errors; machines, however, inevitably fail due to wear and tear or when they become outdated, so that a state of perfection becomes almost impossible. In this sense, failure links the errors of the machine to the state of humans where it is possible to construct nostalgia.

Failure lets us contemplate our normalized desire for progress and to imagine the alternatives to the capitalistic media culture designs. In resonance with Foucault's *heterotopia* (1986) as spaces of difference where ordinary relations within the culture are allowed to be *other*, likewise, failure suspends and disrupts the former and ordinary relations between human and machine. In other words, failure calls on more layers of meaning that immediately meet the eye and brings *other* unexplored relationships toward reality. Technical errors and failure of machines unsettle both ideas of "progress and obsolescence" (Boym 2018, 474) and reveal those technological myths, as Kluitenberg describes in reference to Barthes, "whose original meaning has been erased and onto which new second order significations have been superimposed" (2006, 11–12). For all of the above, failure offers a *what if* view to the world of media, and consequently of nostalgia.

Thing Theory

Failure fractures our conventional relationship with media objects and turns the object of media into a *thing*. When media become things, they gain the potential to raise nostalgia. In this section, inspired from *thing theory* (Brown 2001) and the distinction between objects and things, a term *media-as-things* is developed. Drawing from Heidegger and Lacan, Bill Brown coined the term *thing theory* in 2001 to explain the relationship between human and the abandoned objects.

> We begin to confront the thingness of objects when they stop working for us: when the drill breaks, when the car stalls, when the windows get filthy, when their flow within the circuits of production and distribution, consumption and exhibition, has been arrested, however momentarily. The story of objects asserting themselves as things, then, is the story of a changed relation to the human subject and thus the story of how the thing really names less an object than a particular subject-object relation. (Brown 2001, 4)

For Brown, thing does not belong to the territory of either object or subject, but rather floats in between. In their venture into the unknown trajectories, media-as-things bear a reference to their technique of operation rather than to the date they are manufactured. When our camera stops working, it is the user manual that suggests the device has lost its use and perfection. The history of thing is no longer as explicit as it was before for the object: "we only catch a glimpse of things," and, a thing, as Brown puts it, "can hardly function as a window" (2001, 4). What follows here is the statement that things escape the traditional model of historical time and inhabit the present differently. Indeed, media-as-things require an epistemological investigation into their material aspects. In this sense, the question worth asking is that if media-as-things are aberrant from the history to which media objects pertain, then how do they engender nostalgia?

Humans program media, while media in turn program humans and change social behavior. "[Media] are black-boxes that have history as input and post-history as output. They are programmed to transcode history into post-history, events into programs" (Flusser 2015, 19). To communicate, media must function and translate electrical signals to symbols, signs, and semantics such as text, image, and sound. When the black box is broken, the output is no longer legible for human and thus, cannot mediate human culture as it had done before. Failure disrupts the content and in turn, a new level of relationship between human and media-as-things is shaped. Media-as-things are like alien machines in the human world, and humans' interactions with them is not necessarily historical or cultural; rather, their relationship becomes a private one. In this new relationship nostalgia can be traced out.

Our encounter with media-as-things is an encounter with the intensities of machines that are suddenly amplified through failure, an encounter with a spontaneity dimension. Unlike objects, things reveal "a moment of uncertainty and liminality" as W. J. T. Mitchell argues (2005, 156). Media-as-things are not objects of communication but "[…] play the role of a raw material, an amorphous, shapeless" (156). In this sense, they bear affective intensities that override their communication effects. Media-as-things are suffused with nostalgia as they fail to exchange their former significations.

Obsolete media are valued for their quality of "musealization," a term Böhn uses to describe the proliferation of past media in connection to memory: "objects in a museum which have lost their use value having become mere signs of their former use values, and nostalgia, which can be regarded as a counterpart to the process of modernization" (2007, 145). Today, however, in most people's garage, things are easily and abundantly found. People may avoid discarding things stashed in storage, such as an outdated laptop, a broken camera, aging cassette tapes, or a malfunctioning analog video player. One keeps media-as-things, not because they will ever again prove practical or useful, but because they are drenched in nostalgia. This is not simply a longing for the past. Unlike in museums, where artifacts (are meant to) bear historical references to a linear timeline, our things are museumized in our garage not as historical artifacts but for their affective qualities that ignite nostalgia. Media-as-things are brute and intense materialities that have become nostalgic beyond a specific time and place.

In his installation *Dark Blue* (1989), in Kunsthallen Brandts in Odense, pioneer conceptual artist Jarosław Kozłowski painted all the displayed alarm clocks in the exhibition in black, transforming them to things. Things play a central role in Kozłowski's works. Using objects ranging from alarm clocks and keys to vacuum cleaners and old TVs, Kozłowski breaks the notion of their common functionality in order to challenge human expectations and relationship with them. Kozłowski's black-painted watches are no longer ordinary objects though they may remind us of what they once were. The visitors, noticing a ticking sound, get the impression that the inner parts of the clocks still may work. *Dark Blue* lets us encounter things that cannot serve any of their original function. Highlighting the thingness in Kozłowski's painted clocks, Sabine Folie writes,

> We can't make out the time from their faces and so time is arrested, so to speak, and there suddenly arises a space of freedom that seemingly elevates us out of the temporal continuum, at least as an intellectual experiment. In a stroke, the burden of historical circumstance is temporarily banished and things take center stage in order to speak. (2010, 103)

Dark Blue immerses us in a nostalgia that is not pertinent to any individualized or collective memory. This nostalgia is neither a mourning for the past nor is a simple feeling of regret, but empowers from a material affectivies. *Dark Blue* constructs a desire originated from the intensities of things that are resurfaced and orchestrated to play. It is the brute materiality that works to impregnate nostalgia; and such nostalgia suspends from one's familiar everyday use and practice. Indeed, it is failure that interrupts our everyday relationship with the machine (clocks) and transforms the malfunctioned machine from a product to an archetype—an archetype with aura on which the audience can nostalgically reflect.

Media-as-Things: Broken-Tech Art

To affirm that the failure has the potential to inspire nostalgia, Boym gave an example of Jacques Henri Lartigue's photography, where the artist has benefited from failure in working with technology: "The blurs on the image are photographic errors, nostalgia for what photography could never be, longing for cinema" (Boym 2018, 476). The artists' use of failure in technology is one that Boym called "broken-tech art" (475). Broken-tech art can be a reaction to the acceleration of technology's hegemony in which aura is disappearing. Failure, however, restores aura in media-as-things, and subsequently, nostalgia is inevitable when aura is reinstated. Laura Marks argues in favor of the new identity that dying films can find: "Mechanically reproduced images supposedly lack aura, but as images decay they become unique again" (1997, 97).

Moreover, broken-tech art involves the factor of chance and accident. Boym argues: "If we make failure into an artistic conceit, it can become a form of co-creation or collaboration with chance" (2011, 160). In her series of *Ruined Prints* (2002–2004), Boym interfered and disrupted a working printer while it was in the middle of printing, to intentionally result in errors and imperfect outputs from the device. As the printer could not operate in the expected manner, it created different images and textures each time it performed the act of printing. Failure played a role in creating unrepeatable prints in Boym's project. For engaging chance and accident, *Ruined Prints* are unique, auratic and imbued with nostalgia.

Eventually, broken-tech art shifts our attention from optical depth to the surface: from legible content to the sensing materials within the texture of things. In her project *Unforeseen Past*, Boym used a multiburst mode on a still camera to intentionally blur the images. In her digital re-photography from old photographs, she also purposefully allowed for emergence of errors such as glares and shadows on the surface of images, "all the blemishes that a professional photographer would try to remove," as she described (2011, 159).

Tech errors interrogate the myth of machine and share human vulnerability. Failure in media is "a chance encounter between us and the machines, in which we surprise each other" (73). In listening to a scratched audio CD, hearing a hard drive clicking, or witnessing defective (dead) pixels on a monitor display, our level of consciousness of media's sensing materials increases. Failure breaks the immediacy of media and make us aware of the invisible beholder. In this sense, media-as-things are no longer common vehicles of communication, and the nostalgia they engender is not anchored in the content.

Inspired by Benjamin Franklin's glass armonica, American avant-garde media artist Tony Conrad made *Phonarmonica* as part of his 1960s series of Invented Acoustical Tools. His piece is a combination of four pieces of LP records with a pipe that passes through their center and connects to an electric drill on the top. Records are spun by the power of the drill's spinning head when the player bumps the stylus. Instead of using the pre-programmed speed of a platter, a performer plays the instrument with the headshell in the random speed of the drill. Conrad's *Phonarmonica* is nostalgic for the audience, even those with no experience in listening to such unfamiliar tones.

The time for *Phonarmonica* exists only at the moment that the headshell and the vinyl touch. Conrad's instrument produces unusual sounds through chance and unpredictability that are neither noise nor music. Conrad eradicated the role of sound archive and broke the Pythagorean tuning rules for his record player. *Phonarmonica* changes listeners' expectation of music and brings attention to the working materials of the musical instrument itself—to the temporality of the analog signals. In this sense, *Phonarmonica* embodies the McLuhanian conception that, "The message of the media of modernity is 'acoustic space'" (Ernst 2016b, 25), and not the media's content. Conrad's instrument does not refer to any other musical composition or concern a particular historical context. *Phonarmonica* is an irregular, dysfunctional record player (-as-things) that shares nostalgic qualities for what music has never been.

It is necessary to highlight that the failure discussed in this chapter as an upsurge for nostalgia is an *organic failure* and is distinct from digital media manipulation. Indeed, organic failure in resonance with Boym's concept of broken-tech art marks media-as-things in particular with accidental, unrepeatable and irreversible qualities. Organic failure positions media-as-things in the process of intensive material-mediation outside communication effects when nostalgia emerges. To open up more on this distinction, next section analyzes the body of analog and digital and their functionality through the lens of media archaeology.

A Media-Archaeological Tuned Analysis

Listening to an old record makes one feel nostalgic, but this nostalgia is not entirely connected to the content of the record. The analog tape reel of Martin Luther King's speech, for instance, is nostalgic not just for its historical content, but, as we argue in this chapter, for all of the unwanted cross-talks, flutters, distortions, and noise captured along with his speech on the magnetic tape, as well as the unavoidable decay that its medium bears. Even those unfamiliar with this particular historical context or even with the language may have this nostalgic experience. When listening to a crackling vinyl, one can have nostalgic longing in response to a degree of loss in the materiality of media that makes them affective things: longing for a better quality.

The polysemic description of contemporary nostalgia reminds us of an urge to separate the opposition between old and new media which fuels common media-historical approaches to nostalgia. To concur with this crucial craving, this chapter looks at nostalgia through the lens of media archaeology which is deemed here as an apt approach to study media. Geert Lovink characterized media archaeology as a discipline of reading "against the grain of the past," rather than telling of the histories of technologies from past to present (quoted in Huhtamo and Parikka 2011, 3). Media archaeology aims to subvert the dominant plot of media history and unravel "alternative histories, forgotten paths, and sidekicks of media history" (Parikka 2013, 167). For its impulse to stay anti-hermeneutic, media archaeology emphasizes the "'thinginess' of things and entails not interpretive 'reading' or cultural 'analysis' [of the content] but closely looking at and, when possible, touching, operating, and performing the object of study," as Vivian Sobchack describes (2011, 327–328). In the critique of the idea of technical progress, media archaeologists challenge the divide between old and new media by discovering the "old in the new" and the "new in the old" (Zielinski 2006, 3).

Failure is at the center of attention in media archaeological analysis, owing to the fact that in this perspective, media are studied from a non-communication point of view, and with a "focus on 'what is done' rather than on what is represented" (Sobchack 2011, 324). In this sense, failure, for instance, noise in old phonograph cylinders, is no longer an undesirable byproduct or aftermath, but it importantly alludes to the "media of the real", as Parikka points out, "recording noise in its singularity as well" (2011, 257). In the shift from the narratable world of hermeneutics and semantics to the non-narratable "world of signals that operate beyond and below the cultural symbolism" (Ernst 2011, 242), signal processing is regarded significant to the media archaeological analysis, and this significance, likewise, comes crucial in this chapter in examining nostalgia beyond the content in media. Hence, should we ask, in what way can nostalgia be addressed when one encounters the non-signifying noise in a trash TV?

In the context of the above theoretical framework, the works of artists Wolf Vostell (*Television Décollage* 1963), Nam June Paik (*Zen For TV* 1963), and Aldo Tambellini (*Black TV* 1968), all pioneers in working with television as a *post-medium*, are acknowledged for emphasizing physically real signals in TV rather than the cultural semiotics. Although the goal of these artists was to make critical commentary on the role of television in modern times as a dominant cultural and ideological transmission media in the sixties and seventies, these works also potentially engender nostalgia through failure that occurs in the process of signals. Indeed, it is the encounter with the materiality of noise that affects the audience and leads to nostalgia. With the use of failure, these artists replaced the message in TV with affective noise. As Ernst argues, "Once trash TV is no longer observed as to its content but as to its medium, we see noise" (2013a, 105). In *6 TV De-Col/age* (1963), Vostell desemanticized the work by erasing the message that TV is supposed to transmit. His work is well known for his technique of *decollage* with which he tended to distort the signals. With the use of failure eventually signals are turned into things. In this way, he let the material presence of the electronic media take center stage to speak; it is *signals-as-things* that spark nostalgia in the trashed TV.

Similarly, in his video titled *Information* (1973), Bill Viola constructed a study of electronic signals from a technical mistake in which a videotape recorder accidentally recorded itself. He describes that: "The resulting electronic perturbations affected everything else in the studio. [...] After this error was discovered and traced back, it became possible to sit at the switcher as if it were a musical instrument and learn to 'play' this nonsignal" (quoted in London, et al. 1987, 24). Viola's work, indeed, brings the importance of the materiality of the video to the forefront. The video never plays the same twice, as the tape's disturbed video signals produce random patterns of noise and interference. Noise here equaled information and is granted "not as a mischance but as an aesthetic windfall" (Herzogenrath quoted in Ernst 2013a, 89). The artist's deployment of noise can be discussed in terms of noise's materiality engaged in a process of perpetual transformation; the corrupted signals pollinate nostalgia beyond media's communication effects.

In all the above examples, TV become a thing through conveying noise, and relying on potentials inherent to the video signal. The common cultural communication channel in TV is blocked and we begin to see and hear (sense) the real medium that exists in both optical and acoustic realms (Ernst 2013a). In the moment of signal-to-noise transformation, the connection between signifiers and the signified is dramatically reduced (107). Nostalgia is elicited in the moment of our encounter with noise that is considered nonsignifying by definition in the media-archaeological point of view (Parikka 2011, 259). Disturbing our eyes and ears, noise shares a disregard for the past, building on a sensual materiality of "here and now" (Sobchack 2011, 324) that replaces the content; it is entangled intensely with affect and sensation to engender nostalgia for the audience encountering the artwork. The nostalgia, in this sense, is created by defected signals (noise) which have a metahistorical existence of their own, one we refer to, particularly in its divergence from representational content, as a *nonhistorical nostalgia*.

The Analog and the Digital: What Is New?

Categorizing digital media as *new media* is common practice and has led to misconceptions about analog media. The phrase *new media* has been prevalent in imposing a polarization between analog and digital media. Clarifying the delusions that polarize the analog and digital into the matter of old and new, this chapter aims to build a foundation on which one is encouraged to think about nostalgia beyond the dominance of the content and outside of its common representational contexts. To understand the difference between analog and digital technology or to assess their common ground, we need to know how they work, their materiality, and the process of signals.

In regard to the contemporary shift to the analog mode (Schrey 2014; Stuhl 2014) and the rise of *retro* cultures (Reynolds 2011) within the capitalist media market, nostalgia has been addressed as part of, associating to or arising from the content in media and mainly within the narrative-based mass media. In this sense, nostalgia has been outlined as a tendency to preserve the past memories by artificially restoring them (Niemeyer 2014) through bringing back the imperfection and flaws of analog media into the digital (Marks 2002; Rombes 2009; Schrey 2014). These case studies for nostalgia abound such as examples in *steampunk* cultures (Guffey and Lemay 2014; Sundén 2015), digital retro photography and family videos (Bartholeyns 2014; Sapio 2014), in vintage objects (Niemeyer 2015), and video games (Lizardi 2014), to name only a few.

The term *Analog nostalgia* first was conceptualized by Marks as a desire for indexicality, "a fondness for the 'problems' of decay and generation loss that analog viedo posed" (2002, 153). Marks argues that analog media in comparison to digital media are closer to nature as they provide us with "an indexical representation of reality," and for affording the "Firstness of contact with the world" (149), they have the potential to produce a sense of nostalgic longing in audience. In converting the analog to digital, this direct connection between media and index will be broken. In other words, the digital data loses the connection to the physical reference of the origin of data. In this regard, Brian Massumi particularly explains the analog's primacy in reference to human body and sensation:

> This is the analog in a sense close to the technical meaning, as a continuously variable impulse or momentum that can cross from one qualitatively different medium into another. Like electricity into sound waves. Or heat into pain. Or light waves into vision. Or vision into imagination. Or noise in the ear into music in the heart. Or outside coming in. (2002, 135)

For media archaeologists such as Ernst, the entire distinction between the analog and the digital media drives from their difference in organizing information: the former organizes information based on medium, and the latter does based on format (Ernst 2013a, 89). This view that importantly does not miss media's technicality, can certainly inform the limitation in the content-oriented articulations of media nostalgia. The media archaeological analysis illuminates that the distinction between new and old cannot be referred to the essence of analog and digital media, meaning that there is no "historical difference" in the functionality of these two forms. In reference to a radio built in the 50s, Ernst elaborates on this issue:

> [it] receives radio programs when operated today, since the stable technological infrastructure of broadcasting media is still in operation. There is no "historical" difference in the functioning of the apparatus now and then (and there will not be, until analog radio is finally completely replaced by the digitized transmission of signals); rather, there is a media-archaeological short circuit between otherwise historically clearly separated times. (2013a, 13)

What follows is the argument that we are not yet detached from the analog era. Vitalizing this statement, Jonathan Sterne clarifies that "analog denotes a specific technical process, where one quality used to present another" (2016, 32). In other words, the term analog must not be reduced to just an association with a specific era and a (past) timespan, but rather it needs to be taken more deeply and aligned to the technical specificity of media. Sterne also reminds that "the entire world outside of digital processing is not analog, because analog represents a particular technocultural relationship to nature. Nature may well be conceived as *having* analogs within it, but it cannot *be* analog" (2016, 32). To put it differently, the attribution of analog to everything not-digital is another common false assumption in the digital age that nostalgia studies need to foresee.

To substantiate the above argument, giving some examples is useful here. Considering that analog processing always bears the process of *signal transmission*, it is incorrect to call chemical photography "analog" since it lacks process of electric signals. On the other hand, a video camera can be regarded analog if it relies on signal processing. For instance, Canon AE-1 (1976–1984) and Pentax K1000 (1976–1997) are obsolete cameras that were not analog devices, while Sony Betamovie BMC-100P was the first camcorder with analog signal processing. The examples are plentiful. Not all the past media that have been rendered obsolete were analog, and thus, can be associated with nostalgia.

Moreover, recognizing that in a digital device the functionality of the analog and the digital parts are entangled (Massumi 2002; Sundén 2015; Sterne 2016) is worthwhile, as this chapter holds the view that the analog and the digital should not be separated according to categories of old and new, or past and present in order to be associative to nostalgia. For example, in a digital audio recorder/player, there is an actual reliance on analog signal processing. First, it is ADC (analog-to-digital converter) that converts all electrical signals to binary codes. Then, the signal processing uses DAC (digital-to-analog converter) to transmit the analog signals to headphones. Also, the images one sees on a computer monitor are indeed the digital codes being translated to analog signals. So, analog signal processing exists in both analog and digital media.

As far as the functionality of media is concerned, the media archaeological research prioritizes signal processing over cultural semantics. In this view, temporality of technological media disregards the narratives of the past, as signal processing always takes places in the present time (Ernst 2016a). For media nostalgia, this importantly means that the time for technical media exists only in the moment they are being played, that is in the "here and now" when/where we encounter media-as-things. Ernst explains: "In order for them [media apparatuses] to operate, only electrical energy had to be stored, yet the dependence of electronic presence on stored electricity was not apparent until the moment when the power supply of telegraph, telephones and radios broke down" (2016a, 102). To put it more radically, it can be said that the time in signal processing in a media archaeological perspective is nonhistorical. To justify what nonhistorical nostalgia is, the next section examines the role organic failure plays in analog and digital media.

Failure in Analog and Digital

Organic failure takes place in signal processing and is anticipated in the permeable space between source and destination, depending on several organic factors like weather, humidity, distance, connections, etc. The analog signals always carry noise and decay and have *generation loss* in the process of signal transmission. Since analog signals can have some values in a continuous range, the failure they carry is organic as well. *Generation loss* includes inevitable noise and bandwidth issues that happen in cables, amplifiers, mixers, and recording equipment.

Organic failure gives a way to nostalgia through effecting signals. To put it a bit dramatically, it can be argued that signals, too, can become things due to organic failure. Encountering signals-as-things, one feels nostalgia due to the amplified thingness of the signals that become triggers for nostalgia. The *generation loss* in analog signals is an irreversible phenomenon and impossible to rectify. There exists no exact method to map noise or eliminate it in analog media. Often unexpectedly, the nostalgic experience is a byproduct in artists' works in which generation loss is unavoidable.

Inspired by Nam June Paik's *Magnet TV* (1965), German artist and musician Carsten Nicolai used analog cameras in his installation *crt mgn* (2013) to capture the light of four wall-mounted neon tubes in the gallery. *crt mgn* transmits luminescent neon onto two TV screens whose images are distorted by a swinging, pendulum-mounted magnet. The magnet acts on electromagnetic waves and produces varying imagery and subtle sounds. The audience can trace the path of the signals, as the magnets disturb the image of the light on the TVs. Interactions in the magnetic field are organic and unpredictable, leading to organic failure in signal processing. The distortions are engendered by any accidental alterations in the flow of signals.

The analog circulation among light, image, and sound creates a live loop in Nicolai's work and allows the visitors to encounter a live *generation loss* in the process of signal transmission. When the float of noise on the surface of the TVs becomes visible, the audience notice the relationship between the working parts. The artist's use of organic failure in the signal processing creates an aura of loss and draws the audience into a feeling of nostalgia. When the familiar message of TV is replaced by noise, it is the affective texture of signals-as-things that are at work; it is the nonhermeneutic materiality that takes center stage to let nostalgia upsurge. Signals-as-things become sensory, intense, and affective materialities that engender nostalgia in the course of the audience's interaction with the work of art.

Organic Failure vs. Digital Glitch

What does it mean for nostalgia when it comes to failure in the digital media? The immediate conception of failure in digital media commonly is the digital glitch. In the examples of glitch, however, the issue of noise in digital media (in the level of binary code) is subject to "algorithmic manipulation" and, indeed, is "programmable" (Manovich 2001, 27). Importantly, this means that distortion and noise in digital media can be removed; in other words, the manipulated digital file can be reversed to its original state. In the sense of control, repeatability, and reversibility, digital glitch lacks the aura of loss that media-as-things regain due to organic failure. Thus, the nostalgia that one feels through organic failure is unlikely in digital glitch.

However, digital media can have organic failure as well, and that is only possible in their analog processing. In contrast to organic failure, algorithmic manipulation does not involve entropy in the materiality of digital media. To put it differently, digital failure that engages binary code presents us a different order: a "reordering" rather than a "disorder" as Gregory Zinman puts it (2015, 110). While organic failure offers entropy in things that cannot be avoided and reversed, a manipulated code, assumed as error, can be turned back at the algorithmic level. Hence, in regard to nostalgia, this chapter posits a distinction between the noise-art projects based on algorithm manipulation and the noise in media-as-things that emerge due to organic failure. While the latter is untreatable and entails nostalgia due to thingness, the former is possible to be mapped and recovered to its original state, and in this sense, does not engender nostalgia.

The organic failure in digital media involves the materiality of media and their analog processing (and parts). This issue has been of interest to media artists such as Shinji Toya whose works are related to digital memory and failure. In her project titled *3 Years and 6 Months of Digital Decay*, Toya allows for the construction of nostalgia owing to material decay in digital media. While being screened on an online video streaming website, this project began in 2016 and is expected to be finished in 2019. To examine the idea of "forgetting" in digital data, Toya used CD-R media whose lifetimes are limited because of inevitable *bit rot* (Toya 2016).

Toya's work challenges the statement, "[a]nalogue forgets naturally, yet digital does not" (Toya 2016); it demonstrates that with meticulous observation, we can realize that natural decay is possible in digital media, as well. A CD-ROM is built of various components such as a photoelectric cell, diode laser, and electric motor that work relying on the analog technology embedded in them. The CD-R's lifespan is estimated to be three and half years. The decay in Toya's work happens at the level of materiality in media (not in the digital code) and in that way, it pertains to an organic failure for nostalgia. In encountering with this piece, the audience feel nostalgia as they witness the decomposing pixels, expecting the irreversible disappearance of the video that eventually happens in 2019.

On the other hand, in the context of the above argument, associating digital glitch to nostalgia can be questioned. An example of digital glitch is *Myopia* (2015) by media artist Rosa Menkman whose work mainly investigates different forms of digital glitch, compression and noise artifact. Menkman's work, *Myopia* discloses the glitch in the digital image achieved by compressing the image into a JPEG 2000 coding system. The glitch in Menkman's work is earned at the level of the algorithm. Consider that deleting the original file or overwriting on a JPG file does not cause organic failure. The manipulated digital file can always be corrected back and thus is possible to maintain its original and primary form (see Manovich's Five Principles of New Media 2001). For this reason, through the examination that involves a close look at media in their technical level, it is correct to say that not every error is a potential failure to engender nostalgia.

Dispersion and an Affective Nostalgia

Organic failure is inevitable in the ontological being of media's materiality. Altering media's visual character and coherence, organic failure makes images lose their representational signification. Cassette tapes demagnetize over time, films fade by aging, and optical discs eventually become unreadable due to physical deterioration. A decaying image becomes difficult to see and requires a multisensory and tactile experience associated with a "haptic visuality" (Marks 2002). In contrast to the optical reading of the content, a haptic look rather "tends to rest on the surface of its object rather than to plunge into depth, not to distinguish form so much as to discern texture" (8). This haptic experience, undoubtedly, involves an intensified affect that negates the reading of image (the message). Massumi explains that affect heavily relies on "intensities" which are "embodied in purely autonomic reactions most directly manifested in the skin" (2002, 25). In this way, nostalgia erupts through the skin of things when a dispersed look is facilitated.

In our encounter with media-as-things, we no longer identify signs for they have become illegible, but we immediately begin to *sense* the physically real and affective texture in things. Marks links the nostalgic longing in a haptic image to the anxiety with the historical and cultural dominance of the optical image, that is a "dissatisfaction with the limits of visuality," calling for a desire that seeks "to squeeze the sense of touch out of an audiovisual medium" (2002, 4). Besides image, sound is also subject to failure and can lose its coherence when it becomes noisy. In listening to the distorted sounds of an aging cassette tape, our ears participate in a tactile experience. There are situations in which no individual or collective memories may be recalled, but one still feels nostalgia. When failure occurs, the viewer's body and the materiality of media-as-things interplay. Failure conditions our perception upon a "dispersed look" across the surface of things, as Marks worded in referring to the fading photographs (1997). This dispersion gives us a surprise, shock, or distraction. There is always an encounter between us and media-as-things, an indelible touch but not reading, like a "punctum" in Barthes' words (1981), when dispersion immediately gives a way to nostalgia.

A prominent example in which the artist's use of haptic image is an outset for nostalgia is *Black TV* (1968) by artist Aldo Tambellini from his *Black Video series* (1965–1969). Like other early video artists, Tambellini started to experiment with video technology through manipulation of the internal circuits of the cathode-ray tube of TV to produce scratched spirals and circular forms. The audience are nostalgically drawn into *Black TV* as it eases a dispersed look upon the surface of images. In *Black TV*, Tambellini exposed the materiality of electrons in the surface of TV. *Black TV* is nostalgic as it facilitates an encounter with signals-as-things. The moment the audience become aware of the defected signals (when legibility is disrupted) nostalgia arises. Tambellini's *Black TV* rises to nostalgia beyond a socio-linguistic experience and through a tactile, sensory, and affective interaction with the thingness of the haptic medium itself.

Conclusion

From the Romantic era up to modern and contemporary times, nostalgia has been evolving and posing new implications. Like the other terms that have taken on a multiplicity of meanings, nostalgia, too, has been reborn and has entered new phases. In addition to the effects of digital revolution and archiving, internet and online-access, the growing interest in new materialism, media archaeology, and concepts such as *affect* that have been at stake in media studies during recent years, has bound nostalgia more than ever to its new trends. Among various shifts and analyses that examine nostalgia for the content and situate media as the objects of communication, media archaeology potentially offers a different perspective on media research, in which the concept of nostalgia can be framed within miscommunication and specifically for media in their own nonhistorical laws.

Based on their functionalities and through an attention to the materiality of media, analog and digital media cannot be regarded as binaries of old and new and their temporality in an epistemological level is deemed nonhistorical. If studying media is withdrawn from its ever-historical position, and from a reliance on representational forces, nostalgia can in turn be thought in a different way as well. Nostalgia in the context of failure and in interactions with media-as-things shifts our attention from content to affect and the state of matter that can be sources for nostalgia. Failure as a catalyst allows for affective materialities to take over the meaning and to make one feel nostalgia in encounter with media-as-things.

References

Agamben, Giorgio. 2010. [1993]. "Bartleby, or On Contingency." In *Failure: Documents of Contemporary Art*, edited by Lisa Le Feuvre, 81–84. London: Whitechapel Gallery, Cambridge, MA: The MIT Press.

Barthes, Roland. 1981. *Camera Lucida: Reflections on Photography*. New York: Hill and Wang.

Bartholeyns, Gil. 2014. "The Instant Past: Nostalgia and Digital Retro Photography." In *Media and Nostalgia*, edited by Katharina Niemeyer, 51–69. New York and Hampshire: Palgrave Macmillan.

Böhn, Andreas. 2007. "Nostalgia of the Media/in the Media." In *Self-Reference in the Media*, edited by Winfried Nöth and Nina Bishara, 143–53. Berlin and New York: Mouton de Gruyter.

Boym, Svetlana. 2001. *The Future of Nostalgia*. New York: Basic Books.

Boym, Svetlana. 2008. *Architecture of the Off-modern*. New York: Princeton Architectural Press.

Boym, Svetlana. 2011. "Off-Modern Homecoming in Art and Theory." In *Rites of Return: Diaspora Poetics and the Politics of Memory*, edited by Marianne Hirsch and Nancy Miller, 151–165. New York: Colombia University Press.

Boym, Svetlana. 2018. *The Svetlana Boym Reader*. New York: Bloomsbury Academic.

Brock, Bazon. 2010. [2004]. "Cheerful and Heroic Failure." In *Failure: Documents of Contemporary Art*, edited by Lisa Le Feuvre, 180–182. London: Whitechapel Gallery, Cambridge, MA: The MIT Press.

Brown, Bill. 2001. "Thing Theory." *Critical Inquiry* 28, no. 1: 1–22.

Davis, Fred. 1979. *Yearning for Yesterday: A Sociology of Nostalgia*. New York: Free Press.

Ernst, Wolfgang. 2011. "Media Archaeography: Method and Machine versus History and Narrative of Media." In *Media Archaeology: Approaches, Applications, and Implications*, edited by Erkki Huhtamo and Jussi Parikka, 239–255. London, Berkeley, CA and Los Angeles, CA: University of California Press.

Ernst, Wolfgang. 2013a. *Digital Memory and the Archive*. Minneapolis, MN and London: University of Minnesota Press.

Ernst, Wolfgang, 2013b. "Ernst on Time-Critical Media: A Mini-Interview." Interview by Jussi Parikka. *Machinology*, July 19, 2018. https://jussiparikka.net/2013/03/18/ernst-on-microtemporality-a-mini-interview/.

Ernst, Wolfgang. 2016a. *Chronopoetics: The Temporal Being and Operativity of Technological* media. London: Rowman & Littlefield International.

Ernst, Wolfgang. 2016b. *Sonic Time Machines: Explicit Sound, Sirenic Voices, and Implicit Sonicity*. Amsterdam: Amsterdam University Press.

Flusser, Vilém. 2015. [1983]. *Post-history*. Translated by Rodrigo Maltez Novaes. Minneapolis, MN: Univocal Publishing.

Folie, Sabine. 2010. "LES MOTS ET LES CHOSES." In *Quotation Marks: Jarosław Kozłowski*, edited by Bozena Czubak, 99–103. Warsaw: Profile Foundation.

Foucault, Michel. 1972. *The Archaeology of Knowledge*. Translated by A. M. Sheridan Smith. New York: Pantheon.

Foucault, Michel. 1986. "Of other Spaces." *diacritics* 16, no. 1: 22–27.

Grainge, Paul. 2000. "Nostalgia and Style in Retro America: Moods, Modes, and Media Recycling." *Journal of American & Comparative Cultures* 23, no. 1: 27–34.

Guffey, Elizabeth, and Kate C. Lemay. 2014. "Retrofuturism and Steampunk." In *The Oxford Handbook of Science Fiction*, 434–450. New York: Oxford University Press.

Hertz, Garnet, and Jussi Parikka. 2010. "CTheory Interview: Archaeologies of Media Art." *CTheory*. Accessed May 22, 2018. https://journals.uvic.ca/index.php/ctheory/article/view/14750/5621

Huhtamo, Erkki, and Jussi Parikka, 2011. "Introduction: An Archaeology of Media Archaeology." In *Media Archaeology: Approaches, Applications, and Implications*, edited by Erkki Huhtamo and Jussi Parikka, 1–21. Berkeley, CA and Los Angeles, CA: University of California Press.

Jameson, Fredric. 1991. "Nostalgia for the Present." In *Postmodernism, or, The Cultural Logic of Late Capitalism*, 279–296. Durham, NC: Duke University Press.

Kluitenberg, Eric. 2006. "Second Introduction to an Archaeology of Imaginary Media." In *Book of Imaginary Media: Excavating the Dream of the Ultimate Communication Medium*, edited by Eric Kluitenberg, 7–26. Rotterdam: Nai Publishers.

Krapp, Peter. 2011. *Noise Channels: Glitch and Error in Digital Culture*. Minneapolis, MN and London: Minnesota Press.

Le Feuvre, Lisa. 2010. "Strive to Fail." In *Failure: Documents of Contemporary Art*, edited by Lisa Le Feuvre, 12–21. London: Whitechapel Gallery, Cambridge, MA: The MIT Press.

Lizardi, Ryan. 2014. *Mediated Nostalgia: Individual Memory and Contemporary Mass Media*. Lanham, MD: Lexington Books.

London, Barbara, James Lewis Hoberman, Donald Burton Kuspit, and Bill Viola. 1987. *Bill Viola: installations and videotapes [exhibition, Museum of Modern Art, New York, October 16, 1987 – January 3, 1988]*. New York: Museum of Modern Art.

Manovich, Lev. 2001. *The Language of New Media*. Cambridge, MA and London: The MIT Press.

Marks, Laura. 1997. "Loving a Disappearing Image." *Cinémas: revue d'études cinématographiques/Cinémas: Journal of Film Studies* 8, no. 1–2: 93–111.

Marks, Laura. 2002. *Touch: Sensuous Theory and Multisensory Media*. Minneapolis, MN: University of Minnesota Press.

Marks, Laura, and Dana Polan. 2000. *The Skin of the Film: Intercultural Cinema, Embodiment, and the Senses*. Durham, NC: Duke University Press.

Massumi, Brian. 2002. *Parables for the Virtual: Movement, Affect, Sensation*. Durham, NC and London: Duke University Press.

Mitchell, WJ Thomas. 2005. *What Do Pictures Want?: The Lives and Loves of Images*. Chicago and London: The University of Chicago Press.

Müller, Hans-Joachim. 2010. [2009]. "Failure as a Form of Art." In *Failure: Documents of Contemporary Art*, edited by Lisa Le Feuvre, 200–04. London: Whitechapel Gallery, Cambridge, MA: The MIT Press.

Niemeyer, Katharina. 2014. "Introduction: Media and Nostalgia." In *Media and Nostalgia: Yearning for the Past, Present and Future*, edited by Katharina Niemeyer, 1–23. New York: Palgrave Macmillan.

Niemeyer, Katharina. 2015. "A Theoretical Approach to Vintage: From Oenology to Media." *NECSUS. European Journal of Media Studies* 4, no. 2: 85–102.

Nunes, Mark, 2011. "Error, Noise, and Potential: The Outside of Purpose." In *Error: Glitch, Noise, and Jam in New Media Cultures*, edited by Mark Nunes, 3–24. New York and London: Continuum.

Parikka, Jussi. 2007. *Digital Contagions: A Media Archaeology of Computer Viruses*. New York: Peter Lang Inc.

Parikka, Jussi. 2011. "Mapping noise: Techniques and tactics of irregularities, interception, and disturbance." In *Media Archaeology: Approaches, Applications, and Implications*, edited by Erkki Huhtamo and Jussi Parikka, 256–277. London, Berkeley, CA and Los Angeles, CA: University of California Press.

Parikka, Jussi. 2013. *What is Media Archaeology?*. Cambridge, UK and Malden, MA: Polity.

Parikka, Jussi, and Tony D. Sampson. 2009. "On Anomalous Objects of Digital Culture." In *The Spam Book: On Viruses, Porn, and Other Anomalies from the Dark Side of*

Digital Culture, edited by Parikka, Jussi, and Tony D. Sampson. New York: Hampton Press.

Reynolds, Simon. 2011. *Retromania: Pop culture's addiction to its own past.* New York: Macmillan.

Rombes, Nicholas. 2009. *Cinema in the Digital Age.* New York: Wallflower Press.

Sapio, Giuseppina. 2014. "Homesick for Aged Home Movies: Why Do We Shoot Contemporary Family Videos in Old-fashioned Ways?." In *Media and Nostalgia*, Edited by Katharina Niemeyer, 39–50. New York: Palgrave Macmillan.

Schrey, Dominik. 2014. "Analogue Nostalgia and the Aesthetics of Digital Remediation." In *Media and Nostalgia*, edited by Katharina Niemeyer, 27–38. New York: Palgrave Macmillan.

Seigworth, Gregory J. 2017. "Capaciousness," *Capacious: Journal for Emerging Affect Inquiry*, no. 1: i–v. Web, doi:10.22387/CAP2017.7.

Sobchack, Vivian. 2011. "Afterword: Media Archaeology and Re-presencing the Past." In *Media Archaeology: Approaches, Applications, and Implications*, edited by Erkki Huhtamo and Jussi Parikka, 323–333. Berkeley, CA and Los Angeles, CA: University of California Press.

Sterne, Jonathan. 2016. "Analog." In *Digital Keywords: A Vocabulary of Information Society and Culture*, edited by Benjamin Peters, 31–44. Princeton, NJ: Princeton University Press.

Stuhl, Andy Kelleher. 2014. "Reactions To Analog Fetishism in Sound-recording Cultures." *The Velvet Light Trap*, no. 74: 42–53. Web, doi: 10.7560/VLT7405.

Sundén, Jenny. 2015. "Technologies of Feeling: Affect between the Analog and the Digital." In *Networked Affect*, edited by Ken Hillis, Susunna Paasonen, and Michael Petit, 135–149. Cambridge, MA: The MIT Press.

Tambellini, Aldo, 2015. "An Autobiography." In *Black Zero*, edited by John Wronoski, Heide Hatry, Christopher Shultz, Anna Salamone, and Joseph D. Ketner, 51–95. New York: Boris Lurie Art Foundation.

Toya, Shinji. 2016. "*3 Years and 6 Months of Digital Decay.*" Accessed May 22, 2018. http://cargocollective.com/stoya/3-Years-and-6-Months-of-Digital-Decay

Zielinski, Siegfried. 2006. *Deep Time of the Media: Toward an Archaeology of Hearing and Seeing by Technical Means.* Cambridge, MA and London: The MIT Press.

Zinman, Gregory. 2015. "Getting Messy: Chance and Glitch in Contemporary Video Art." In *Abstract Video: The Moving Image in Contemporary Art*, edited by Gabrille Jennings, 98–115. Oakland: University of California Press.

10. *Making Sense of Cultural Crisis: Radical Nostalgia, Iconic Representations, and Popular Culture*

EMILY TRUMAN

Popular culture is a symbolic space in which the social dynamics of systems of power are explored through practices of representation (Fiske 2010). Further, "revolutionary symbols," and the counter-cultural narratives they represent, are common themes in North American popular culture, with familiar signifiers such as the raised fist or the silhouette of Cuban revolutionary Che Guevara used to evoke the idea of socio-political shifts. While the continued popularity of such symbols is commonly attributed to the promotion of the "radical chic" aesthetic in marketing and advertising,[1] thus framing their use as ironic and de-politicized, to explain their significance in this way obscures their potential to contribute to popular understanding of the political. Instead, framed through the conceptual lens of *radical nostalgia*, this chapter explores the role of popular representations of revolutionary symbols as unique visual modes of expression informing public conceptions of political ideologies and ideals.

In the wake of the 2008–2009 financial crisis, images of revolutionary symbols emerged in North American popular culture to make sense of the changing political, economic and social climate. Three popular "revolutionary icons" linked to this conjunctural moment of crisis included Marie Antoinette, Rosie the Riveter, and Barack Obama, images of which circulated widely in the form of highly visible visual texts (both material and digital) including, t-shirts, collectible toys, posters, magazine covers, newspaper editorial cartoons, blogs and other forms of digital media. Images of these icons displayed unique visual properties: they were linked together through the use of *radical nostalgia*, a theme and motif of radical leftist politics that established itself as an *aesthetic expression* at the historical juncture in question. Counter to radical chic's focus on ironic (de-politicized, de-contextualized) consumption, *radical nostalgia* emphasizes the importance of *context* in questions of significance pertaining to popular visual phenomena. This opens up the conceptual space to consider how popular cultural texts offer insights into cultural anxieties that arise in relation to historical moments of change, and how these may inform public conceptions of cultural/political values.

In this chapter, the underpinnings of *radical nostalgia* as a theoretical concept are examined, illustrating its significance as an aesthetic mode in relation to iconic representations in North American popular culture. Additionally, the chapter explores the visual characteristics of the *radical nostalgia* aesthetic through compositional interpretive methods (Rose 2007) and analyzes its meaning using a discursive analytical framework for the study of visual texts called iconography (Panofsky 1970). Following the visual analysis of three key examples, the remainder of the chapter examines the findings in relation to the importance of context, cultural anxieties and attitudes, and the politics of progressivism.

Examining Radical Nostalgia*: Theoretical Origins, Characteristics, Examples*

The concept of nostalgia has a three hundred year history, over the course of which its meaning has shifted significantly from that of a seventeenth-century medical term to describe the physical condition of home-sickness (physical longing for another space) to that of a nineteenth-century psychological term to describe the emotional experience of wanting to return to a past experience (mental/emotional longing for another time).[2] Over time the meaning of nostalgia has shifted away from the idea of *the spatial* towards the idea of *the temporal* (Hutcheon 2000; Blunt 2003; Ladino 2012; Bonnett 2016). Thus, being afflicted with nostalgia, or feeling nostalgic, indicates a search for lost time (rather than lost place) that is inaccessible but that we continually try to revive or retrieve (Hutcheon 2000).

Nostalgia is primarily seen as a mode of forgetting, and studies of the concept have explored different dimensions of its expression of longing for the past. This includes approaches examining nostalgia as innately tied to narratives of loss and alienation (Hutcheon 2000; Boym 2001); nostalgia as a stylized cultural mode detached from historical experience (Jameson 1991), and drawing attention to the artificial construction of "the past" (Grainge 2002); nostalgia as an individual, mediated experience disconnected from shared cultural history (Lizardi 2015); the commodification of the material past in advertising/marketing and in consumer culture (Cross 2015; Jezinski and Wojtkowski 2016; Keller 2016); and nostalgia as a mode of thinking about the (political) future (Pickering and Keightley 2006; Bonnett 2010, 2016; Keightley and Pickering 2012). It is to this last conceptualization of nostalgia that I now turn.

Contrary to the dominant view of nostalgia as a sentimentalized, and thus de-politicized, view of the past, Michael Pickering and Emily Keightley (2006) argue for its potential as a dynamic shaping force in relation to the politics of the everyday. In support of this argument, they propose the idea of multiple modes or "modalities" of nostalgia, enabling multiple interpretations of its uses and functions, such as shifts in meaning according to context by different social actors. This is a re-conception of nostalgia as a state in which one interacts with the past: "the desire [is] not to return but to recognize aspects of the past as the basis for renewal and satisfaction in the future" (921). Here, nostalgia is not a *literal* desire to return to the past, but a *metaphorical* desire to use the past as a model for the future: "nostalgia can then be seen as not only a search for ontological security in the past, but also a means of taking one's bearings for the road ahead in the uncertainties of the present" (921). This can be achieved by using the past as "a reference point for critique of the present and a result of this, for possible transformation in the future" (Keightley and Pickering 2012, 118).

Similarly, Alistair Bonnett (2010, 2016) argues for a conceptualization of nostalgia firmly rooted in the political. In his work *Left in the Past: Radicalism and the Politics of Nostalgia* (2010), Bonnett applies the concept of *radical nostalgia* to the re-labelling of a longstanding contradiction in leftist politics in the West: namely that a false dichotomy has been set up between "radicalism" and "nostalgia," whereby one is the antithesis of the other.[3] He argues that while nostalgia has been criticized by radical political movements as a desire to return to the status-quo of the past (and as inherently subjective), it has in fact always been an important tool in the process of imagining the radical future. He argues that "one of the most prominent narratives found within radical movements is the attempt to apply the movement's past to the movement's present" (40). Bonnett (2016) also stresses the "active nature of nostalgia" (7) in order to advance an understanding of the sentiment of loss as linked to power and agency. Thus framed, "melancholic ideas and practices are not just reactive responses to change but can also be forms of action and activism" (7).

Although Bonnett is primarily interested in the notion of *radical nostalgia* as a political attitude, the concept is used here to describe an *aesthetic*, or visual mode of expression, related to the appearance and circulation of revolutionary symbols in contemporary popular culture. This aesthetic mode represents the visual meeting space between two political symbols, one past and one present, in which they overlap in composition and content. While Bonnett does not examine popular mediated texts or objects in relation to radical political attitudes, as is proposed here, he does reflect on the potential significance of objects in relation to nostalgic experience. Specifically, he argues that while we tend to criticize or denigrate nostalgia in the public realm, we "tacitly indulge" in it in private (2010, 6). This reflection about the potential dichotomy between publicly experienced nostalgia versus the privately experienced, raises questions about how *radical nostalgia* specifically, is encountered, carried out, or performed given its direct ties to the political, and thus public, realm. Ryan Lizardi (2015) points to similar concerns about the lack of potential for nostalgic objects/texts to belong to a shared cultural experience of the past, given that the modality of mediated nostalgia produces individually curated media experiences of history (34). As an aesthetic mode of expression, *visual radical nostalgia* offers conceptual space to consider how nostalgia objects/texts which may be linked to private experience (i.e. acquisition, display, consumption, etc.) are also fundamentally connected to notions of the popular, the public, and the political. As the main subject of this chapter, the cultural texts examined here featuring representations of "revolutionary icons" are linked to both the private and the public in content, use, and meaning. Thus, they offer an example of nostalgia with the possibility to intervene in the idea of the individualized mediated past that Lizardi describes.

Radical Nostalgia in Popular Culture

In light of the popularity of radical chic marketing/advertising in North American popular culture, it is not surprising that examples of the *radical nostalgia* aesthetic are also prevalent. However, *radical nostalgia* is a distinct popular visual phenomenon because it superimposes progressive political symbols of the past onto present historical events/figures. Some notable examples from the past decade include the following: book cover images of former Venezuelan President Hugo Chavez invoking Cuban revolutionary Che Guevara (2009),[4] the raised fist of resistance pictured within a stylized Egyptian eye on the cover of *Time* (2011),[5] a Bernie Sanders campaign t-shirt featuring re-claimed artwork from a Franklin D. Roosevelt social security program poster (2016),[6] and the re-imagined contemporary female figure of the "We Can Do It!" labour poster wearing a pink pussyhat on the cover of *New Yorker* magazine (2017).[7] These examples showcase a connection between past and present which is pictured in the overlap between the visual foreground and background of the images (including their histories). This distinct aesthetic style uses a form of nostalgia to frame the significance of the media/cultural texts in relation to the past: *radical nostalgia* encompasses a sentimental longing for the past and, at the same time, a hopeful vision of the progressive political future *through the visual practice of representation.*

The significance of the interconnectedness of past and present to the *radical nostalgia* aesthetic is highlighted in the example of the *Occupy Wall Street* protest movement (2011–2012) and its central symbol of the Guy Fawkes mask. While the physical occupation of New York City's Zuccotti Park in September 2011 generated international media coverage, the driving motivations behind the protest were not initially clear. The mask, worn by the protesters, and then documented and editorialized by journalists, became a key symbol through which central issues of income inequality and socio-economic status were tied to the movement. The visuality of the mask was significant: it inscribed a more coherent referent upon a movement that had been strategically "quiet" about its specific purpose and political objectives, providing a useful symbol for the characterization of the movement as a whole by outsiders and observers (such as journalists, political pundits, and spectators). Although a largely "visible" movement in terms of its public presence, the *Occupy* protests appeared to confound observers who wished to define, explain, and codify it in order to understand its significance. A prime example of this practice is the October 31, 2011 cover of the internationally distributed American magazine *Bloomberg BusinessWeek*, which features the Guy Fawkes mask (smiling white face with black eyebrows, eye outlines, moustache, goatee, and rosy cheeks) against a black background, covered in red spray paint that reads "Occupy Wall St.," accompanied by the small caption in white "Who's behind the mask".

The layering of the words over the mask inscribed a comprehensible narrative on the movement, linking it to a symbol already previously associated with anti-establishment politics. Significantly, the symbolism of the Guy Fawkes mask borrowed from three previous contexts: as a symbol associated with the hactivist movement *Anonymous* (Walker 2011; Coleman 2014); as an appropriation from Alan Moore's 1982 comic *V for Vendetta* and the 2005 Warner Bros. film adaptation of the same name (Moore 2012); and as a representation of the historical figure Guy Fawkes, the anti-authoritarian who plotted to overthrow the English government in 1605 (Soncul 2014). Whether inferred by protesters themselves, or suggested by journalists in stories about the movement, all of these references are present to some degree in the association of the mask with the *Occupy* movement.[8] As framing narratives, these symbolisms contribute to the exploration and understanding of the meaning of the Occupy movement in the present. *Radical nostalgia* is a project of "picturing" the unfamiliar present in relation to the past in order to contextualize its meaning.

Radical Nostalgia and Revolutionary Icons

The potential for the *radical nostalgia* aesthetic to re-orient conceptions of the past to inform the political future stem not only from its progressive roots, but also from its subject matter: revolutionary symbols. And, more specifically, from the symbolic status of this group of symbols as *cultural icons* in North American popular culture. Popular icons function as a "visible, concrete embodiments of the myths, beliefs, and values which form a culture's mind set" (Nachbar and Lause 1992, 170–1). As key cultural representations, popular icons not only express intangible ideas, they also contribute to the cultural significance and legitimacy of those ideas (Nachbar and Lause 1992). Revolutionary icons function in this way: they are used to signify past revolutionary events, and used as frames to make legible present moments of social change that are in the midst of unfolding. Icons do not have fixed narratives: they can be evoked in a variety of contexts at different historical moments and used to communicate various messages. However, they are often employed in the telling of narratives, specifically those of revolutionary movements, or moments of significant social change that produce uncertainty. As Nachbar and Lause (1992) note: "Popular icons ... help us find order in the midst of the chaos of life, and they provide a comforting, reassuring element of familiarity and predictability" (177). Paradoxically, revolutionary icons provide this "familiarity and predictability" through symbols of change, that is, emblems and figures that are associated with *both* particular political events *and* a broader ethos representing a break with the status quo, and a movement away from established social, cultural, and political conditions towards a different future. The quintessential example is Cuban revolutionary Che Guevara, a figure who has achieved iconic status internationally as a symbol of revolution, dissent, protest, and social change, as evidenced by his omnipresent image. Indeed, the famous red and black portrait poster image of Che created by Irish artist Jim Fitzpatrick in 1968 (based on Cuban photographer Alberto Korda's original image "Guerrillero Heroico" taken in 1960) is often referred to by academics and popular writers as one of the most reproduced images of the twentieth century.[9]

Revolutionary icons are used to symbolize social, cultural and political abstractions (such as difference, equality, fairness, hopefulness, etc.) in popular culture, and as such, they are fundamentally *public* texts in terms of both their subject matter and their visibility. They are a form of *public icon*, as articulated by Robert Hariman and John Lucaites in *No Caption Needed: Iconic*

Photographs, Public Culture, and Liberal Democracy (2007). In this work, the authors examine the role that popular American journalistic photographs, such as Dorthea Lange's *Migrant Mother*, play in constituting the ideas of civic duty and the formation of public identity. They present a detailed framework to explain the significance of the iconic photo in contemporary popular culture, arguing five vectors of influence which situate it as a central element of public culture: "reproducing ideology, communicating social knowledge, shaping collective memory, modeling citizenship, and providing figural resources for communicative action" (9). Ultimately, they position the iconic photograph as a "form of civic performance," which they theorize helps public audiences to deal with cultural and political contradictions and crises (29).

Like the photographic icon, revolutionary icons popularly appear in relation to particular moments of crisis (such as recessions, depressions, health care crises, unemployment, political instability, etc.), which give rise to the production of social uncertainty. Generally, moments of social rupture result in heightened use of symbols to communicate meaning because they recall past moments of collective unity. As a notable example, the events of 9/11 saw the (re)production of a visual lexicon of American patriotism, referencing and recycling iconic image elements into newly relevant ones, such as the reconstitution of the World War II photo "Raising the Flag at Iwo Jima" into the photo "Ground Zero Spirit," featuring New York Fire Fighters raising the American flag amidst the World Trade tower rubble (Hariman and Lucaites 2002; Sturken 2007). Thus, revolutionary icons are potent symbols that signify immediate moments of historical change as they occur, and over longer periods of time they also act as symbolic markers of the ripple effects of crisis moments.

Against the broader context of the North American financial collapse of 2008–2009, here I will examine representations of three revolutionary icons that appeared in popular cultural texts, and were used to signify various dimensions of the socio-political environment created by the crisis. They are: Marie Antoinette, the privileged "old regime" queen of the French Revolution; Rosie the Riveter, the enduring World War II feminist heroine; and Barack Obama, the new icon of social-democratic "hope." The term "revolutionary icon" is used here to describe a popularly recognizable figure that is strongly associated in Western popular consciousness with a historical event that witnessed great social, cultural and/or political change. Revolutionary icons are not necessarily leaders or heroes of social and political movements (although they may be); above all, they are highly recognizable cultural symbols so strongly associated with a perceived key moment of historical change that their image is popularly employed to symbolize the moment of change itself. The purpose of the analysis that follows is to examine in detail the visual characteristics of the texts in some key examples that feature the above figures, in order to identify key attributes of the *radical nostalgic* aesthetic.

Image Analysis: Methods, Image Selection, Findings

This analysis uses in conjunction two frameworks for the study of visual texts, both rooted in a critical approach emphasizing in-depth observation, one focusing on visual composition and the other on visual discourse. The first, *compositional interpretation* (Rose 2007), explores in detail the configuration of the visual object through its individual parts through five key compositional elements: content, colour, spatial organization, light, and expressive content. It provides a specialized vocabulary for describing the form of images, and is particularly useful for exploring image effects, or *how* representations work to produce particular results (Rose 2007). Compositional interpretation is carried out through the application of a set of questions to the cultural texts under study:

1. *Content*: What is shown, or pictured?;
2. *Colour*: What colours are present? (i.e., hues), How are the colours used? (i.e., saturation—the purity of a colour, and value—the lightness or darkness of a colour);
3. *Spatial organization*: How are the elements of the image positioned in relation to each other and to the framing space? (i.e., width, depth, interval, distance, perspective), What is the logic of the composition? (i.e., angle, height, distance, structuring of the viewer's gaze);
4. *Light*: What type of light is present? (i.e., daylight, candlelight), What is the source of the light? What does the light emphasize or highlight?;
5. *Expressive content*: What is "the feel" of the image? What are its affective characteristics?, What is the combined effect of subject and form? (Rose 2007, 40–49)

Building upon the results of this compositional analysis, a second visual framework is then applied to assess the discursive content of the images under study. Borrowed from art history, *iconography* (Panofsky 1970) is a detailed methodological approach to the study of the content, rather than form, of visual imagery (51). It examines three different, but interrelated, aspects of visual phenomena: a) *primary/natural subject matter* (factual and expressive), such as shapes, forms, poses, and gestures which are referred to as *motifs*; b) *secondary/conventional subject matter*, such as themes and concepts (communicated through motifs) which are referred to as *images, stories or allegories*; and c) *intrinsic meaning or content*, such as cultural attitudes (related to political, religious, philosophical, or social historical viewpoints) which are referred to as *symbolical values* (53–57). A key strength of this approach is its emphasis on the importance of context surrounding an image, or the "historically specific intertextuality on which meaning depends" (Rose 2007, 151).

This approach is carried out by recording visual elements/devices (or motifs) present in the image, coding them in order to identify key themes (or stories, allegories) present, and then interpreting their significance (or cultural symbolism) in relation to historical context (or cultural attitude). It should be noted that there are overlaps between compositional interpretative methods and the first dimension of Panofsky's model. In the present analysis, the compositional interpretation replaces the first level of the iconography model because it provides a more comprehensive approach to visual dimensions of the image, the nuances of which are especially important in relation to this analysis of an aesthetic mode of expression. However, all three aspects of the iconography model are also critical to this analysis because it is in their interaction that the complex meaning of an image is assessed. Overall this model (in conjunction with compositional interpretation), outlines a unique understanding of *how* images work as they do, enabling a critical assessment of the mechanics of *visual radical nostalgia*.[10]

Image Selection

Three key images selected for analysis emerged from the prolonged context of general cultural anxiety in North American popular culture following the economic crisis of 2008–2009. They were chosen for their depiction of *radical nostalgia*, that is, their subject matter concerns the visual overlapping of a "revolutionary icon" of the past, and a socio-political figure of the present. More broadly, these images were chosen to represent three significant categories of revolutionary figures represented in the time period (2009–2011) following the crisis period of the economic collapse: Marie Antoinette, Rosie the Riveter and Barack Obama.[11] The examples were located using targeted online searches for electronic images of cultural texts, specifically news images, magazine covers, and editorial cartoons, which were located on media organization websites and professional blogs. The selected images are an editorial cartoon featuring Michelle Obama (as Marie Antoinette),[12] a newspaper front page image featuring Sarah Palin and Michele Bachman (as Rosie the Riveter),[13–14] and a magazine cover featuring Barack Obama (as Che Guevara).[15] Their visual, cultural and symbolic content is presented in detail in Table 10.1.

Table 10.1: Image analysis findings.

		Marie Antoinette Image	“We Can Do It!” Image	Obama Image
Compositional Analysis	Content	Female figure of colour in elaborate Baroque-style white gown and pompadour hairstyle, on a white balcony in front of an open set of white doors, with red curtains, and pink walls, sign on the wall indicates “Ritz, Marbella Spain”. Facial expression is neutral, mouth is slightly open. A speech bubble to the right says: “Let them eat gulf shrimp”.	Two white female figures standing back to back, wearing blue shirts with the sleeves rolled up and red scarves over their hair, posing with one arm flexed against a yellow background. Facial expressions are happy, featuring smiles. The large overhead caption reads: “TOUGH LADIES!”.	Stylized silhouette of a male figure pictured in shades of blue, red and white, wearing a blue suit, white shirt and red tie, against a half blue, half red background. Facial expression is contemplative, eyes stare out into the distance, mouth closed. Large caption beneath reads “WHAT NOW?”.
	Colour	White, pink, red	Blue, yellow, red, white	Blue, red, white in various shades
	Spatial Orientation	-Figure is centered, foregrounded against frame of open doors in background. -Viewer looks straight at figure who looks back out at viewer (and/or slightly to the left)	-Figures are offset to the left and right, mirror imaged in their raised arm poses -Viewer looks straight at figures who look off to the left and right	-Figure’s body is positioned on an angle to the left, with face upturned to the top right -Viewer looks up slightly at figure, who gazes out over the top of the viewer into the distance
	Light	Simulated sunlight source from the left as the right side of the figure’s face and hair are shadowed	Simulated light source from above, as bodies under the arms are shadowed	Simulated light source from the left as the right side of the figure’s face and top of right shoulder are shadowed
	Expressive Content	Small, distanced figure produces detached feeling, cool colours produce serious tone	Smiling facial expressions and warm primary colour tones produce pleasing, positive tone	Serious, thoughtful facial expression, and predominantly blue shades, produce calm tone

		Marie Antoinette Image	"We Can Do It!" Image	Obama Image
Discursive Analysis	Primary or natural subject matter (motifs)	-Cartoon illustration -princess/royalty motif	-Photo-realist illustration -labour motif	-Stylized lithographic illustration -visionary/leader motif
	Secondary or conventional subject matter (stories, allegories)	Dress, hairstyle, and text evoke Marie Antoinette in the era of the French Revolution (eighteenth century). In the context of the events of Michelle Obama's private trip to Spain (August 2010), and the BP Oil Spill in the Gulf of Mexico (Apr.-July 2010): *Michelle Obama is superimposed onto Marie Antoinette*	Clothes, hairstyle, and pose evoke female figure of the "We Can Do It!" poster in WWII era America (mid-twentieth century). In the context of the growing popularity of Tea Party politics (2011): *Sarah Palin and Michele Bachman are superimposed onto Rosie the Riveter*	Image style, pose, colours evoke internationally popularized image of Che Guevara (mid-twentieth century). In the context of growing doubt about the idealized vision of President Obama in the famous "HOPE" poster by artist Shepard Fairey: *Barack Obama is (still) superimposed onto Che Guevara*
	Intrinsic meaning or content (cultural attitudes, symbolical values)	Michelle Obama is elitist, privileged, and out of touch with the American people. ***Elitist behaviour is undesirable**	Sarah Palin and Michele Bachman are strong, hard-working, female politicians. ***The ability to labour is a desirable attribute**	Barack Obama remains a symbol of the hope for social unity and equality. ***Social unity and equality are desirable states**

As the rows of the table above illustrate, each stage of the analysis, from the compositional elements to the discursive categories, builds upon the proceeding step in order to move from a basic description of content, toward a more detailed understanding of the symbolic subject matter contained within the images. This process encompasses the movement from iconography, the process of describing and classifying images, to iconology, a level of interpretative synthesis made possible by the first (Panofsky 1970, 57–58). Panofsky (1970) argued that the ability to move from one level of analysis to another was dependent upon "correct" readings of each, the analysis of which were to be supplemented with literary sources, expert opinions, oral traditions, and (cultural) intuition. Additionally, he argued, a "corrective principle" must be applied at each stage to counter the potential bias of the researcher: knowledge of the history of style (in relation to motifs), the history of types (in relation to stories/allegories), and the history of cultural symptoms/symbols (in relation to cultural attitudes) (61). These different forms of knowledge provide the context needed to interpret the potential meaning(s) of the images under analysis. Indeed, the meanings above are interpreted in relation to several layers of context: first, the situational circumstances of each image/case; second, in relation to the history of the icon's meaning and representations; and third, against the general background of socio-cultural crisis. Thus, in order to read the meaning of an image of Michelle Obama pictured as Marie Antoinette as it has been done above, it is necessary to know more about the history of the image itself in order to better understand what it references: a political controversy about public figures taking private vacations with perceived public money, coinciding with an environmental disaster threatening a popular US tourist destination. It is also necessary to know more about the history of the icon and its symbolism over time, in order to ascertain which "version" of the icon is being referenced. For example, Marie Antoinette's iconicity has, over time, symbolized different things, from elitist political figure to a recuperated symbol of neoliberal feminism. Finally, it is instructive to consider the cultural ethos informing the period of crisis in which the image is situated, and the potential "cultural attitudes" that may be associated with economic crisis. Here, three predominant themes are recognized as a crisis of egalitarian ideals, a crisis of labour, and a crisis of democratic equality, which are reflected in the three revolutionary icons examined: Marie Antoinette as an icon of excess, Rosie the Riveter as an icon of (female) labour, and Barack Obama as an icon of unity.[16]

While cultural icons have preferred meanings at specific historical moments, this does not mean that their analysis produces "correct" (i.e., singular) readings of their representation (Truman 2014, 2017). Instead, the selected images are used to highlight how popular visual imagery embodies cultural values that contribute to public conceptions of political ideologies. Thus, another layer of context may be added to the analysis above: the ideological positioning of the viewer, which impacts the reading of the *radical nostalgia* aesthetic. As explained earlier in the chapter, *radical nostalgia* is a theme and motif specifically representing radical leftist politics, which is also been described here using the terms counter-cultural, revolutionary and progressive. As a political label, the term "progressive" is defined as one who holds "avant-garde or liberal views," and one who is a "supporter of social, religious, or political progress or reform" (Progressive 2013). As the term's core meaning centres around the favouring or promotion of change, the label "progressive" has much in common with the idea of the revolutionary as both are terms used to describe reactions to social uncertainty. Thus, the *radical nostalgia* aesthetic is theoretically rooted in progressive ideologies. However, this does not mean that revolutionary icons can only be used and interpreted according to progressive viewpoints, as the transposing of Republican politicians Sarah Palin and Michele Bachman onto the liberal-feminist symbol of the "We Can Do It!" poster evidences. In fact, examples of contestation or controversy (which can be traced through news content, blogs and social media content) surrounding the preferred meaning of a revolutionary icon from a particular ideological viewpoint, (such as the 2009 *New York* magazine Obama "Hate" cover), can reveal the complex ways in which political meaning(s) are generated in popular culture through different ideological interpretations of *radical nostalgia*.

Returning to **Radical Nostalgia:** ***Human Figures, Cultural Anxieties, and Progressive Politics***

While the image analyses above highlight the differences in composition between the three examples of *radical nostalgia*, they share a significant commonality in form: the focus on a human figure (whether real or imaginary). At the center of visual *radical nostalgia* is a human face with the ability to evoke a historical figure of the past in order to represent the current moment of crisis. The ability to superimpose one face upon another, infers a connection or narrative between two figures. A key example of this are the visual references in Shepard Fairey's Obama "HOPE" Poster to Jim Fitzpatrick's famous image of Che Guevara (Wortham 2008; Margolin 2009; Oray 2012). These include: facial positioning, outward eye gaze, and stylized silhouette. Drawing upon such recognizable visual elements increases the symbolic status of the superimposed contemporary figure through comparison. However, the layering of human figures also adds to the complexity of analysis, as these are images in which representations of gender, race and ethnicity, and sexual identity are being produced and reproduced. The overwriting of contemporary political figures with those of the past suggests the potential for a kind of visual erasing or silencing of the former's politics, identity, and social positioning, which must then be recuperated in the analysis of *radical nostalgia*'s effects.

Significantly, the centrality of the human figure to *visual radical nostalgia* is tied to its intrinsic meaning, which Panofsky (1970) defined as "the underlying principles revealing the basic attitude of a nation, a period, a class, a religion or philosophical persuasion" (55). These principles, or "cultural attitudes," are revealed in the attribution of particular attitudes and behaviours to the central figures of the images of *radical nostalgia*. They manifest as desirable or undesirable characteristics of people and/or systems, so in the examples above: elitist behaviour is undesirable, the ability to labour is a desirable attribute, and social unity and equality are desirable states, in relation to the 2008–2009 economic collapse. In this way, specific sets of cultural values are revealed as associated with the historical moment of socio-cultural crisis in question; revealing general cultural anxieties, and functioning as symbolic discussions of what counts as ideal in terms of progressive (and other) cultural values. Further, the presence and circulation of images featuring *visual radical nostalgia*, contribute to the project of defining the parameters of social connection between citizens. This claim echoes Hariman and Lucaites (2007) in their assessment of the iconic photograph as a symbolic entity with the ability to "define relationships between civic actors" (11). This is because iconic photos both produce and draw upon social knowledge (a "web of social connections") to contextualize a historical event, opening up the space to analyze it from multiple perspectives (10). Thus, the symbolic order that surrounds cultural icons presents them with the ability to depict democratic ideals for civic actors: "From an intermediate position within the social order, the icon provides a reflexive awareness of social forms and state actions that can lead to individual decisions and collective movements on behalf of democratic ideals" (3). As the authors argue, this process takes place through "modes of representation" which are central to the process of political meaning-making, in particular in the modern liberal-democracy because the modern, ambiguous, abstract state has become disconnected from the individual (17). In light of this, "citizenship might depend on modes of representation that can enact the relationship of the abstract individual to the impersonal state" (17).

To be clear: the use of *visual radical nostalgia* will not result in total social, cultural, or political transformation caused by revolutionary action. As John Fiske (2010) argues, the model of social change associated with popular culture does not take place through revolutionary breaks in history, but is rather "an ongoing process, aimed at maintaining or increasing the bottom-up power of the people within the system. It results in the softening of the harsh extremities of power, it produces small gains for the weak, it maintains their esteem and identity. It is progressive, but not radical" (148). Exploring the transformative potential of popular cultural texts, such as blue jeans and television soap operas, Fiske claims: "we are wrong to expect popular culture to be radical (and thus to criticize it for not being so). Radical political movements neither originate nor operate at the level of representation or of symbolic systems" (148). However, the radical and the popular are not opposing categories, but complimentary ones: the former must engage popular support, and the latter must connect with political movements in moments of historical crisis, in order to be effective (Fiske 2010). The concept of *radical nostalgia* occupies the overlapping symbolic space between these two positions, offering representations of progressivism and testing their validity against others.

Conclusion

As a theoretical concept, *radical nostalgia* sheds light on the process of the formation of public discourse related to politics, and identifies cultural anxieties linked to moments of socio-cultural crisis and contextualizes them historically. More practically, it functions as an educational tool in the pursuit of political literacy, by highlighting the critical analysis skills needed to identify and challenge how nostalgic mediated representations frame (and possibly limit) the discussion of the meaning of events/crises. Further, the example of *radical nostalgia* offers useful images for exploring and criticizing the concept of authenticity or "visual truth" in an era of digital image manipulation, "fake news", and networked social media sharing practices. These implications are in line with Hariman and Lucaites' (2007) assessment of the three key purposes of iconic images as a distinct visual practice: to communicate about 'the public', to socialize the viewer, and to educate them about how to deal with social change (18). Critically, the study of *radical nostalgia* sheds light on the importance of popular culture as a symbolic site for understanding politics and its visual representations.

Notes

1. In the context of consumerism, "radical chic" is a term that describes the manifestation of rebellion (and/or the rebellious attitude) as a theme or aesthetic in the marketing material and strategies of various popular consumer brands and their goods. On the origins of the term, see Hartle (2012). For a discussion of the commodification of counter-cultural attitudes, see Heath and Potter (2004).
2. The first recorded use of the term dates from 1756 as a medical term to describe home sicknesses or the "melancholia caused by prolonged absence from one's home or country" (Nostalgia 535). The term was coined slightly earlier in 1688 by Swiss Physician Johannes Hofer while "examining the particular kind of melancholy experienced by Swiss mercenaries when removed from their homeland. … Drawn from the Greek *nostos* (meaning "return home") and *algos* (meaning "pain"), nostalgia described the homesickness … that soldiers could suffer and even die from when fighting away from their native land. Symptoms involved despondency, weeping, and sometimes suicide" (Grainge 2002, 19).

3. While Bonnett outlines broadly the source of the term "radical nostalgia" as originating in response to political theory in the modern era, he does not offer a specific defining source for the term. He does however briefly discuss Peter Glazer's book *Radical Nostalgia: Spanish Civil War Commemoration in America* (2005) which employs the term in a similar fashion in his study of performative commemorative practices in American culture.
4. See U.K. cover of Bart Jones' *Hugo!: The Hugo Chavez Story* (2009) by Vintage, and cover of Barry Connon's *Hugo Chavez and the Bolivarian Revolution* (2009) by Manchester University Press.
5. See April 18, 2011 cover of *TIME* magazine (European & Asian Edition), cover illustration by Cecila Wong for *TIME*.
6. No longer available on the Bernie Sanders campaign website, the "FDR Throwback T-shirt" was sold in 2016 and can be seen here archived in a public Pinterest account: https://www.pinterest.ca/pin/489273946998413182/
7. See the February 6, 2017 cover *The New Yorker* magazine.
8. For examples of news coverage of *Occupy Wall Street* examining the source of the symbolism of the Guy Fawkes mask, see Jones (2011); Thompson (2011).
9. For explorations of Che Guevara's iconicity, see Ziff (2006); Casey (2009).
10. It is worth noting that the focus of this analysis on the question of *how* images work, rather than *why* images work as they do as explored by semiological approaches (i.e., Charles Sanders Pierce, Roland Barthes) (Rose 2007, 145), is the reason why it does not employ the specialized language of semiotics (i.e., sign, signifier, signified) to explore the imagery in question.
11. These case studies are central to my doctoral dissertation project. For a more detailed discussion of each, including collections of examples, see Truman (2014).
12. "Let them eat gulf shrimp", editorial cartoon by Pulitzer Prize winning cartoonist Michael Ramirez, featured online in *Investor's Business Daily*, August 9, 2010.
13. For ease of discussion, here I am associating the two cultural entities of the "We Can Do It!" poster and the cultural figure of "Rosie the Riveter". However, I acknowledge their conflation in American history, and thus the importance of examining them as unique cultural texts/narratives. For an excellent exploration of their intertwined history, see Kimble and Olson (2006).
14. "Tough Ladies!", cover of the *Boston Herald*, July 20, 2011.
15. "What now?", cover of *Esquire* magazine for February 2009, artwork by Shepard Fairey.
16. For a detailed historical examination of each figure's iconicity, see Truman (2014).

References

Blunt, Alison. 2003. "Collective Memory and Productive Nostalgia: Anglo-Indian Homemaking at McGluskiegani." *Environment and Planning D: Society and Space* 21 (6): 717–38.

Bonnett, Alastair. 2010. *Left in the Past: Radicalism and the Politics of Nostalgia*. New York: Continuum.

———. 2016. *The Geography of Nostalgia: Global and Local Perspectives on Modernity and Loss*. New York: Routledge.

Boym, Svetlana. 2001. *The Future of Nostalgia*. New York: Basic Books.
Casey, Michael J. 2009. *Che's Afterlife: The Legacy of an Image*. Toronto: Vintage.
Coleman, Gabriella. 2014. *Hacker, Hoaxer, Whistleblower, Spy: The Many Faces of Anonymous*. New York: Verso.
Cross, Gary. 2015. *Consumed Nostalgia: Memory in the Age of Fast Capitalism*. New York: Columbia University Press.
Fiske, John. 2010 [1989]. *Understanding Popular Culture*, 2nd edition. New York: Routledge.
Glazer, Peter. 2005. *Radical Nostalgia: Spanish Civil War Commemoration in America*. Rochester, NY: University of Rochester Press.
Grainge, Paul. 2002. *Monochrome Memories: Nostalgia and Style in Retro America*. Westport, CT: Praeger.
Hariman, Robert and Lucaites, John Louis. 2002. "Performing Civic Identity: The Iconic Photograph of the Flag Raising at Iwo Jima." *Quarterly Journal of Speech* 88 (4): 363–92.
———. 2007. *No Caption Needed: Iconic Photographs, Public Culture, and Liberal Democracy*. Chicago, IL: The University of Chicago Press.
Hartle, Johan Frederik. 2012 March 23. "Radical Chic? Yes We Are!" *Eurozine*. https://www.eurozine.com/radical-chic-yes-we-are/
Heath, Joseph and Potter, Andrew. 2004. *The Rebel Sell: Why the Culture Can't be Jammed*. Toronto: Harper Collins.
Hutcheon, Linda. 2000. "Irony, Nostalgia and the Postmodern". *Methods for the Study of Literature as Cultural Memory, Studies in Comparative Literature* 30: 189–207.
Jameson, Fredric. 1991. *Postmodernity, or, the Cultural Logic of Late Capitalism*. Durham: Duke University Press.
Jezinski, Marek and Wojtkowski, Lukasz. 2016. "Nostalgia Commodified: Towards the Marketization of the Post-communist Past Through the New Media". *Medien & Zeit* 4: 96–104.
Jones, Jonathan. 2011 November 4. "Occupy's V for Vendetta Protest Mask Is a Symbol of Festive Citizenship." *The Guardian*. Last edited November 7, 2011. https://www.theguardian.com/commentisfree/2011/nov/04/occupy-movement-guy-fawkes-mask
Keightley, Emily and Pickering, Michael. 2012. *Mnemonic Imagination: Remembering as Creative Practice*. New York: Palgrave Macmillan.
Keller, Mario. 2016. "Experienced Mood and Commodified Mode: Forms of Nostalgia in the Television Commercials of Manner". *Medien & Zeit* 4: 61–71.
Kimble, James J. and Olsen, Lester C. 2006. "Visual Rhetoric Representing Rosie the Riveter: Myth and Misconception in J. Howard Miller's "We Can Do It!" Poster." *Rhetoric and Public Affairs* 9 (4): 533–70.
Ladino, Jennifer. 2012. *Reclaiming Nostalgia: Longing for Nature in American Literature*. Charlottesville: University of Virginia Press.

Lizardi, Ryan. 2015. *Mediated Nostalgia: Individual Memory and Contemporary Mass Media*. New York: Lexington Books.

Margolin, Victor. 2009. "Obama Sightings." *Journal of Visual Culture* 8 (2): 183–89.

Moore, Alan. 2012 March 8. "Viewpoint: V for Vendetta and the Rise of Anonymous." *BBC News Online*. http://www.bbc.com/news/technology-16968689

Nachbar, John and Lause, Kevin. 1992. *Popular Culture: An Introductory Text*. Madison, WI: The University of Wisconsin Press.

Nostalgia. 1989. *Oxford English Dictionary*, vol. 4, 2nd edition, 535. Oxford: Clarendon Press.

Oray, Patrick B. 2012. "Myth, Symbol, and the Branding of an American Presidency." In *The Iconic Obama, 2007–2009: Essays on Media Representations of the Candidate and New President*, edited by Nicholas A. Yanes and Derrais Carter, 28–42. Jefferson, NC: McFarland & Company, Inc.

Panofsky, Erwin. 1970[1955]. "Iconography and Iconology: An Introduction to the Study of Renaissance Art." In *Meaning in the Visual Arts*, edited by Erwin Panofsky, 51–81. Harmondsworth: Penguin.

Pickering, Michael and Keightley, Emily. 2006. "The Modalities of Nostalgia." *Current Sociology* 54 (6): 919–41.

Progressive [B1a]. 2013 September. *Oxford English Dictionary Online*. http://www.oed.com/view/Entry/152244?redirectedFrom=progressive

Rose, Gillian. 2007. *Visual Methodologies: An Introduction to the Interpretation of Visual Materials*, 2nd edition. Washington, DC: Sage.

Soncul, S. Yigit. 2014. "From Screens to Streets: The Dissemination of Guy Fawkes Image in Physical and Living Media." *Between IV* (7): 1–9.

Sturken, Marita. 2007. *Tourists of History: Memory, Kitsch, and Consumerism from Oklahoma City to Ground Zero*. Durham, NC: Duke University Press.

Thompson, Nick. 2011 September 5. "Guy Fawkes Mask Inspires Occupy Protest Around the World." *CNN Online, U.S. Edition*. https://www.cnn.com/2011/11/04/world/europe/guy-fawkes-mask/

Truman, Emily. 2014. "Back to the Political Future: Coping with Crisis Through Radical Nostalgia for Revolutionary Icons." PhD diss., Carleton University. https://curve.carleton.ca/c50d2586-0c62-4f04-93a3-b5fe2b0168d6

———. 2017. "Re-thinking the Cultural Icon: Its Use and Function in Popular Culture." *Canadian Journal of Communication* 42 (5): 829–850.

Walker, Rob. 2011 December 8. "Recognizably Anonymous." *Slate Magazine*. http://www.slate.com/articles/arts/design/2011/12/guy_fawkes_mask_how_anonymous_hacker_group_created_a_powerful_visual_brand.html

Wortham, Jenna. 2008 September 21. "'Obey' Street Artists Churns out 'Hope' for Obama." *Wired Magazine*. http://www.wired.com/underwire/2008/09/poster-boy-shep/

Ziff, Trisha. 2006. *Che Guevara: Revolutionary & Icon*. New York: Abrams Image.

11. *Assessing the Political Possibilities of Interactive Nostalgia*

SALLY J. SPALDING

In the first issue of *Interactions: Studies in Communication and Culture*, Mark Andrejevic poses a powerful question: “What are we to make of the fact that the advent of ‘bottom-up’ media production amidst celebratory claims about the democratizing power of interactivity have coincided, arguably, with increasing economic and political inequality” (2009, 35)? His question echoes similar concerns from a number of critical voices about the nature of civic engagement and the possibility of progressive politics in the age of late capitalism and interactive social media. This anxiety over the relationship between interactive media and democratic engagement is felt all the more acutely in ongoing conversations about the role of emotion as instigator and mediator of interactivity and civic engagement. Anne Bartsch and Mary Beth Oliver offer a concise recounting of the manifold voices who fear that “emotional involvement with media content comes at the expense of cognitive depth and rational scrutiny” (2011, 12). This fear of emotion and affect as overwhelming and undermining democratic participation and progressive politics is clearly explained and justified in a series of works from a number of academic disciplines; particularly cultural and rhetorical media criticisms (Berlant 1997; Cloud 2003; Sturken 2007, 2011).

In recent years, these concerns about the political possibilities of emotion have developed with specific regard to nostalgia. In the aftermath of the U.S. financial crisis of 2008, several critics’ analyses of nostalgic discourse and visuals began to reiterate the concerns of those critical of emotion more broadly. Such scholars argue that nostalgia is being used to depoliticize the public by encouraging uncritical consumption and a fixation on a distorted vision of the past as the means to assuage the insecurity and deflect the pain of an uncertain future (Hasian 2001; Von Burg and Johnson 2009; Wood

2010). In her critique of post-financial crisis American films, Elena Oliete-Aldea argues that not only did the financial crisis instigate "a nostalgic search for the shelter of a cohesive community" (2012, 348), but that in the era of late capitalism nostalgia itself has become more economic. This search for identity through nostalgic consumption is indicative of what Gary Cross dubs "consumed nostalgia," a new form of nostalgia that has "emerged in the twentieth century" (2015). This new nostalgia attempts to assuage the stress of living in the time of "fast capitalism" by consuming products from their childhood. Specifically, Cross argues "today's nostalgia is rooted in special emotions linked to recovering memories distinctive to the objects of modern childhood and consumerism" (2015). By connecting certain commodity forms to nostalgic sentiment through advertising, producers are able to "sell" nostalgia (Oliete-Aldea 2012, 351). Nostalgia, then, becomes a form of commodity itself that in turn "likely heals the sense of insecurity and marginalization felt by alienated individuals" (Merchant and Rose 2013, 2621).

In spite of the evident value of these contributions, these readings of the depoliticizing uses of nostalgia should not be taken to mean that nostalgia is deterministically linked with depoliticization. Recent scholarship in cultural and communication studies complicates attempts to reduce nostalgia to an emotional means of enforcing conservative ideology (Atkinson and Rosati 2012; Bonnett 2010; Pickering and Keightley 2006; Smith 2000; Tannock 1995). These authors argue that nostalgia can harness collective memory for progressive ends. It is this potential to foment progressive, even radical, resistance that lead Micheal Pickering and Emily Keightley to argue that nostalgia holds a positive dimension, "one associated with desire for engagement with difference, with aspiration and critique, and with the identification of ways of living lacking in modernity" (2006, 921).

These critical engagements, which argue both for and against the political possibilities of nostalgia, indicate the need for a clear theory on the persuasive efficacy of nostalgia beyond its effect on collective memory and a method for critiquing the modes of political action encouraged by nostalgic appeals (and emotional appeals, more broadly). This chapter offers one such method by arguing for a renewed attention to the ways that specific emotions encourage individuals to act and the affiliative possibilities they invite. Specifically, I argue that, by attending to the action tendencies—the "particular ways in which bodies are predisposed to be moved by specific emotions" (Condit 2013, 6)—and affiliative possibilities nostalgic appeals invite, it becomes possible to distinguish between affective appeals that have greater and lesser tendencies to depoliticize or repoliticize the public. In the case of nostalgia, I argue that those who experience the emotion are set off on a two-step action tendency sequence that may predispose them to interaction with others and thereby be used to strengthen and/or extend affiliations with others. However, the political potential of nostalgia to advance progressive ends depends largely on the particular structuring of participants' interactions with imagined and real others and the types of affiliation those interactions enable.

To provide this illustration, I turn to the ways in which nostalgia is deployed by two public interactive art pieces critical of late capitalism in the years following the financial crisis of 2008. In the case of the art installations under review, both use the form of the carnival game to evoke nostalgia and incite participatory action tendencies. Nonetheless, one installation's mode of participation reifies long-standing pro-capitalism and anti-capitalism affiliations and depoliticizes the engagement it seeks to foment. The other encourages an extension of affiliative empathy toward the working class, which effectively troubles the pro/anti binary and its entrenched politics of animosity. Through comparison of the two pieces, I show that a method that accounts for the action tendencies of a given emotion, in addition to the trajectories of affiliation and action promoted by individual emotional appeals, can better discern depoliticizing appeals to emotion from those that encourage broadening affiliation and action.

This study begins with an overview of existing literature on nostalgia as an embodied emotional experience, as well as the action tendencies and affiliations that are likely to attend one's experience of nostalgia. I then turn to an explanation of how the two interactive art installations use the form of the carnival game to evoke nostalgia, activate approach action tendencies, and thereby encourage participation in critiques of capitalism. I next assess the political efficacy of the two installations by highlighting the ways in which the various modes of engagement in the interactive art pieces may encourage stabilization or undermining of existing affiliations and emotional investments in capitalism. I conclude with a reflection on the ways this mode of criticism can complicate existing literature on nostalgia and offer new avenues to effectively critique the political possibilities of public appeals to emotion.

Nostalgia, Action Tendencies, and Affiliation

At its most simple, nostalgia has been defined as "the longing for one's remembered past" (Batcho 2013, 357). However, Ulrich R. Orth and Steffi Gal recognize that nostalgia may correspond to "a past actually lived by the person" *or* vicarious nostalgia "which deals with a period outside of the individual's living memory" (2014, 162). Regardless of whether nostalgia is experienced personally or vicariously, Orth and Gal argue that the experience of nostalgia occurs through a two-part partially involuntary and partially voluntary mental process that can influence an individual's behavior. The first part of nostalgia's two-step process is interaction with a nostalgia-inducing image that invites the experience of an involuntary memory. Their research indicates that viewing particular images causes people to experience "visually induced involuntary memories." Involuntary memories are "spontaneous" and activated with little to no "executive control." The experience of involuntary memories:

> Typically depends on a distinct feature-overlap between the remembered and the current situation ... The implicit memory system allows representations of past experiences to persist and thereby influence current feelings, preferences, and decisions, even when there is no recollection of the original experience. (162)

In other words, particular forms or visuals—"features"—which are present in both the remembered and current situation, instigate the involuntary memory and "influence" decision making and action behaviors.

The second step of nostalgia's action tendency sequence involves both voluntary and involuntary elements. As Orth and Gal state, the involuntary memories evoked by nostalgia-inducing images influence the viewer's feelings in the present (164). This occurs through a process in which participants reproduce the emotions associated with that memory: joy, comfort, sadness, anxiety, happiness, etc. (162–63).[1] In other words, while nostalgia is itself an emotional state, its influence on behavior is mediated by another emotion, such as joy, comfort, sadness, wistfulness, etc. These secondary emotions, induced by the nostalgic-evoking image, influence behavioral intention and instigate or deter the second step of nostalgia's action tendency, approach or retreat from the visual and the proposed action (Levine, Lench, and Safer 2009; Orth and Gal 2014). For example, in the case of marketing, if a customer saw a label that reminded the customer of their childhood, they would involuntarily recall a childhood memory. In turn, the associative emotions of that memory would influence the customer's likelihood of buying that product. If the secondary emotion was a pleasurable one, then the individual might be persuaded to purchase the item so that the experience of the pleasurable emotion could be recreated with each subsequent use. If the secondary emotion was negative, then the customer might be compelled to retreat from the item.

While this example may seem to reify critiques of nostalgia as inherently consumerist and individualistic, additional contemporary research shows that nostalgic action tendencies tend to prime individuals to engage with others and problem-solve rather than isolate and retreat into the past. The memories of the past become the foundation for social interaction and the (re)constitution of a troubled identity, particularly in times of crisis. In her study of the correlations between nostalgia and coping strategies, Krystine Irene Batcho found that, even when faced with a social or financial crisis, participants primed with nostalgic recall of positive childhood events displayed "greater attention to thinking and strategizing and then taking action to improve the situation" (2013, 364). This scholarship shows that while nostalgia may lead to comfort or other positive emotions, these emotions *can* influence and induce action tendencies that promote affiliative ties and pro-social behavior.

To illustrate how attending to the affiliative and action tendencies of nostalgia can reveal the ways in which emotional appeals may either depoliticize or repoliticize a public, I analyze two interactive art pieces designed in the wake of the United States' financial crisis of 2008: "Capitalism Works for Me! (True/False)" by Steve Lambert (hereafter, CWFM) and the "Minimum Wage Machine" by Blake Fall-Conroy (hereafter, MWM). Both art pieces have travelled domestically and internationally and invited structured forms of participation. An analysis of the art installations highlight how, first, the forms of visual rhetoric, like the carnival game, can instigate the action tendencies of particular emotions and, second, how those action tendencies can be put to work to broaden or narrow affiliative possibilities. In the following section, I look to the formal features of the carnival game and its associated emotional repertoire to reveal how visual rhetoric installations could invoke personal or vicarious nostalgia for an ideal, playful past and in turn influence participant behavior.

Nostalgia-Evoking Carnival Games and Participatory Action Tendencies

In the wake of the financial crisis, artists critical of late capitalism and its potential role in the financial crisis have, intentionally or not, used visual forms to incite nostalgia. Fortuitously, two of these interactive art exhibits appropriate the form of the carnival game to incite nostalgia and thereby encourage participants, primed by positive emotions, to interact with their art. In both instances, the carnival game symbolizes the promise of a temporary reprieve from the present crisis and indeterminate future through a return to the emotional pleasures of an idealized past. While the carnival game will not transport one physically back and forth in time, its visual forms can evoke nostalgia—personal or vicarious—through involuntary memories of a moment of childlike pleasure. This moment of pleasure encourages viewers to participate in the carnival "game" that might allow us a brief connection to the pleasures of our (imagined) emotional past.

This move to utilize nostalgia as a means of provoking action has been theorized and corroborated in the field of consumer research. In their summary of past consumer research on nostalgia, Merchant and Rose find vicarious nostalgia can influence the purchase of a myriad of products including cars, clothing, food, and even banks (2013, 2620). Rhetorical scholars echo Merchant and Rose's findings, arguing that nostalgic images can encourage individuals to act, primarily through consuming the product—be it movie, book, or beer—that displays a nostalgia-evoking image (Dickinson 1997, 1; Oliete-Aldea 2012, 351).

In the same way that nostalgia-inducing images can encourage enjoyment-seeking actions such as consumption, the use of the carnival game form invites participation in the game-like critique of capitalism. CWFM is an apt example. If you had walked through Times Square in New York City during the Fall of 2013 and Spring of 2014, you would have seen a temporary addition to the larger than life billboards and flashing lights of the surrounding businesses. Perched in the center of the square, and thereby slightly offset from the expansive advertisements that reach from ground to sky, cocooning the visitors in capital, sat a new billboard. This one is also larger than life—though less grandiose when compared to its surroundings—standing nine feet tall and twenty feet long. In white letters, accented by lightbulbs and red trim, the billboard lights up the word "CAPITALISM." Below the lighted letters, on a blue background the words "works for me!" are painted in white. On either side of "works for me!" are lit LED screens: one labeled "True" and the other labeled "False." Off to the right of the billboard is a silver podium with two buttons: a green button labeled "True" and a red button labeled "False" along with a timer that counts down. As is implied by the buttons, this billboard attempts to compel a different form of participation than those advertisements that flash around it. CWFM asks individuals to step up to the podium and respond true or false to the prompt "Capitalism Works For Me!"

It is specifically the nostalgia evoking form of the carnival game that invites and frames audience participation.[2] In the case of CWFM, individuals are invited into a familiar game-like atmosphere—facilitated by the format of the billboard and its accompanying podium—and encouraged to cast a vote as well as a justification for that vote. The brightly colored, lightbulb—rather than fluorescent—lit billboard painted in red, white, and blue, the LED screens that recall a traditional scoreboard, the podium where participants push an overly large red or green button before the time runs out, all signal the form of a leisurely, yet exciting carnival game.

Responses by art critics reveal that CWFM's aesthetic is read as its creator intended—as a seemingly vintage carnival game. Jennifer Schuessler of *The*

New York Times describes CWFM as "a 20-foot by 9-foot red, white and blue retro-styled illuminated scoreboard" (2013), Mark Brown of *The Guardian* and Laura Davis of *The Liverpool Post* highlight its carnival-like features describing the billboard as "like a huge carnival sign" and "a cheerful, carnivalesque sign," respectively (Brown 2013; Davis 2013). The carnival game is the form through which participants understand the means of interaction. According to Schuessler, while the initial response to CWFM in Times Square was trepidation, Lambert's art installation quickly inspired diverse participants to stand in line in order to "play" (2013). Images of the "scoreboard" after a "completed" game speak to its success in garnering participation: in Boston, 690:546 for, in New York City, 217:247 against, in Los Angeles's Charlie James Gallery, 339:346 against.

In a fashion similar to CWFM, the MWM uses the form of the carnival game to encourage participation. The MWM is a simple box filled with shiny pennies: the bottom half is made of unfinished wood and the top half is made of glass. The box sits on top of a simple unfinished wood stool and stands six feet tall. At this height the bright pennies sit at eye level for most adult participants. The MWM "allows anybody to work for minimum wage" by turning a large metal crank on the exterior of the box (Fall-Conroy n.d.). If a participant turns the crank fast enough to generate sufficient energy, they will receive one penny "every 4.97 seconds" from a slot at the front of the box. At this rate, a participant could earn the national minimum wage of $7.25 an hour were they to turn the crank at a sufficient speed for a full hour.[3]

The construction of the piece recalls the construction of toy claw machines popular at fairs, carnivals and arcades. Similar to the toy claw machines, participants can see the spoils of their efforts through the glass that forms the top half of the box. Instead of toys or candy, participants encounter a box full of thousands of pennies; instead of a joy stick to maneuver the claw inside the machine in an attempt to claim a toy, participants encounter a simple crank on the right side. For visitors with more mature inclinations the MWM might more closely resemble a slot machine, albeit a bland one. Because of the resemblances between the two machines, participants are able to associate the MWM with the pleasure of nostalgia through the consumption and the challenge the toy claw game and slot machine impose. While the MWM has received considerably less press and the absence of the scoreboard prevents any concrete tally of participants, some reviews include photos of several individuals interacting with the MWM. Thus, despite a lack of instructions, participants already know how to interact with the MWM presumably because of its similarity to the carnival game form.

While the carnival game form may evoke nostalgia and its accompanying action tendencies, it does not follow that participation in CWFM or the MWM will lead to deliberation or undermine participants' emotional investment in capitalism. The visual form of the carnival game may trigger nostalgic action tendencies and inspire social interaction; however, the modes of participation structured by the artist and followed by the participants determine the *kinds* of social interactions, affiliations and deliberative opportunities available. As Carole Blair reminds us, monuments and memorials, and arguably other instances of interactive art, "do perhaps even more obvious work on the body. They direct the vision to particular features, and they direct—sometimes control—the vector, speech, or possibilities of physical movement" (1999, 46). These modes of interactivity, in turn, affect how we understand and interact with the world around us. Therefore, an effective critique of appeals to emotion must attend not just to the ways the rhetoric invites an emotional response, but to the ways in which the structure of the appeal directs an emotion's action tendencies toward or against others through its manipulations of the participant's body. In the case of CWFM and the MWM, the particular performances each installation allows in turn determines the political possibilities of its emotional appeal by narrowing the forms of sociality and modes of activity the action tendencies of nostalgia may take. To argue for how the two pieces individually enable particular performances of sociality and affiliation, I attend to the ways that action tendencies and modes of participation structured by the artists reinscribe or reorient affiliations to others under capitalism.

CWFM, the Ticking Clock, and Limited Affiliations

Steve Lambert (n.d.) started the CWFM as a way to start a conversation about the taboo subject of capitalism and its viability as an economic system in the modern era. He states:

> I'm excited that this piece takes on what for most Americans is a taboo, or even nonexistent subject; whether global, hegemonic capitalism actually works for most people. But whew, talking about that is boring! And telling people what to think is worse! This sign gets passers by to participate in deceptively simple vote [sic] (True/False) which only pretends to offer resolution. Every aspect of the interaction draws them in to more complex questions and conversations, leading to new thoughts and ideas about a better world!

Lambert hopes that his project will allow for new imaginings of the future; imaginings that derive from and drive collectives to a renewed belief that they "can intervene and somehow steer social development." Arguably, CWFM and its "deceptively simple" performative, game-like components and flashy billboard presentation succeed in its task to compel participation largely through its retro carnival game aesthetic and the feelings of nostalgia for an idealized, playful past that the stylization invites. Even more important to the political project Lambert envisions is that the nostalgia evoked and participation encouraged extends to those generally disenfranchised in public policy debates. Anyone who is moved to participate can step up and vote regardless of their citizenship status or whether or not they have any ownership to the surrounding commercial, local, or national space. This performative casting of a vote, then, might compel a diverse group of participants, some perhaps for the first time, to vote on whether or not the economic system under which they dwell is personally viable. In this way, it is clearly possible that "Capitalism Works For Me! True/False" and its deceptively simple performative components and flashy billboard presentation effectively utilize nostalgia and the pro-social behavior it tends to encourage to incite thought and discussion about capitalism.

Despite its success in evoking nostalgia and instigating participation from a wide swath of demographics, I argue that CWFM's participatory structure is more likely to deter deliberation and broaden affiliation in favor of reinforcing participants' existing feelings about capitalism and strengthening existing affiliations. This structure, then, fails to reorient emotional investments in capitalism. Rather, the art installation's modes of engagement—the ways that participants' bodies interact with the game and others—counteract its resistive potential by encouraging participants to draw a false analogy between the voting power of citizens in a democracy and the consumptive power of individuals under capitalism. In other words, the formal similarities between CWFM, the carnival game, and the voting booth reify the depoliticizing belief that capitalism is beholden to and can be modified by a compilation of individual choices rather than a concerted movement against its more insidious practices.

If the goal of CWFM is to start a conversation about capitalism then Lambert's decision to include a timer as part of the piece, while true to the form of the carnival game, discourages extended dialogue or reflection. When participants walk up to the podium they are immediately faced with a timer that begins counting down the time they have before their choice must be made and their place at the podium taken over by the person standing close behind them. This ticking clock echoes what Roger Stahl names the post-Cold War "rhetoric of the deadline," through which the mass media marks the time between the present and an impending and traumatic deadline (2008, 81).

This countdown and implied deadline effectively limit democratic debate due to both the restriction of the time available for deliberation as well as the perceived inevitability of the deadline and its attendant outcomes. Rather than take time to discuss the pros and cons of capitalism, participants are encouraged to make a decision motivated in part by the anxiety of the ticking clock. Therefore, while CWFM uses the nostalgic form of the carnival game to draw in participants, its amplification of the countdown and deadline, and its concomitant experience of anxiety, limit the opportunities for participants to develop "the complex questions and conversations" Lambert hopes to inspire.

In addition to the limited time for deliberation, the push of the button and the associated tally of votes projected onto the LED screen allow participants to feel as though their voices have been heard because their vote has been cast and counted. Having the power to physically express their choice and then have that choice projected publicly allows individuals to feel as though their opinion has been counted, even if that opinion proves to be politically irrelevant. This feeling of validation, of doing one's part and speaking one's mind, is a public expression of depoliticized citizenship. Sturken argues that the United States is inculcated in a culture of comfort where practices of consumption act as a means "to confront loss, grief, and fear through processes that disavow politics" (2007, 6). As an exemplar of this culture of comfort, Sturken analyzes the rise of the memorial teddy bear—teddy bears given to children who have experienced trauma, teddy bears sold in gift shops at national monuments and sites of trauma, etc. She argues that the selling of memorial teddy bears at the site of the Oklahoma City Bombing:

> Aims to allow visitors to leave the memorial feeling positive about the good that the bombing brought out in the people who suffered loss, rather than come away concerned by what the bombing meant. Importantly, the teddy bear doesn't promise to make things better; it promises to make us feel better about the way things are. (7)

The pushing of the green or red button and the visual recognition of that engagement in the LED screen tally works in a similar way. CWFM allows participants to *feel* like they have contributed to a conversation about capitalism; but, their vote and the tally that represents it have little to no effect on the way things are nor do they offer concrete opportunities to "make things better" through additional forms of affiliation and action.

This failure to extend participation beyond the temporary space of the CWFM "game," is evidenced by the limited scope of the CWFM's virtual presence. Despite Lambert's website dedicated to the piece, a number of news stories and interviews chronicling the installation's travels (Adler 2013;

Brown 2013; Campbell 2013; "Capitalism Works for Me" 2015; Davis 2013; Lambert 2014; Schuessler 2013), as well as a presentation given by Lambert at the 2012 Creative Time Summit (Lambert 2012)—a conference held on "the one-year anniversary of the birth of the Occupy movement … focusing specifically on wealth inequity and the ways in which it erodes democracy" ("About the 2012 Creative Time Summit"), there is a dearth of responses to the installation beyond those formally requested of immediate participants by Lambert, journalists, or art critics. The comment sections and discussion boards dedicated to the piece remain relatively empty; rather, the discussion appears to begin and end with the immediate participants or second-hand viewers' encounter with the installation.

That is why CWFM, rather than invite substantial critique, may deter critical action. The casting of the vote encourages participants to draw a false analogy between the contract between citizen and state in a democracy and the relationship between citizen and economy under capitalism. While in a democracy it is possible to conceive of a vote as influencing the future of societal contracts, Jean Baudrillard reminds us, "Capital … has never been linked by a contract to the society it dominates" (1983, 29). In other words, capitalism does not aspire to answer to the demands of those who function within it. When the participants vote they are not being commissioned into a potentially resistive collective or space of imagining as Lambert hopes; rather, they are being drawn into the idea that capitalism is subject to a moral and democratic regime that can be easily overturned through an accumulation of individual choices. The performance of a "deceptively simple vote" asks participants to engage in a performance of citizenship that reduces citizenship to consumption and encourages participants to believe that capitalism is "linked by a contract to the society it rules" (Baudrillard 1983, 29). In casting a vote for or against capitalism, participants are being deterred from the fact that a vote on capitalism is insufficient for substantive change.

Were the modes of participation and engagement not enough to invite skepticism of CWFM resistive potential, the affiliative possibilities of CWFM should. Although the vote encourages participants to act, the prescribed actions fail to shift participants' affiliations with capitalism or other subjects under capitalism. CWFM's most glaring blockage to new affiliative possibilities lies in its insistence that participants gauge their answer based solely on their personal experience. The question posed is "does capitalism work for *me*," not "us," "most people," "everyone," "the poor," etc. To their credit, many respondents vacillated back and forth between a simple true and false because of their affiliative ties to others for whom capitalism did or did not work (Lambert). However, the installation's explicit question encourages participants to determine their answer based on their individual experiences or those of their immediate family or friend groups. Thus, the critical eye Lambert hopes to inspire is turned inward to oneself and one's familiars, rather than actively spurring new affiliative ties to or engagement with others.

Employing a methodology that accounts for both the action tendencies of a given emotion (here, nostalgia) and the ways that interactive structures dictate the manifestation of those tendencies, it becomes apparent that, while Lambert's CWFM successfully evokes nostalgia and compels participation, the options for affiliative ties are significantly reduced. As a result the action tendencies of nostalgia are constrained to reify pre-existing affiliations rather than convincing those who currently believe that capitalism "works for me" to question the sufficiency of that assumption.

The MWM and New Affiliations

In contrast to Lambert's CWFM, Blake Fall-Conroy's MWM offers modes of participation that can appropriate nostalgic action tendencies to undermine participants' positive emotional investment in capitalism and facilitate new relationships across existing affiliative lines. This shift occurs in two ways: first, by troubling participants' emotional investment in the capitalist ideal of meritocracy and, second, by facilitating an affiliative relationship across class lines. These new emotional and affiliative relationships to capitalism and those that dwell within it undermine the rhetorics of hard work and deservingness that bolster antagonisms between the "hardworking" middle and upper-class and the "lazy" working class. As a result of its particular modes of interaction, the MWM uses the nostalgia-evoking carnival game form to encourage participation in an art piece that offers new affiliative possibilities across class lines.

Unlike the CWFM, the MWM does not encourage participants to interact with others, and Fall-Conroy does not espouse a particular agenda for the installation apart from a brief speculation about how the machine could be used across the nation to enable more individuals to work. Fall-Conroy simply provides directions for reproducing his machine so that more people can share this experience. His comments about the project stick strictly to the issue of labor. They may or may not be read as satirical:

> In the future, I see possibility in a lot of these machines hooked into a grid, with people performing basic human labor for money. Perhaps a new form of renewable energy generation? A new kind of supercomputer with thousands of people performing basic calculations at minimum wage "stations" across the world? Who knows? (Mets 2009)

This focus on the reproduction of the machine, rather than discourse about the types of interaction the machine compels, is exemplified by the fact that of what little Fall-Conroy says publicly about the MWM the vast majority is about the way the machine works. He outlines the building process in detail, arguably so that the machines can be replicated.

While at first this focus on individual interactions with the MWM might be counterintuitive to crafting affiliations or disrupting the depoliticization of emotion, the modes of physical interaction the MWM requires work to direct participants' behavior in ways that shift participants' emotional relationship to meritocracy. This shift in participants' investment in meritocracy is encouraged through perspective by incongruity; the "strategic juxtaposition [that] highlights tension between two groups by placing artifacts/elements of each side by side" (Demo 2000, 147). In particular, the MWM adopts the form of the carnival game, invites a nostalgic recollection of a real or imagined past of merriment and play, and juxtaposes it to the banality of minimum wage labor. This stark juxtaposition between the carnival game form's promise of reenacting past pleasures and the MWM's reality of monotonous repetition makes more visible the fallibility of late capitalism's meritocratic guarantee that with enough hard work and a little luck, anyone can reap the financial benefits and enjoy the emotional pleasures of capitalism.

Unlike its associated carnival games—the slot machine or toy claw machine—the MWM does not place any limits on the time participants can "play" nor does a participant's performance or prize improve based on the time "playing." When a person steps up to a slot machine and pulls down the lever they take a risk that they will win, that their investment—financial, physical, and temporal—will pay off as a windfall of clinking coins tumble down into the trough in front of them. However, when participants begin to turn the crank on the MWM, to pull the lever, they are met with a consistent and underwhelming "clink" every 4 … 3 … 2 … 1. It does not matter how fast the participant turns the wheel. For the MWM, faster does not equal better. In fact, faster means that you might expend too much energy and wear out too quickly or jam the machine. Thus, the meritocratic belief that with sufficient effort menial labor can turn into meaningful (in both the financial and emotional sense of the word) labor is undermined by the MWM's imposed incongruity between the carnival game form and the prize of minimum wage labor.

In the same way that the MWM undermines the anticipated limits of "play" time, it undermines the valorization and excitement of risk. The toy claw machine promises a prize for labor if one is willing to take the risk of wasted finances and labor. The toy claw machine promises that with enough practice and hard work a participant can become "good enough" to win. The ever-present risk that the number of tries paid for will outweigh the value of the eventual prize drives the excitement of the game. However, the MWM reveals that there is no secret to success nor is there any excitement to the repetition. The enjoyment of repetition and risk is undermined by the banality and consistency of the pennies' clink into the trough. Rather than succeed through personal initiative and experience the enjoyment of the challenge, the MWM guarantees a minimum of success and what begins as a fun game quickly becomes a mundane activity where payoff is woefully inadequate for the labor it requires. In other words, the physical performance of minimum wage labor with the MWM teaches those without a minimum wage job what minimum wage is, by arguing—through their own performance—what minimum wage labor is not: a game. In these ways, the MWM undermines participants' emotional investment in meritocracy.

Not only does the structure of the MWM use nostalgia to encourage participation and perspective by incongruity to trouble participants' emotional state, it also encourages new affiliations between participants and the minimum wage laborer. If nostalgia's action tendencies drive individuals to seek social interaction and affirmation, then the MWM's structure channels the possibilities of that interaction and affiliation to just one: the minimum wage worker. Where participants in CWFM have to grapple with a countdown, a line of people, the crowded, animated space of Times Square, and the creator, participants in the MWM are left with far fewer distractions. The only communication the participant receives, apart from the carnival game form, is a sign that reads "Minimum Wage Machine." Furthermore, the positioning of the crank, on the right hand side and traveling in a clock-wise motion, encourages participants to face the machine rather than stand to the side of it. As a result, participants are focused on the machine rather than other potential participants, other visual features in the environment, or persuasive messages.

This isolation from all possible others is then coupled with the structured participation of the MWM to engender a new affiliation between the participant and the minimum wage laborer. The MWM places the participant into the role of minimum wage laborer. Participants who interact with the MWM must physically engage with the machine to make it work. In fact, the participant's body is the primary means of interacting with and making sense of the MWM. They are the sources of energy. While in CWFM voters must press a button, CWFM works independently of their physical labor. In contrast, the MWM's focus on labor increases "higher levels of interactivity … making the user more disposed to persuasion" (Carnegie 2009, 166). This mode of interactivity opens up the participant to the persuasive message and affiliative possibilities of the MWM. Vassilis Sevdalis and Markus Raab argue:

> Recent approaches within an embodied cognition framework provide evidence that the capacity to understand an individual's cognitive and affective states depend on the observer's sensorimotor experience and seek to identify the factors influencing this process. … Empathy, as a means of embodying another individual's states, may be particularly potent in situations that involve the trained human body in motion. (2014, 174)

In other words, physical embodiment and performance facilitates affiliations and better understanding of others. It is for this reason that Shannon Walters argues that touch functions rhetorically "as a crucial vehicle for resisting these limiting emotions [pity, inspiration, sympathy] and catalyzing new emotional transactions" across lines of privilege and difference by facilitating new means of identification (2014, 169). By encouraging participants to embody minimum wage labor and attaching that labor to negative, rather than positive feelings, the MWM can begin to shift participants' understanding of minimum wage workers from lazy and undeserving to persons burdened by the banality of minimum wage labor and the empty promises of meritocracy.

Given the MWM's potential to establish new affiliations between different classes, it is unfortunate that Fall Conroy did not go further to exploit those possibilities for more long-term or substantial political goals. After all, if the MWM does anything it is at the level of one individual's emotional experience. Attaching these new feelings of unrest or empathy to new economic policies that advocate for an increase in minimum wage or humane working conditions, or to new charitable giving opportunities, or new volunteer and membership opportunities with working class organizations might lead to a more substantial shift in financial, emotional, and time investments among participants. However, the MWM does offer a new repertoire of emotions that skilled rhetors and activists can now draw upon. Even if participants do not cognitively make the link between minimum wage labor and the banality and inequity of modern capitalism, participants have had the experiences of poorly requited, boring labor and had that experience linked to minimum wage. Even if they turn rapidly away from the experience, they do so because boredom and labor and money have been linked as a repulsive assembly.

Conclusion: The Political Possibilities of Nostalgia

While in many instances, emotional appeals, like nostalgia, may lead some to distance themselves from and disavow the troubling national and global politics of the present, I have argued that assessment of the depoliticization and/or (re)politicization encouraged by a particular deployment of an emotion requires more than blanket deterministic dismissal. It requires attending to a given emotion's action tendencies, the affiliations these action tendencies encourage, and how the particular deployments of each emotion encourage the structuring of participants' affiliative options.

The differences between CWFM and the MWM's use of the carnival game form and the implications of those differences in terms of promoting and precluding new affiliations and actions across class lines are indicative of the wide spectrum of political possibilities that attend any emotional appeal. For instance, scholars in multiple disciplines have advanced considerable work determining the cognitive appraisals, physiological responses, and action tendencies that distinguish closely linked emotions—like empathy/sympathy/compassion/pity or shame/embarrassment or guilt/sadness—from one another. While on the surface these emotions may seem interchangeable and the distinctions between them minor, the nuances between these emotions substantially change how individuals are predisposed to act and relate to others as a result of each emotional experience. Attending to the nuances of each emotion used in an emotional appeal and the ways the structure of the appeal influences that emotion's affiliative and active potential can allow critics to better theorize the difference between depoliticizing and repoliticizing emotional appeals, thereby allowing activists insights into the construction of emotional appeals that may animate public deliberation, promote affiliations across differences, and lead to productive social change.

Notes

1. There is debate on whether or not emotions are stored in the memory itself. General agreement is that they are not. Rather, nostalgic images allow for the recreation of the emotional experience of the past adapted to the context of the present.
2. Suominen provides a similar assessment of the ways in which past gaming experiences inform when, how and with whom individuals engage in gaming in the present.
3. The MWM can be recalibrated to deposit pennies at a rate based on the different minimum wage rates of various locations.

References

"About the 2012 Creative Time Summit." n.d. Creative Time Summit. Accessed October 11, 2016. http://creativetime.org/summit/about-the-summit/overview-2012/.

Adler, Margot. 2013. "Does Capitalism Work? A True/False Quiz in Times Square." *NPR.Org*, October 5, 2013, Weekend Edition Saturday edition. http://www.npr.

org/2013/10/05/229192177/does-capitalism-work-a-true-false-quiz-in-times-square.

Andrejevic, Mark. 2009. "Critical Media Studies 2.0: An Interactive Upgrade." *Interactions: Studies in Communication & Culture* 1 (1): 35–50.

Atkinson, Joshua, and Clayton Rosati. 2012. "DetroitYES! And the Fabulous Ruins Virtual Tour: The Role of Diffused Intertextual Production in the Construction of Alternative Cityscapes." *Critical Studies in Media Communication* 29 (1): 45–64. https://doi.org/10.1080/15295036.2010.516002.

Bartsch, Anne, and Mary Beth Oliver. 2011. "Making Sense of Entertainment: On the Interplay of Emotion and Cognition in Entertainment Experience." *Journal of Media Psychology* 23: 12–17.

Batcho, Krystine Irene. 2013. "Nostalgia: Retreat or Support in Difficult Times?" *The American Journal of Psychology* 126 (3): 355–67. https://doi.org/10.5406/amerjpsyc.126.3.0355.

Baudrillard, Jean. 1983. *Simulations*. Translated by Paul Foss. United States of America: Semiotext[e].

Berlant, Lauren. 1997. *The Queen of America Goes to Washington City: Essays on Sex and Citizenship*. Durham, NC: Duke University Press.

Blair, Carole. 1999. "Contemporary U.S. Memorial Sites as Exemplars of Rhetoric's Materiality." In *Rhetorical Bodies*, edited by Jack Selzer and Sharon Crowley. Madison, WI: University of Wisconsin Press.

Bonnett, Alastair. 2010. "Radicalism, Antiracism, and Nostalgia: The Burden of Loss in the Search for Convivial Culture." *Environment and Planning A* 42: 2351–69.

Brown, Mark. 2013. "Indoor Fracking Installation Seeks to Provoke Debate." *The Guardian*, June 17, 2013.

Campbell, Phil. 2013. "Capitalism Works for Me … ?" *The Huffington Post*, June 10, 2013, sec. Entertainment. http://www.huffingtonpost.com/phil-campbell/capitalism-works-for-me-steve-lambert_b_3052401.html.

"Capitalism Works for Me. TRUE/ FALSE." 2015. *A(r)CT: Art Can Act* (blog). June 8, 2015. https://artforwhat.wordpress.com/2015/06/08/capitalism-works-for-you-true-false/.

Carnegie, Teena A. M. 2009. "Interface as Exordium: The Rhetoric of Interactivity." *Computers & Composition* 26 (3): 164–73. https://doi.org/10.1016/j.compcom.2009.05.005.

Cloud, Dana L. 2003. "Therapy, Silence, and War: Consolation and the End of Deliberation in the 'Affected' Public." *Poroi* 2 (1): 125–42.

Condit, Celeste M. 2013. "Pathos in Criticism: Edwin Black's Communism-As-Cancer Metaphor." *Quarterly Journal of Speech* 99 (1): 1–26.

Cross, Gary. 2015. *Consumed Nostalgia: Memory in the Age of Fast Capitalism*. New York: Columbia University Press.

Davis, Laura. 2013. "Birthday Exhibition Looks to the Future; Fracking, Virtual Reality Sky-Writing and a Giant Ear - It's Got to Be FACT's 10th Anniversary Show. Laura Davis Takes a Look." *Liverpool Post*, June 13, 2013, 1; National edition, sec. Post Culture.

Demo, Anne Teresa. 2000. "The Guerrilla Girls' Comic Politics of Subversion." *Women's Studies in Communication* 23 (2): 133–56.

Dickinson, Greg. 1997. "Memories for Sale: Nostalgia and the Construction of Identity in Old Pasadena." *Quarterly Journal of Speech* 83 (1): 1–27.

Fall-Conroy, Blake. n.d. "Minimum Wage Machine." Blake Fall-Conroy. Accessed October 13, 2016. http://blakefallconroy.com/18.html.

Hasian, Marouf. 2001. "Nostalgic Longings, Memories of the 'Good War,' and Cinematic Representations in "Saving Private Ryan"." *Critical Studies in Media Communication* 18 (3): 338–58.

Lambert, Steve. 2012. "Tactics." Presented at the 2010 Creative Time Summit, NYU Skirball Center, October 12. http://creativetime.org/summit/2012/10/12/steve-lambert/.

———. 2014. "Is Capitalism Working for You?" *Creative Time Reports.* April 7, 2014. http://creativetime.org/reports/2014/04/07/does-capitalism-work-for-you/.

———. n.d. "Capitalism Works for Me! True/False." Steve Lambert. http://visitsteve.com/made/capitalism-works-for-me-truefalse/.

Levine, Linda J., Heather C. Lench, and Martin A. Safer. 2009. "Functions of Remembering and Misremembering Emotion." *Applied Cognitive Psychology* 23 (8): 1059–75.

Merchant, Altaf, and Gregory M. Rose. 2013. "Effects of Advertising-Evoked Vicarious Nostalgia on Brand Heritage." *Journal of Business Research* 66 (12): 2619–25. https://doi.org/10.1016/j.jbusres.2012.05.021.

Mets, Matt. 2009. "Minimum Wage Machine." *Makezine.Com*, November 30, 2009. http://makezine.com/2009/11/30/minimum-wage-machine.

Oliete-Aldea, Elena. 2012. "Fear and Nostalgia in Times of Crisis: The Paradoxes of Globalization in Oliver Stone's "Money Never Sleeps" (2010)." *Culture Unbound: Journal of Current Cultural Research* 4 (3): 347–66.

Orth, Ulrich R., and Steffi Gal. 2014. "Persuasive Mechanisms of Nostalgic Brand Packages." *Applied Cognitive Psychology* 28 (2): 161–73.

Pickering, Michael, and Emily Keightley. 2006. "The Modalities of Nostalgia." *Current Sociology* 54 (6): 919–41.

Schuessler, Jennifer. 2013. "Keeping Score on Capitalism." *The New York Times*, September 24, 2013, sec. The Arts/Cultural Desk. http://artsbeat.blogs.nytimes.com/2013/09/21/times-square-art-project-keeps-score-on-capitalism/.

Sevdalis, Vassilis, and Markus Raab. 2014. "Empathy in Sports, Exercise, and the Performing Arts." *Psychology of Sport & Exercise* 15 (2): 173–79. https://doi.org/10.1016/j.psychsport.2013.10.013.

Smith, Kimberly K. 2000. "Mere Nostalgia: Notes on a Progressive Paratheory." *Rhetoric & Public Affairs* 3 (4): 505–27.

Stahl, Roger. 2008. "A Clockwork War: Rhetorics of Time in a Time of Terror." *Quarterly Journal of Speech* 94 (1): 73–99.

Sturken, Marita. 2007. *Tourists of History: Memory, Kitsch, and Consumerism from Oklahoma City to Ground Zero.* Durham, NC: Duke University Press.

———. 2011. "Comfort, Irony, and Trivialization: The Mediation of Torture." *International Journal of Cultural Studies* 14 (4): 423–40. https://doi.org/10.1177/1367877911403250.

Suominen, Jaakko. 2008. "The Past as the Future? Nostalgia and Retrogaming in Digital Culture." *The Fibreculture Journal*, no. 11. http://eleven.fibreculturejournal.org/fcj-075-the-past-as-the-future-nostalgia-and-retrogaming-in-digital-culture/.

Tannock, Stuart. 1995. "Nostalgia Critique." *Cultural Studies* 9 (3): 453–64.

Von Burg, Ron, and Paul E. Johnson. 2009. "Yearning for a Past That Never Was: Baseball, Steroids, and the Anxiety of the American Dream." *Critical Studies in Media Communication* 26 (4): 351–71. https://doi.org/10.1080/15295030903176641.

Walters, Shannon. 2014. *Rhetorical Touch: Disability, Identification, Haptics*. Columbia, SC: University of South Carolina Press.

Wood, Andrew F. 2010. "Two Roads Diverge: Route 66, 'Route 66,' and the Mediation of American Ruin." *Critical Studies in Media Communication* 27 (1): 67–83. https://doi.org/10.1080/15295030903554375.

Contributors

Alexandra Bardan earned a B.A. in Fine Arts from the Art Academy, Bucharest and a Ph.D. in Information and Communication Sciences at Université Sorbonne-Nouvelle Paris 3. She is a lecturer at the Faculty of Journalism and Communication Studies, University of Bucharest, where she teaches courses in editorial design, photojournalism, digital image production, and desktop publishing. Her research interests cover visual communication, post-communist nostalgia, social history, and everyday life in communist Romania.

Raymond Blanton is Assistant Professor of Communication Arts in the School of Media and Design at the University of the Incarnate Word in San Antonio, Texas. His research is primarily concerned with the civic and religious dimensions of rhetoric, communication, and media in intellectual history and American culture, particularly the mythology of the road in the Delta blues, in Martin Luther King, Jr. and the American civil rights movement, and the history of cinema.

Jonathan M. Bullinger, Ph.D., is a collective memory scholar specializing in late-20th U.S. culture around commemorative issues of war and popular culture. His doctoral work focused on the remembrance of World War II in the U.S., 1984–2012, and he is currently working on a project focusing on the historicization of post-war popular culture products during the '80s and '90s. He has also published on the topic of World War II, historical representation, and video games.

Sebastian Felzmann, M.A., studied German Literature and Journalism at the KIT (2003–2009) and worked as a research assistant and project manager at the University of Arts and Design in Karlsruhe (2008–2014), followed by a brief employment at a marketing agency with the focus on infotainment games and apps (2014–2017). Since April 2017 he holds the position of Research Manager at the Cologne Game Lab/TH Köln. He loves retro games and old gaming devices so much, that he had written a book about that subject and several scientific papers and even held various lectures about Media Nostalgia and Gaming History.

Ashley P. Jones is a Ph.D. student in the Moving Image Studies program at Georgia State University. Her research interests include representation and aesthetics in digital gaming, feminism in transmedia texts, and critical/cultural studies. She has presented work on the monstrous body of Lara Croft, gender dichotomy in the *Tomb Raider* game series, and black feminism in the post-colonial film *Les Saignantes* (2005). Her current research has her exploring the aesthetics of the digital game Tacoma and the role of authorship in digital gaming.

Carson S. Kay is a doctoral student in Communication Studies at Ohio University. Raised among the Blue Ridge Mountains of North Carolina, Kay contemplates how race, space, and political partisanship function within the Southern States. As a nationally awarded speaker, Kay uses her extensive public platform experience to advocate for social change; Her manuscripts may be found in the Interstate Oratorical Association's Winning Orations.

JeongHyun Lee is a doctoral candidate in Communication, Rhetoric, and Digital Media program at North Carolina State University. Her research areas are critical media studies, cultural studies, memory studies, and post-human media studies. Her research focuses on digital media, technology, temporal experiences, and memory practices. She is currently exploring the intersectional temporal experiences between bodies and machines in memory practices.

Alexandra Lippert is a doctoral student in Communication Studies at Ohio University. As a former teacher in inner-city under resourced schools in Cincinnati, Ohio and the mother to a bi-racial son, her research interests have a continued commitment to issues of social justice and the missing narratives of marginalized communities. She has published several pieces of work in both popular media and academic journals, such as the Journal of Health Communication.

Ryan Lizardi is assistant professor of digital media and humanities at SUNY Polytechnic Institute. He focuses his research on media encouraged nostalgia, including his books *Mediated Nostalgia* (2014) and *Nostalgic Generations and Media* (2017), explorations of television remakes, and representations of time travel in media.

Mani Mehrvarz is a media artist and filmmaker, currently a Ph.D. candidate in the Department of Media Study at the University at Buffalo. His principal topics of interest are nostalgia, archives, German media theory, and post-history. Mani received his Master in Intermedia Arts from University of

Arts in Poznan, where he focused his study and art projects on the intersection of moving-image and nostalgia. His video-arts and films have received recognition and awards and have been exhibited and screened worldwide since 2004.

Maryam Muliaee is a multimedia artist based in Buffalo, New York. Currently, she is pursuing her Ph.D. at the University at Buffalo, in Media Study, a practice-based program in media arts and technology. Her current research and practice focus on media archeology and archiveology, mapping and locative media arts. Maryam's art has been exhibited in national and international juried exhibitions, festivals and screening programs since 2007.

Sally J. Spalding is an assistant professor at Southeast Missouri State University. Her current research focuses on the role of emotion in constituting social movements and driving public deliberation on issues related to healthcare, gender parity, and social justice.

Emily Truman is a postdoctoral fellow in critical communication in the department of Communication, Media and Film at the University of Calgary. Her program of research questions the form and function of cultural icons in relation to specific historical, social, cultural, and political contexts. Previous work in this area examines the conceptual category of the cultural icon, and the public figure of the graffiti artist, while current projects explore food and nutrition icons.

Natalia Vasilendiuc has a B.A. in Journalism and a Ph.D. in Information and Communication Sciences from the University of Bucharest. She is an associate professor at the Faculty of Journalism and Communication Studies, University of Bucharest, where she teaches courses in sociology of journalists, media sociology, project management, and research methods. Her research interests are focused on media professional culture, post-communist nostalgia, gender equality, and the Media.

Index

C

D

E

N

O

P

www.ingramcontent.com/pod-product-compliance
Ingram Content Group UK Ltd.
Pitfield, Milton Keynes, MK11 3LW, UK
UKHW021837100926
8556IPUK00004B/396

9 781433 162428